CROOKS
THE STORIES BEHIND
THE HEADLINES

ALSO BY PAUL WILLIAMS

Gilligan

The Monk

Almost the Perfect Murder

Murder Inc.

Badfellas

Crime Wars

The Untouchables

Crimelords

Evil Empire

Gangland

Secret Love (ghostwriter)

The General

CROOKS

THE STORIES BEHIND THE HEADLINES

PAUL WILLIAMS

ALLEN&UNWIN

First published in Great Britain in 2024 by Allen & Unwin, an imprint of Atlantic Books Ltd.

A CIP catalogue record for this book is available from the British Library.

Trade paperback ISBN 978 1 80546 119 7
E-book ISBN 978 1 80546 120 3

Printed by CPI Group (UK) Ltd, Croydon CR0 4YY

10 9 8 7 6 5 4 3 2 1

Allen & Unwin
An imprint of Atlantic Books Ltd
Ormond House
26–27 Boswell Street
London WC1N 3JZ

*Dedicated to my family, friends and colleagues
who provided love, support and encouragement.
And to the many unnamed gardai whose
interventions saved my life and protected my
loved ones on more than a few occasions.*

CONTENTS

PROLOGUE

The memory of covering my first crime story forty years ago has not faded with time.

It was a cold afternoon on a bleak windswept mountainside in Leitrim in mid-December 1984. I was standing frozen to the spot, arms in the air, staring down the two long, shiny barrels of the old shotgun pointing straight at me from a few feet away.

My startled gaze met the owner's razor-sharp eyes as they peered unblinking between the two silver hammers at the operational end of the ancient weapon.

'I shot Black and Tans with this and I'll do the same to you, ya tinker.'

The hard edge to the pensioner's voice left no doubt that he and his trusted gun had indeed dispatched a few of the hated British paramilitaries over sixty years earlier.

The situation wasn't helped by the fact that the stranger who'd called to his door was a dishevelled looking nineteen-year-old in faded jeans and an old combat jacket. I had no doubt that he could do it again. The veteran of the War of Independence assured me the weapon was loaded. I believed every syllable he uttered as he sat in a chair facing the door in the modest, white-washed cottage on *Sliabh an Iarainn* – the mountain of iron – in whose shadow I had grown up.

Fresh out of college and full of enthusiasm I was four months into my first staff job as a cub reporter with my local newspaper, the *Leitrim Observer*. I had come looking for a scoop, not expecting the prospect of getting a belly full of buckshot instead. In those unforgettable few moments of pure fear it looked like my career was about to end before it even got started. It was a baptism of fire in a job where threats of being shot would become an occupational hazard in the years ahead.

The antique shotgun and its owner John Bernard Keaney, the eighty-two-year-old warrior, were the reason I was there in the first place. My initial foray into crime reporting involved chronicling a terrifying phenomenon which suddenly emerged in the winter of 1984 and has haunted rural Ireland ever since. Four decades later it has effectively become normalized and is euphemistically categorized as 'rural crime'.

It involved gangs, mostly from the Travelling community, who began specializing in targeting the most vulnerable people in society – elderly folk living in isolated areas in the north-west of rural Ireland. The counties worst hit were Leitrim, Roscommon, Sligo and Mayo. At the time the sudden upsurge in rural crime shocked the entire nation. Pensioners living alone were being robbed and beaten in their homes. I didn't know it at the time but I was witnessing a watershed moment in our social history which shattered Ireland's pastoral tranquillity and left people living in fear. A career in journalism is a constant learning curve and this was my stark introduction to a dark side of life I knew nothing about.

In November and December 1984 the number of raids had reached epidemic proportions. Over a number of weeks the owner of the *Leitrim Observer,* Greg Dunne, and legendary photographer Willie Donnellan took turns driving me the length and breadth of the county to interview the growing number of victims. I found it truly shocking. I grew up in a close-knit, peaceful, law-abiding rural community where keys were left in the door and our elderly citizens were treated with the utmost respect. Crime was practically non-existent in lovely Leitrim.

It was deeply upsetting to see and hear the fear in the faces and voices of people like my beloved granny Ellie who had passed six years earlier. I will never forget the sense of despair in the people whose trust in the world had been shattered in their twilight years. The old folks who had lived through the worst and poorest of times didn't trust banks and believed in keeping their savings under the mattress. The money was for the 'rainy day' and to ensure there was enough for a funeral so that they would not be a burden on anyone. Our proud older generation wanted dignity in death. For that they were robbed and, in some cases, beaten and terrorized. It left me with a lifelong detestation of so-called 'Travelling gangs'.

But there was one good news story on the back of the crime surge which was why I was trembling in front of John Bernard's shotgun. I had heard on the bush telegraph that two weeks earlier he had sent a gang of thieves running for their lives in much the same fashion as I was now experiencing. I wanted to tell his heroic story.

He had plenty of reason to be on high alert. The week before my visit the crime spree had claimed its first murder victim when an eighty-two-year-old woman was beaten to death in her home in neighbouring County Roscommon. Brigid Cummins was fatally attacked with a broken chair when she and her elderly sister Mary confronted a burglar who had entered their bedroom in the middle of the night.

When I knocked on the door of the isolated cottage it was answered by John Bernard's charming seventy-one-year-old wife Bridget. I remember her smile as I asked to speak to her husband. She said something like 'he is here' before calmly standing to one side to reveal the same double-barrelled shotgun I came to talk about. I instinctively hoisted my arms in surrender realizing that I could not move either forward or backwards without being caught in the blast.

I excitedly explained that I was from a few miles down the road in Ballinamore 'and there's no tinkers there'. I also told him I was with the *Observer* although I looked nothing like a reporter. I could hear Willie Donnellan's car starting up as if he was about to leave. I have slagged my old friend about that ever since. I told John Bernard that Willie was – I hoped – with me. Willie has always been a household name in Leitrim.

After a few tense moments the mood suddenly changed and John Bernard and his wife broke into smiles. The reliable old gun was placed to one side and I was invited to 'pull up close to the fire, son' as they told their story over cups of piping hot tea. The thieves' modus operandi was to arrive pretending to sell blankets and other goods. Then they either stole the money surreptitiously or terrorized their victims to hand it over. The gardaí later confirmed to me that the men who called to the Keaney's isolated home were suspected of carrying out dozens of similar burglaries over the previous months.

They had arrived after dark. Two men approached the front door while the third remained in the car with the engine running. They were offering to sell blankets and were attempting to move into the house when John went on the defensive.

'I got suspicious because it was the first time anyone came to sell blankets to me on a Sunday night,' he recalled. It was then he introduced them to his reliable old war companion. Facing the double-barrel shotgun, the thugs vanished in seconds.

'We weren't afraid of the "Tans" and we'll surely not be afraid of a bunch of boyos,' said the former guerrilla soldier.

When I asked if he would have used the lethal weapon the veteran didn't hesitate. 'I haven't got the gun for fun,' he smiled.

John and Bridget posed for pictures after the tea, with him brandishing the fearsome weapon of war.

I was so proud as I watched the front-page story trundle off the ancient printing press on 15 December 1984. I felt that it would do some good, which is what it's about for all journalists.

In the story the local garda superintendent warned of the result if people were prepared to protect themselves with guns. In a message clearly intended for the bad guys he told me: 'At present we have an explosive situation if someone is forced to use a gun. It could have tragic consequences.'

In the days before the politically correct era of bullshit we now live in, the superintendent had no intention of depriving John Bernard Keaney of his shotgun. He wanted to inform the ruthless thugs – labelled 'granny bashers' by the rest of the Travelling community – of what might happen if they kept up their activities. Today, if a farmer or elderly person uses a gun to protect themselves it is automatically confiscated by the police.

Forty years later I am still highlighting the problem of rural crime. The more things change the more they stay the same. I have written many stories about innocent, decent people like John Bernard Keaney who have been murdered or left seriously injured when predatory monsters entered their homes.

Whenever I hear of another brutal crime committed against vulnerable rural dwellers I always get damned angry – and think of a gutsy old veteran who fought for a free Ireland and stood up for himself.

That experience on the side of the mountain coloured my view of the world. It launched my career writing about crime, criminals and their despicable acts.

CHAPTER ONE

————

CRIME REPORTING

It has been said that if journalism is the first rough draft of history then crime journalism has a habit of being rougher than most. I have spent the past forty years chronicling the roughest draft of history in the making – the evolution of organized crime in Ireland. From the front seat of what was often a white knuckle ride I have witnessed firsthand a lot of the seminal events which changed the face of the gangland that first absorbed me as a junior reporter. When I moved from the much more tranquil world of provincial journalism to the big city I realized that rural crime was only a small part of the complex picture.

My journey in crime reporting began while I was studying for the Leaving Cert. As an idealistic youngster looking for adventure I wanted to become a war correspondent. In 1983 I was accepted onto a two-year course in the School of Journalism at the College of Commerce in Rathmines, then part of the Dublin Institute of Technology, now known as Technical University of Dublin. It was the only journalism course in the country at the time and each year twenty-five candidates were selected out of about 300 applicants. To qualify for a place students had to get at least two honours in their Leaving Cert subjects, including English, and be successful at an interview in front of a three-person panel, consisting of the course supervisor David Rice, the then editor of the *Irish Times* Douglas Gageby and, appropriately enough for the profession concerned, a psychologist. When compared to other occupations journalism tends to attract a disproportionate number of eccentric people.

The panel picked the applicants who they reckoned were suited to the job of a hack. What many journalists of a certain age refer to as 'Rathmines' was the bedrock of Irish journalism. Amongst its alumni are several of the top names in Irish broadcasting and print media, international bestselling authors and several well known newspaper editors. My class included long-time friends John Burns and Stephen Rae. As deputy editor of the *Sunday Times* Burns made it one of Ireland's biggest selling papers, and Stephen became the editor-in-chief of the entire Independent News and Media (INM) group. Another classmate was Orla Guerin, the BBC's intrepid and much respected international correspondent. Then there was me, the guy who wanted to go to war.

I didn't think that I had much of a chance of getting a place, especially when I had to explain why I had three secondary schools on my CV – as a rebellious kid I was expelled from two and finally settled down in the third, Carrigallen Vocational School, which, my long suffering parents reminded me, was my last chance of a formal education. The principal was Mick Duignan, an old family friend who decided to take a risk. Having to cycle ten miles a day to get there certainly focused me on my studies. I told the panel the unvarnished truth. One of the principles I always stuck by in my life and career is to tell the truth whatever the consequences. As a journalist the people you deal with must have trust in you. I said that my parents were both relieved and surprised that I had actually managed to do my Leaving and had then come out with good results.

Then there was my explanation to the panel as to how I came by the still bandaged nasty head wound. I had sustained it a few weeks earlier when I stole my mother's new car and went for a joyride one night with a group of friends. My reckless escapade came to an abrupt end when I wrote it off after ploughing into a telegraph pole. We had a miraculous escape from what criminologists would describe as my primary act of law-breaking deviance.

To cap it all off when the interviewers asked me what kind of journalism I fancied I remember the look on their faces when I said war correspondent: This kid is mad.

My dad Benny drove me up to Dublin in the dusty pick-up truck he used in the family business which was quarry drilling. We looked a right pair of local yokels from the bog. Thanks to me the pick-up had become our primary mode of transport. Dad asked how I did. I said I had done shite and as we drove back to Leitrim we discussed what I was going to do next. I had already decided on a strategy in the likely event that I was rejected – I was determined to get a start in journalism. I had compiled a list of the names and telephone numbers of every provincial newspaper editor in the country. I planned to start at the top and work my way down. I was certain one of them would have a job for an enthusiastic rookie. Provincial newspapers have always provided the best training ground for journalists, before they can look to joining the nationals.

The telegram informing me that I had been successful was one of the most momentous experiences and biggest surprises of my life – there were no texts or emails in those archaic times.

After my first year I spent the summer on work experience at the *Longford News* but before I was due to go back to college I was offered a job on my local newspaper, the *Leitrim Observer,* by the owner Greg Dunne. The *Observer* had been the starting ground for David Walsh of the *Sunday Times,* the journalist who exposed Lance Armstrong as a doping cheat. I dropped out of my second year and my graduation. The summer months had convinced me that I could learn more on the actual job than in a classroom. In those days of high unemployment even David Rice advised that I should take the job when it presented itself.

I found myself in the strange position of reporting the news from my home town of Ballinamore. The *Observer* was one of the oldest papers in the country and one of the last still using the hot metal system. I loved the smells of the molten lead and the printing ink and the sound of the big very old printing press. I was witnessing a piece of publishing history which would shortly give way to new technology.

Rural crime was my first big story. However, I left the *Leitrim Observer* six months later when Derek Cobbe, the colourful owner of the *Longford News,* offered me a staff position. It was no reflection on the *Observer* – the *News,* based in a big town, was more exciting. It was one of the only full-colour newspapers in Ireland at the time. Derek Cobbe was an amazing, inspiring boss. A magician, hypnotist and artist, he was – and still is – a legendary figure in Irish newspaper history. His extraordinary flair for presentation and layout made him a pioneer. His deputy was another journalistic titan, John Donlon, a Rathmines alumnus, whose writing first attracted me to the paper. Four decades later he lives close by and still reminds me, 'I taught you everything you know gosson, not everything I know'. In 1988 Donlon was appointed the first news editor of the *Irish Star* newspaper which was based close to the *Sunday World,* so he could keep an eye on me. Sixteen years later he became my news editor in the *Sunday World* where the sports editor, the late and much loved Pat Quigley, acknowledged his role in my career with the nickname 'Bram', as in Bram Stoker who also created a monster!

Donlon had previously trained another journalist – my future partner in life, Anne Sweeney – who was also from Ballinamore and a few years ahead of me in the business. She went on to earn numerous awards for her work and later worked for a time with the *Irish Press*. We met when she joined the *Longford News*. The paper was also the training ground of a number of renowned journalists who had departed for the bright lights of Dublin – Alan O'Keefe and Liam Collins. I always wanted to follow in their footsteps.

I had two wonderful years in the *Longford News*. We had a great editorial team, Donlon, Anne, me, the late Joe Donlon and photographer Willie Farrell, under the leadership of Derek Cobbe. The weekly routine included covering the local district courts and meetings of the county council, the urban council, the VEC, the agriculture committee and even local parish committees. Ciaran Mullooly was a junior reporter in the *Longford Leader* at the time, and would help me navigate the bewildering maze of EU-imposed agricultural acronyms. In 2024 Ciaran, who spent thirty years as an RTÉ correspondent, was elected as an independent Irish MEP.

In those years if there was a meeting the junior hack was dispatched to cover it. A lot of them were boring and it challenged our reporting skills to eke out the newsworthy angles and produce readable copy for the public. In summer there were agricultural shows, ploughing matches and festivals. I liked the festivals the best. I also did plenty of human interest stories about ordinary people's lives. My first campaign, apart from covering rural crime in the

Leitrim Observer, was highlighting the appalling living conditions of Travellers on the halting site at the edge of Longford town.

In 1986 I answered an advert looking for two junior reporters with the *Sunday World*. I jumped at the chance of joining the country's most exciting tabloid. In many ways the broadsheet *Longford News* was as close to a tabloid as a provincial newspaper could get. I was told that a few hundred aspirant hacks had applied but in the end, much to my surprise, I got one of the jobs. I joined the paper in February 1987 with Cathy Kelly, a dear friend, who went on to become an international bestselling author. Under the guidance of our news editor, Sean Boyne, it was where I started the reporting on crime which has dominated my life ever since.

One of the unique features of working as a reporter is that you witness all human life in its most unvarnished form. It is a constant learning curve. Unlike any other area of the media crime reporters get close up and personal with the dark side of human nature. At the rough edge of history we see humanity at its rawest and most evil, reporting on violence, murder, tragedy, atrocity, greed and betrayal. Through the decades I investigated and exposed a fascinating and fearsome cast of characters – killers, paedophiles, rapists, armed robbers, drug traffickers, money launderers, fraudsters, extortionists and terrorists. To get around legal hurdles I started the tradition of giving them exotic sobriquets which contained a strong hint to their actual identities. In the process I made the criminals household names much to their often extreme annoyance.

I spent much of that time recording dramatic changes and seminal events as the underworld morphed from a motley collection of armed robbery gangs into a vast, multi-billion euro drug trafficking industry. Irish Crime Inc. is now a thriving international entity, with Irish narcos now dealing directly with the leaders of the most notorious cartels in the world, including those in Colombia and Mexico. When I joined the *Sunday World* in 1987 armed robbery was the stock and trade of organized crime. Within a decade it was exclusively narcotics, particularly cocaine, the Devil's Dandruff, which continues to be the fastest growing commodity on the market – either illicit or otherwise.

In the process I observed the old gangland ethics of the so-called 'ordinary decent criminal' being swept aside by a much more violent and treacherous breed of gangster for whom life was as cheap as a bag of cocaine. With so much money at stake, greed, treachery and betrayal replaced the concept of honour amongst thieves. All gangsters by their nature tend to be social Darwinists who believe that only the fittest, strongest and most ruthless get to survive and prosper.

When I started out there were three main Irish criminal gangs led by the General, the Monk and 'Factory John' Gilligan. Today there are at least thirty large narco groups at the apex of a hierarchy consisting of scores of smaller outfits in a sophisticated and well organized international distribution network. At the top of the pyramid are the cartels run by Irish ex-pats Christy Kinahan and his sons, and George Mitchell, the Penguin. In the process the narco virus has seeped out beyond the cities and poisoned the countryside. Drug dealers now sell their wares in every village and town across Ireland. Crime has become part of the fabric of society.

I discovered early on that the lynchpin of organized crime is the symbiotic relationship that exists between civil society and the underworld. The dangerous latter could not prosper without the ambivalent former. Law-abiding citizens' insatiable love of cocaine has generated an alternative economy and a new criminal subculture that has brought carnage and savagery in its wake. The drug dealer's customers, who comprise a large cohort from all walks of life, are cognitively detached from their inadvertent role in the rise of the godfathers and the violence that they abhor and fear. The problem has created another disturbing social phenomenon whereby the families of drug takers are intimidated into paying their children's debts.

The transition to the era of the narcos can be quantified in blood and misery. It created the new phenomenon of the gang war as the gun became the corporate tool of choice for the entrepreneurs vying for a share of the spoils.

In 1987 I covered my first gangland murder, that of a scrap dealer called Mel Cox who crossed swords with the family of Gerry Hutch, the Monk, whose life and crimes I have chronicled in articles and books. The criminal mastermind's rise to gangland infamy coincided with the start of my career in national journalism. He and his gang pulled the biggest armed robbery in the history of the State a few days before I was given a desk in the *Sunday World*. They hit a cash-in-transit security van and made off with the equivalent of €3.3 million today. From that point on I developed an enduring interest in the enigmatic godfather and his crimes.

Of the cast of characters I encountered through my journey covering crime, Gerry Hutch stands out as being the nearest thing to being honourable and decent you can get in the underworld. It doesn't mean he is clean as he has been connected to three gangland murders spanning forty years. Then there are the victims, mostly security staff, who were terrorized at gunpoint in the various heists. But I like to describe him as the least worst of them all.

The Cox murder, which had nothing to do with drugs, was the only gangland killing recorded in 1987. At the time I had no contacts to speak of as I was only finding my feet in a new world of cops and robbers. But from then on I gradually got to know gardai on the frontline, the people who knew better than anyone else what was actually going on. I met them in the courts and at conferences. In 1990 I was granted exclusive access to spend a fascinating day with the gardaí based at Store Street Station. I rode along in their squad cars as they raced between reports of robberies and assaults in and around O'Connell Street. When darkness fell I was in the local garda van as it was pelted with stones and bricks from the now demolished Sheriff Street flats. Some of the most remarkable and decent people I have met are members of An Garda Síochána. It helped get me hooked.

I also got to know criminals at the various levels of the gangland hierarchy. As I got better known on the crime beat, sources would make contact with information. People came forward for myriad reasons, from jilted lovers to gang members bearing grievances against their fellow mobsters. People would also come forward after reading a particular story to reveal other details.

In journalism protecting sources is sacrosanct. In crime journalism the responsibility is the difference between life and death. One of the criminals in this book, P. J. Judge, the Psycho, once plotted to have me kidnapped and tortured in order to identify who amongst his mob had been giving me inside information. Sources involved with gangsters put their lives and the security of their families at risk by telling what they know. The new murderous era of gangland has made it more hazardous than ever.

A decade after the Cox murder there was an average of twenty murders per year. By then I was immersed in the world of crime. Over that period I noticed a predictable pattern emerge in the life cycles of the average hoodlum. Ambitious low-level gang members who shoot their way to the top of the pile and become major players don't often retire at the top or die in their sleep. If they don't get busted by the police and sent to jail, they stay at the top for five or six years before falling foul of an even more violent and ambitious pretender to the throne. It is a paradigm for the dynamics of succession in a world where the only rule is that of survival.

The primal instincts of treachery and betrayal tend to be the root of most gang wars. Those same instincts sparked two of the worst gangland conflagrations I witnessed in all my years as a crime reporter.

The most recent was the mismatched Kinahan/Hutch feud in Dublin which claimed a total of eighteen lives, including two innocent bystanders. The vast majority of the killings, sixteen, were the work of the Kinahan cartel and their allies, in their attempt to wipe out the Hutch clan. It began in 2014 when Gary Hutch, the Monk's nephew, double-crossed his boss Daniel Kinahan by trying to have him whacked. When the assassination attempt failed a peace deal was hammered out between the cartel and Gerry Hutch so that his nephew's life was spared.

A year later Daniel Kinahan reneged on the agreement when he had Gary Hutch shot dead in Spain. The same day his sicarios went to kill Gary's gangster father, Patsy Hutch, but failed. Then Kinahan stepped over the line when he sent his hit men to execute the Monk. Cops and crime reporters knew that a seismic eruption of violence was inevitable. When it came, however, everyone was stunned by the ferocity of the unprecedented attack on the Kinahan cartel at the Regency Hotel, north Dublin, in February 2016. It included a five-man hit team, three of whom were dressed as Emergency Response Unit (ERU) cops brandishing AK-47 military assault rifles.

The equivalent of a terrorist spectacular was intended to wipe out the entire top tier of the cartel. However, the planned massacre turned out to be a failure when Daniel Kinahan and his top lieutenants escaped. One gang member, David Byrne, was shot dead. Equally unprecedented and shocking was the bloodbath that followed over the next two years. Kinahan and David Byrne's brother Liam – the gang leader in Dublin – unleashed a small army of hit men who murdered fourteen people. The people living in Dublin's north inner-city community where the Hutch family came from were terrorized in the process and the real ERU were deployed on the streets to keep the peace.

The Monk was acquitted in 2023 of involvement in the Regency attack and David Byrne's murder. He has resumed his carefree life in retirement which the row with the Kinahans had interrupted so violently but the madness has cost him dearly. He lost his brother, three nephews and his two closest friends.

The ongoing savagery of the Kinahans has proved another defining feature of the story of crime, which seems to get lost on even the cleverer godfathers: murders are bad for business. Gangland violence attracts more heat from the police than any other crime because it terrifies society and undermines the public's faith in the State's ability to protect them. The extraordinary garda response during the feud led to the imprisonment of over eighty members of the cartel in Ireland. Many of them were convicted on their own words as secret garda bugs recorded them plotting murders. The leadership of the gang's UK operations were also busted and locked away. Ultimately it focused international attention on the Kinahans' billion euro operation and their corrupt influence over international professional boxing.

They became pariahs confined to their desert bolthole in Dubai after the US authorities offered a bounty for information leading to the arrests and apprehension of Christy Kinahan and his two sons. It placed them at the top of the world's most wanted list of narcos. In September 2024 the Irish State was using diplomatic and police connections to secure the extradition of Daniel Kinahan and at least one other member of the cartel. I look forward to writing the end of that story when it inevitably arrives.

The war that raged for over ten years between the sadistic McCarthy/Dundon mob and the Keane/Collopys in Limerick was even more horrendous than the Kinahan/Hutch feud. I spent a lot of time in Limerick over the years and at one point the wry joke in the *Sunday World* newsroom was that I had achieved my initial ambition of becoming a war correspondent.

In the midst of the mayhem the Dundons earned the deserved distinction of being the most savage creatures in gangland history. I labelled them Murder Inc., and wrote a book of the same name. As part of their campaign of terror they deliberately murdered five innocent people either because they got in their way or, with the shocking execution of young mother Baiba Saulite, simply as a personal favour for another gangster pal. I was covering a real life horror show. The murder spree claimed over twenty lives. In both cases whole communities were terrorized and scores more adults and children were left injured and psychologically traumatized. The war also produced an accidental hero in Steve Collins, the extraordinarily brave father of Roy Collins, another innocent victim who was murdered by the Dundons in 2009. The murder was revenge for Steve testifying in court against Wayne Dundon, jailed for seven years for threatening to kill Steve's nephew in the family pub in 2004. Steve galvanized the people of Limerick when he organized a huge march, demanding an end to the mobsters' grip on the city. His actions forced the Government to introduce a raft of hard-hitting anti-gang legislation and moved gangland cases into the non-jury Special Criminal Court to avoid the intimidation of jurors. I was honoured to have been able to help Steve by highlighting his campaign. He and his family remain dear friends.

The murder of entirely innocent, decent people was the starkest example of how the new breed no longer observed behavioural boundaries and didn't care who they hit. The gangs are no longer afraid of the public being part of the collateral damage.

The journey through the evolving crime world has been fascinating and rewarding. It could also be emotionally disturbing, depressing and angering, especially to hear the harrowing stories of the innumerable, often forgotten, victims whose lives were irrevocably devastated by evil deeds inflicted by bad people. I also got to shine a light into the other dark recesses of society where evil hides, through the experiences of victims of domestic abuse, rape and child abuse.

The most disturbing story I ever covered about child sex abuse happened in 1992. A private investigator, Liam Brady, had been hired by a company to secretly record phone calls made by an employee, a seemingly respectable man, that they suspected of being involved in fraud. What the tapes revealed was much more disturbing – the man was part of a paedophile ring. In the recorded conversations he could be heard talking to another man as they discussed abusing children as young as two and three years of age. The subject matter was the most vile and depraved that I have ever encountered.

The gardaí launched a major investigation after Brady reported his findings to them. In one particularly creepy recording the man was talking to his teenage daughter. And while there was nothing explicitly said in the conversation I still recall instantly thinking that he was also abusing her. It was sickening. A file on the case was later sent to the DPP by gardaí attached to a special unit in Garda HQ but it was decided that there wasn't enough evidence to sustain a criminal charge. The secret recordings could not be used in the case.

A few days after we published the story I was a guest on a popular late-night radio phone-in show with Chris Barry on FM104 where we ran a few clips from the tapes but with the voices disguised. The lines to the show were jammed as hundreds of men and women called to relate their own horrific stories of being abused as children. It was a steep learning experience for me. I remember standing in a queue in the bank a week later when it suddenly dawned that any one of the respectable looking men in front of me could also be child abusers hiding in plain sight. As a parent the experience made me very protective of my kids.

Another investigation which I am most proud of was exposing as a serial paedophile a major godfather called Stephen 'Rossi' Walsh in 2006 by telling the stories of his terrified female victims who he raped as children. Walsh was a dangerous criminal who had been a member of the General's gang. He had also been involved in arson, extortion and accident fraud. Everyone was terrified of him. The publicity gave the victims the courage to testify against him. He was subsequently convicted and sentenced to over twenty years in prison. Writing about the stories of such cruelty and desolation made it hard to remain impartial or detached. And there were other reasons why it became more personal than business.

———

Since the mid-1990s Irish crime journalism has become a hazardous profession, following the gangland murders of two colleagues and friends, Veronica Guerin and Martin O'Hagan. In 2019 the name of journalist Lyra McKee was added to the list. The threat of violence, intimidation and death became the popular course of action for criminals like John Gilligan who sought to silence the messengers.

The crime beat is the only area of the media where journalists run the risk of being targeted by dangerous people as a result of what they write. On more than a few occasions the menace of gangland violence came too close for comfort to my own door, as it has done to other crime reporters. I had a few close shaves but thanks to a combination of survival instincts, luck and timely interventions and protection from the gardaí, I lived to tell the story. I hold the rather dubious distinction of being the only journalist in the country to receive permanent police protection for over a decade. (See Chapter 14.)

Crime journalists, myself included, have also come in for more criticism than any other area of the trade: from politicians, academics, other (begrudging) journalists and, of course, the criminals themselves. Vincent Browne once wrote: 'crime journalism is the lowest form of the species.' At the time he was upset by the fact that we'd accused Patrick 'Dutchy' Holland of being the hit man who murdered Veronica Guerin without any evidence. Holland *was* the assassin. The only reason there was no evidence was that witnesses were too scared to testify.

The most common quibble is that we glamorize the mobsters and the mobs. It is nothing new. In 1837 Charles Dickens, one of the first journalists to write about crime, was castigated when he published *Oliver Twist*. The critics accused the greatest literary genius in history of glorifying crime. It's nice company to be in.

Criminals by their nature prefer to reside in the shadows, well out of the spotlight of media attention. One of the lessons I first learned in the years spent covering the story of the General, Martin Cahill, is that gangsters will do anything to preserve their anonymity and avoid exposure in the media. Cahill never went anywhere without his mask.

Being unidentifiable and anonymous provides a layer of protection to the gangster. Like vampires being caught in the sunlight, media coverage can be potentially disastrous. Exposing crime and criminals has an important role in a free society. Public attention on a criminal and their exploits makes life difficult and gives the police greater impetus to come down hard on them. By and large most of the leaders of the gangs are men. There are no known godmothers in Ireland. Testosterone is an important ingredient in the criminal psyche.

When intimidation doesn't work they resort to their lawyers or complain to the Press Council about some perceived infringement of the codes of ethics. I've lost count of the number of threatened legal actions and complaints I've received. The vast majority of them went nowhere. Over the years a number of major criminals applied unsuccessfully to the High Court seeking gagging orders against me. They attacked me on websites, in poster campaigns and even on RTÉ's *Liveline*. (See Chapter 15.)

These days criminals mostly scurry around like rats in the sewers of social media from where they spew lies and attack the credibility of their accusers. When they go on the offensive you know that you have done something right. As a crime journalist I have always believed the old adage: you only get flak when you're over the target.

Daniel Kinahan was a prime example of using the social media platforms to spout lies. He even made a ludicrous YouTube 'movie' to claim that the 2016 attack on the Regency Hotel by the Hutch gang was the product of a grand conspiracy involving the Irish Government, the gardaí and the media to keep the Kinahans' favourite political party, Sinn Féin, out of power. Sinn Féin has always wanted to abolish the Special Criminal Court because over the years it was the State's main weapon against their terrorism. Kinahan even commissioned an online 'book', written by some anonymous individual, in which amongst others, I was named as being one of the conspirators. At the time he was particularly exercised by a story I had written for the *Sunday Independent*. It came from the Hutch clan and outlined Gary Hutch's knowledge of how Kinahan had double crossed and murdered former business associates in Europe. Daniel had tried to cover up the killings as the work of Russian mobsters.

I have also learned a lot about the psychology of gangsters over the years. One of the things that always fascinated me is how men who control criminal organizations through fear and violence can be terribly thin-skinned when it comes to media coverage. It is a trait shared by every villain I ever encountered, regardless of whether he is a street-level thug or a clever international crime lord. If they can't lash out physically or issue death threats the vast majority of criminals will instinctively play the victim. Criminal psychologists would describe it as the process of rationalizing their behaviour and the classic defence mechanism of a narcissist.

Daniel Kinahan's father Christy Kinahan was, like his son, a self-pitying mobster. But even the imperious, well-educated, self-styled gangland sophisticate who speaks several languages proved to be a sensitive soul. I bestowed him with the sobriquet the Dapper Don, in recognition of his dress sense and elevated position in the hierarchy of mobsters. For several years I tracked his trajectory as he became one of the top drug traffickers in the world, highlighting the cartel's controlling role in organized crime and its international operations.

Kinahan had proved to be an elusive target over the years as he went to great lengths to avoid reporters. I was the first journalist to doorstep the international mob boss when I finally caught up with him in Belgium in 2009. I was waiting for him with a photographer as he emerged from a court in Antwerp. He had just been released on bail after being held in custody for a year while the authorities investigated money laundering offences. A year earlier I had gone to Antwerp to exclusively cover the story of his arrest. The conspiracy included a football club and a number of Belgian police officers. The court had found him guilty and sentenced him to four years. We had been tipped off that he was going to be released because, in the strange Belgian justice system, a felon only has to serve a third of his sentence and Kinahan had served most of that already. The deal was that the authorities would contact him when it was time for him to go in and finish the final months of the sentence.

As he walked with his lawyer on the street I sidled up and introduced myself. The Dapper Don went white in the face but showed no other emotion. He was much taller than me and a known expert in judo so, in the event that he knocked me unconscious, I warned photographer Padraig O'Reilly to 'get the picture, then call the ambulance'.

As I walked alongside I asked Kinahan what he thought of being classified as one of Europe's biggest cocaine dealers. Clearly angry at the unwarranted intrusion, he sullenly replied in a cultured European accent: 'You do not tell the truth. You take information from the police and then write false stories based on that information about me. Therefore I will not be giving you an interview.'

Then he began accusing me of being a drug abuser and hiring prostitutes in some part of Spain I had never heard of. Criminals have a narrow imagination when it comes to hurling abuse and project their own moral code. In a spontaneous reaction, and a moment of madness, I shoved the godfather of international crime with my shoulder to see how he'd take it. I was recording him on my phone as I said: 'Christy, for all your sophistication you're no different from all the other scumbags... can you not come up with something more original?' My life has been punctuated with reckless moments.

I said I wasn't there to hear about my imagined bad habits, I was there for his side of the story, asking him: 'Isn't it time that you put the record straight?'

The Dapper Don said nothing more and walked off. I was delighted that I got what I came for. His pictures were plastered all over the front page of the *Sunday World* the following weekend.

Eamon Dunne, the serial gangland killer I dubbed the Don was another mobster who felt terribly sorry for himself. Over a period of four years Dunne waded through a river of blood to become one of the most feared figures in gangland. The Don was directly responsible for fifteen murders during his strike for power, including that of his former boss Martin 'Marlo' Hyland and of innocent trainee plumber Anthony Campbell, who was in the wrong place at the wrong time. Dunne had also been involved in the organization of the murder of Baiba Saulite.

On 20 January 2009 the paranoiac murdered his best friend and fellow gangster Graham McNally. It was the third murder in the space of a few weeks that he had either ordered or done in person. By that stage he had slain ten former associates and enemies. As gangland's most prolific killer he was certainly worth an interview. The following day I phoned him to ask about his role in McNally's killing and the other murders. I'd got his number from a source and decided to chance my arm.

The Don was furious at the intrusion into his privacy and demanded to know where I got his number. I glibly explained that I couldn't reveal my sources lest they suffer the same fate as his other victims which of course was perfectly true.

Surprisingly he opted to stay on the line as I recorded his every word. Dunne's responses were typically defensive and evasive. He denied any involvement in the murders and diverted to complain bitterly about the media coverage of his activities, especially the stuff that had appeared in the *Sunday World*.

Dunne, the serial killer and most feared gangster in the country at the time, put on a human mask and accused me of putting his life at risk. I got a very illuminating interview which bordered on parody. 'I feel that I am now a target over all of this. I feel unsafe. I don't know anything about anyone getting clipped,' Dunne moaned, as he blamed the media and the cops for his predicament.

When I asked if he was aware that his name had been linked to the various murders Dunne angrily replied in a self-pitying rant:

> I didn't murder anyone. What do you mean my name is coming
> up everywhere as a suspect? I am aware that I am hurt and
> upset over my friend being killed. I think it is very insensitive
> of you to be ringing me today after my friend has been killed. I
> am fearful for myself and my family. I don't want my friends or

his [McNally's] family to think that I had something to do with it. No one has come to me and said to my face: 'I am accusing you.' I didn't clip [shoot] anyone. I did not murder my friend Mr McNally. He was a good personal friend of mine. How did you get my number and where did you get all the information about me?

Dunne eventually agreed to a face-to-face meeting with me but he wouldn't take any other calls. A few days later he went to the courts seeking an injunction to stop the gardaí leaking stories about him to the media. Dunne, who fancied himself as a barrack room lawyer, claimed that there was a conspiracy between the press and the police to damage his 'safety and integrity'. I ran our interview with Dunne on the front page and catalogued his astonishing death toll in the same week. I gave him the nickname the Don and was glad to have contributed to his woes.

In the months following the call the Don ordered the murder of another five associates. The dead included Christy Gilroy, one of his own hit men who vanished in Spain in February 2009 after carrying out the double murders of Dunne's rival Michael 'Roly' Cronin and his friend James Maloney on 7 January. I broke the story of how Gilroy was shot dead and buried in an unmarked grave on the Costa del Sol. He had been killed by another notorious hit man I later exposed, Eric 'Lucky' Wilson.

In the stories I revealed how the Don was becoming more unhinged and unpredictable. When he took the macabre, prophetic step of ordering his own casket and grave I got the tip off and shared the news with the readers. Some of my information came from garda sources and also from lower ranking criminals in Dunne's orbit who were frightened and sick of him. Even criminals like to use the media sometimes to get the story out. My experience told me the Don was running out of road.

Dunne had been an important business partner of the Kinahan cartel and their large Dublin network. But gardaí were clamping down hard on the drug trafficking operation as a result of his murder rampage. Dunne was becoming a pariah in the underworld. His mentor at the time, Eamon Kelly, stood away from him. The veteran gangster, who was one of the pioneers of the original gangland and also a mentor to the Monk as he started out, knew that his protégé was running out of friends. I had been covering the story of Kelly's life ever since I first began reporting crime. He was the first Irish gangster to be convicted of importing a large quantity of cocaine in the early nineties, long before the drug became universally popular. Around the same time I tried to get an interview with him but he walked away. When I became crime editor of the *News of the World* in 2010 I had Kelly photographed in the street and named him as the Don's top advisor.

It was only a matter of who got to Dunne first: the cops or his own ilk. I later revealed how the Don crossed the line when he began threatening people like Gerry Hutch's best friend Noel Duggan, a likeable rogue who was the top tobacco smuggler in the country, suitably dubbed Mr Kingsize. The Kinahans and their associates, including Gary Hutch, had resolved that Dunne would have to be stopped before he tried to kill one of them. In the traditions of gangland people like Eamon Dunne don't get sacked, locked away or banished. To borrow a phrase often used by Gerry Hutch, Dunne 'had to go'. On 23 April 2010 a hit man shot him three times in the face and head as he sat with friends in a pub in Cabra, north Dublin. In a completely separate set of circumstances his mentor Eamon Kelly was gunned down by a dissident republican gang two years later.

The deaths of the veteran villain and his savage protégé exemplified the predictable nature of life and death in gangland in the roughest draft of history, especially the one that has evolved since the start of the twenty-first century. Gangland has an alternative ecosystem where there is no governance or central authority. Although it did not exist in the seventeenth century, the writings of Thomas Hobbes, the father of modern political philosophy, can be interpreted through the prism of modern gangland. In his book *Leviathan,* published in 1651, Hobbes postulated that in the absence of a lawful authority, where each person would have the right to everything they wanted, civil society would descend into a 'war of all against all'. In such a world life would be one of 'continual fear and danger of violent death' where the life of man would be 'nasty, brutish and short'.

Over the decades I have chronicled the nasty, brutish and short lives of many criminals who lived outside the realms of civil society. The most infamous anarchist of them all was also the one who confirmed my chosen route in journalism.

His name was Martin Cahill, the crime boss they called the General.

CHAPTER TWO

───

UNMASKING THE GENERAL

We had been sitting in the van for what felt like an eternity: watching and waiting, poised for action. Several hours had dragged by since the commencement of the secret surveillance operation at 4 a.m. on a chilly October morning. As dawn broke and the south Dublin suburb came to life, its citizens were oblivious to our presence as they hurried past, distracted by the cold and the humdrum routine of life.

Being unobtrusive was central to the plan. Attracting unwanted attention would blow our cover, especially if someone called the cops to report two men lurking suspiciously in a van for hours on a quiet leafy side street. Since taking up position on Oxford Road in Ranelagh close to the target's home, neither of us had dared move even for a coffee or a toilet break – it wasn't an option. To mitigate the basic necessities we had come equipped – with a hot flask and a plastic bottle.

Experience had taught us that a momentary lapse in focus could result in missing the most elusive of targets – one who possessed an uncanny sixth sense for secret watchers. The self-inflicted privations and the monotonous hours spent sitting in the same cramp-inducing positions would be worthwhile if we bagged the one scoop that had eluded the Irish media for years – to unmask the hooded bogeyman of organized crime.

That was exactly what I planned to do that day along with my colleague and long-time friend Liam O'Connor – aka the Loc. O'Connor was a tough, experienced snapper who had been working for the *Sunday World* since shortly after the country's home-grown cheeky tabloid rolled off the presses to shake up the stuffy Irish newspaper industry.

Liam's first ever assignment was to capture the horrific carnage and devastation left in the immediate wake of the Dublin bombings of 1974 that left twenty-three dead and hundreds injured and maimed. O'Connor had no compunction doing tricky, dangerous jobs or spending long hours on surveillance which was why we partnered together throughout my career with the paper. Photographer Padraig O'Reilly would also become an integral part of our small, three-member team. Over the decades we unmasked many godfathers.

The target of our clandestine escapade this time was one Martin Joseph Cahill, the undisputed godfather of the Irish criminal underworld, public enemy number one, better known by his sobriquet, the General – and one of the reasons why I became immersed in crime reporting.

It was two years since Cahill had first become a household name after a groundbreaking TV documentary on RTÉ's *Today Tonight* introduced the Irish public to the General. It exposed him as the ruthless boss of the most prolific armed crime gang yet to exist in Ireland. The programme was the first time that organized crime had been placed so dramatically front and centre in the public spotlight. Cahill and his associates were filmed in the streets being followed by the masked cops from a special overt surveillance unit called the Tango Squad. The criminals all wore masks too. The scenes were unprecedented on Irish TV. It was watched by over a million people, turning the hooded gangster into a household name overnight – and I was hooked on the story.

When he was confronted by reporter Brendan O'Brien, Cahill was surprisingly loquacious and mischievous. He denied he was the General. When O'Brien asked who he thought the General was, the eponymous anti-hero replied: 'Some army officer maybe… sure the way the country is these days ya wouldn't know.' From then on he was referred to as 'Martin Cahill, who denies he is the crime boss known as the General'.

The documentary's release coincided with an unprecedented high-profile police surveillance operation by the Tango Squad that had played out on the streets of Dublin's southside over several months in 1988.

In January 1988 Cahill and six of his top lieutenants – Eamon Daly, Martin Foley, Seamus 'Shavo' Hogan, Noel Lynch, Christy Dutton and John Foy – had been targeted by the new Tango Squad. The unit derived its name from the radio phonetics for T (target). Cahill was Tango One. The maverick garda unit consisted of young enthusiastic cops with orders to antagonize and harass the mobsters around the clock. Everywhere the General and his men went, each one was closely followed by up to six hooded cops. When the seven targeted villains were on the move at the same time over forty cops went with them. Any time Cahill was at home the Tango Squad members would sit outside while others would loiter on the walls at the back.

The mob, Irish society or even the gardaí had never seen the likes of the Tango Squad before. Rather than going to ground Cahill, true to form, had gone on the offensive once the operation started. Despite the intense police attention he ordered the murder of Ned Ryan, the senior detective, who had been a thorn in his side throughout his criminal career. Cahill blamed Ryan for the Tango Squad's interference in his life. Two hitmen were sent to murder the officer on the night of 29 January 1988 but aborted the mission when they spotted a detective in the house brandishing an Uzi submachine gun. Gardaí had received information about the hit in the nick of time and prevented the murder.

Members of the Tango Squad were openly threatened by Cahill's mob and some were forced to move their families for safety at the height of the operation. In one altercation Martin 'the Viper' Foley smashed the jaw of a detective and was later jailed for two years. The greens at the garda golf club in Stackstown in Rathfarnham, south Dublin, were dug up and tyres were slashed on several cars belonging to club members who were all cops. Cahill later openly taunted the cops in the street, saying he had no problem 'getting a hole in one in Stackstown'.

After four months of high drama the surveillance operation was stood down and switched to undercover, led by the Serious Crime Squad. By then gardaí had effectively smashed the General's gang.

I had joined the *Sunday World* as a junior reporter a year before Cahill's exposure as the *capo dei capi* of Ireland's gangland and the establishment of the Tango Squad. The General had me captivated. His story exemplified the theory that crime reporting certainly is the roughest draft of history. The more I learned about him and the underworld he controlled, the more I wanted to know. It became addictive and all consuming. The godfather had effectively opened a portal that led me into an alien subterranean world full of drug dealers, killers, cops and robbers. Crime would dominate the course of my life and career after that.

Pursuing the General's story would also lead to the first death threats I was to receive over the years that followed. From then on threats from criminals became an occupational hazard.

My rapt interest in Cahill and crime also influenced my enduring interest in criminology. I wanted to better understand the sociology of crime and the environmental and psychological factors that had created such a bizarre and terrifying character. A month before our stakeout in Ranelagh I had started a post-grad diploma in criminology and many years later went on to do a masters.

Finding out everything I could about the General fuelled my interest. By 1990 the ruthless crime boss had been responsible for some of the most brutal and outrageous offences yet recorded in Ireland. To the police, who had been on his trail for many years, Cahill was the most hardened, sadistic gangster they'd ever encountered, while for his victims the General was synonymous with violence, intimidation and fear. In the underworld he was seen as an inspiration and a hero.

Cahill was one of the founding godfathers of the new gangland; the *eminence grise* of a generation of opportunistic young villains who emerged in the early 1970s to become professional armed robbers and international drug traffickers – people such as the Dunnes, John Gilligan, the Hutches, the Mitchells, the Cunninghams and Christy Kinahan. The Dunne brothers had first introduced Cahill to armed robbery in 1974 and he never looked back. Up to then he and his brothers had been prolific burglars.

In the pantheon of infamous villains Cahill still stands out as the one who singlehandedly ushered in a new era of violent organized crime in Ireland, long before senior police had begun to acknowledge that the phenomenon even existed.

Always pushing at the edges of what he could get away with, Cahill set a high bar for others who followed in his footsteps. He preserved his position as an untouchable gang boss by inflicting violence on other criminals or anyone else, including State officials, who dared cross paths with him. In one particularly infamous case Cahill nailed a gang member to a floor because he suspected the minion of stealing some of the proceeds from a heist.

The eccentric gangster was also unique amongst his peers in that he deliberately set out to do battle against the gardaí and the State. His campaign against the Irish authorities included bombing, shooting and attempted murder. Cahill was Ireland's first narco-terrorist.

Thirty years after his violent demise at the business end of an IRA assassin's gun the Irish public still recognize his name. The notorious hood was immortalized in popular culture after his life and crimes were portrayed in no less than three major movies. I also wrote the bestselling biography of his life and crimes, *The General*, which was adapted for a movie by John Boorman featuring Brendan Gleeson. No other Irish criminal has ever attracted so much interest.

The public's fascination with Cahill was initially prompted by the way that he always hid his face behind balaclava masks. When the glare of the media spotlight focused on him in 1988, Cahill, a portly figure in his trademark anorak, turned it into a comic spectacle to demonstrate his defiance and contempt, dropping his trousers and showing off his *Mickey Mouse*™ shorts. Cahill was ensuring that no one, apart from his family and inner criminal circle, could recognize him in the street.

I was one of the many reporters who pursued Cahill for an interview in the late 1980s. I had approached the masked joker several times on the street but without success. I was told to fuck off or had the door slammed in my face on the numerous occasions that I called to his front door. Letters sent to him requesting a meeting went unanswered.

On one occasion, however, that I approached him for an interview I asked, as Cahill walked away, what he thought a criminal was. He stopped and thought for a moment. 'The only real criminal is a man who abuses kids,' he replied from behind the hand covering his face, before walking on in silence. Together with Liam O'Connor and Padraig O'Reilly, I had followed him in the hope of getting his picture without the mask but to no avail.

By the time of our latest attempt to secure his picture, the image of Cahill in the trademark anorak and balaclava had burned into the national psyche as a symbol of the new world of organized crime. He personified Carl Jung's observations on the public's fascination with criminals:

> With what pleasure we read newspaper reports of crime. A true criminal becomes a popular figure because he unburdens in no small degree the consciences of his fellow men, for now they know once more where evil is to be found.

In 1990 the only picture of Cahill in the public domain was a photocopy of an out of focus black and white image which had been taken several years before. His hidden face created the aura of sinister mystique that underlined his status as gangland's bogeyman-in-chief. In many ways the picture *was* the story. Everyone wanted to see the face of the elusive General. I was determined to be the first.

The only chance we had of getting the picture was to catch the ever-vigilant mobster completely off guard. Having consulted garda contacts in the famous Tango Squad, we reckoned we had only one opportunity of getting the scoop that everyone wanted. The key lay in his tangled love life which, like every other aspect of Cahill's anarchic character, was complex. While he no more resembled an ardent lover than he did a swaggering gang boss, he shared the love of two women – his wife Frances and her younger sister Tina Lawless. The bizarre three-way consensual relationship ultimately produced nine children. Small, chubby and bald with a comb-over and wearing dirty jeans and stained tee-shirts, Cahill was no Dapper Don or designer-clad Monk but the sisters were happy to share the man they both loved. As far as the participants in gangland's strangest love triangle were concerned there was nothing complicated about their domestic arrangements.

Cahill never masked the fact that he lived in his own parallel universe, a sub-cultural world with its own set of rules and standards. From the early stages of my research it became apparent that rejecting society's codes of behaviour was integral to Cahill's philosophy in life, which was best summed up by his favourite song – 'Que Sera Sera!' In his world view social morals were dictated by a hypocritical establishment ruled by corrupt politicians and a perverted church. In any event Cahill, his wife and his sister-in-law never broadcast their relationship and were intensely private and protective of their offspring. In the years before his violent demise in 1994 I found that other gangsters were particularly coy when it came to talking about the bizarre relationship. Other criminals knew better than to pry and treated it as a taboo subject for health and safety reasons.

Members of the Tango Squad had discovered the unorthodox living arrangements two years before as they followed Cahill around every day. Information about the bizarre *ménage a trois* had inevitably leaked out to journalists. For legal reasons none of the media had written about it until after his death when underworld sources were finally brave enough to confirm the story. One of them was John Traynor, Cahill's confidant, friend and adviser who later became one of my sources for *The General*. An accomplished fraudster and career criminal, Traynor had been a friend of Cahill's from childhood. Nicknamed the Coach by Veronica Guerin, the duplicitous Traynor conspired with John Gilligan when he plotted her murder in 1996. Traynor recalled how he once mentioned to Cahill that his love life was the subject of gossip amongst journalists and cops. The eccentric gangster said that he was happy to use it as a psychological tool to confuse his enemies. 'The thing is that it has fucked up the Guards' heads and they don't know what's what or who's who,' he grinned broadly.

The only predictable pattern in Cahill's daily routine was dividing his time between the two women. His wife Frances, neé Lawless, resided in a four-bedroom detached house in upmarket Cowper Downs in Rathmines, south Dublin, which Cahill bought with cash stolen in a bank robbery. The quiet estate was close to where the Lawless and Cahill families had grown up next door to each other in a rundown flats complex called Hollyfield Buildings that had been demolished years before. Tina Lawless lived one mile down the road in a cluster of corporation houses at the end of a small cul de sac called Swan Grove, off Oxford Road in Ranelagh.

To confuse matters even more, the corporation house was officially rented to Cahill and his wife Frances. The home in Cowper Downs was in Tina's name. When he wasn't out robbing

Cahill spent the night in Swan Grove with Tina and the rest of the day with Frances at Cowper Downs. The *Today Tonight* TV crew had followed Cahill as he moved between the two addresses. We knew from our contacts that he normally left Swan Grove around midday but the time could vary.

That October morning, the plan was pretty straight forward. We hired a red Hiace van and parked it on Oxford Road so that the side door faced the entrance to Swan Grove. Liam sat in the back with a long lens at the ready. I took up position in the front passenger seat watching the entrance over my left shoulder. We placed reflective silver film over the glass in the doors to prevent unwanted inquisitors looking in, and the side door was left slightly ajar for a quicker opening. When Cahill appeared I would alert Liam when the moment was right to open the door and take the snap. If all went to plan Cahill would be looking straight into the camera lens – hopefully maskless.

The difficulty was that Cahill's house was out of sight from our position which meant that once he drove out of the cul de sac and turned onto Oxford Road we would have as little as twenty seconds to snap him. But it was also an advantage. Before he emerged into the sunlight the shadowy godfather always checked for watchers. If no one was there he tended to get into the car without the balaclava, although it was always in his pocket. In fact he carried several of them just in case the cops swiped it off his head, as they often did.

I had done a discreet recce up the cul de sac when we'd arrived at 4 a.m. and confirmed that Cahill's red Honda car was parked outside. Now all we had to do was sit and wait. Although still the country's most wanted gangster Cahill had not been active for several months and had dropped out of the headlines. He was keeping a low profile and therefore unlikely to be on his guard against journalists trying to get his picture. The fall off in his activity had been due to the success of the garda operation two years earlier which resulted in the capture of all of his key lieutenants. By October 1990 over a dozen members of Cahill's gang were serving long prison sentences.

The last time Cahill had been involved in a major crime was ten months earlier on 8 January 1990, when he and two accomplices robbed the Allied Irish Bank branch in Ranelagh village, a short walk from Swan Grove. Cahill shot an unarmed garda who was pursuing him on foot after the raid. Garda John Moore was hit in the arm by one of Cahill's bullets. The officer also suffered a flesh wound to the leg when he was shot by Cahill's brother, Eddie, before the pair made good their escape. The young cop had been extremely lucky. I later interviewed the injured garda about his near death experience. Some years later while I was researching Cahill's biography it emerged how lucky John Moore had actually been. The General had aimed to fire another shot at the garda's chest but the gun's trigger broke off just as he squeezed it. If it hadn't malfunctioned the General would have added capital murder to his expansive criminal CV.

There was no evidence to charge Cahill or his accomplices. There wasn't even enough on which to justify arresting him for questioning. Eddie Cahill, who was on bail at the time, was subsequently jailed for possession of heroin. John Traynor would later tell me how the crime boss confided to him that the close call had convinced him it was time to stop taking part in robberies and confine himself to the planning instead. While desperately trying to outrun Garda Moore, Cahill said he'd promised himself: 'I'm packin' in this fuckin' game. If I get away I'll never rob a fuckin' bank again.'

The years the General had spent gorging himself on cakes, fizzy drinks and curries had taken a toll on his health. Even though he didn't drink, smoke or take drugs, he was unfit, overweight and suffering from diabetes. Aged forty he realized it was a younger villain's game. Events elsewhere had also given him reason to believe that his life as a 'blagger' or armed robber was coming to an end. In the months before the stakeout I had witnessed another piece of Irish history with the violent debut of a deadly new garda squad called the Emergency Response Unit (ERU) which shot dead three armed robbers following bank heists. It convinced Cahill and his fellow blaggers that holding up banks was too dangerous and marked the beginning of the shift from armed robberies to narcotics as the stock and trade of organized crime. (See Chapter 4.)

Martin Cahill didn't need his wily sixth sense to figure out that it was time to retire. In his paranoia he began to believe that if he ever came face to face with the ERU they'd shoot first and ask questions later. Perhaps he was right.

It was little wonder that Cahill had been keeping his head down by the time we were holed up trying to get his picture. Having lost so many of his top men and with mounting garda successes against the armed robbery gangs Cahill had been taking time out to reorganize his business in light of the new world order. As we waited for him we hoped that the hiatus had lulled him into a false sense of security.

Cahill finally emerged from Swan Grove around 2 p.m. – ten hours into our surveillance when we were about to abort. His car turned out of the cul de sac and slowly came towards us. I could see the outline of his head and his hair jutting out around his head – he wasn't wearing a mask. When Cahill stopped to check for oncoming traffic he was a few feet away from us.

Liam opened the door, the camera clicking feverishly. For a brief moment Cahill appeared to freeze behind the wheel – perhaps initially believing that some old enemy had come to close his eyes. It would have been a perfect ambush. But he quickly composed himself and drove off at speed down Oxford Road.

In the excitement of the moment we decided to give chase. I jumped into the driver seat and quickly turned the van around. At the junction with Charleston Road Cahill stopped for oncoming traffic, giving us enough time to catch up with him. He then drove up Charleston Road towards Rathmines. At the next junction he jumped the traffic lights, turning onto Palmerston Road in a bid to lose us. We stayed with him. He jammed on the brakes a number of times to force us to rear-end him, a stunt he had often pulled with the police. It would have been a wonderful opportunity to sue us and the *Sunday World* for whiplash – and also to get to know us for future reference.

As the small convoy continued up the road I drove alongside Cahill's car as the Loc hung out the side door, snapping away. Cahill had donned his balaclava and pulled the hood of his anorak over it for good measure. On at least three occasions the General suddenly swerved towards us to force a collision with oncoming cars. The chase continued until he turned into Cowper Downs, heading for his second home. We broke off and returned to the office in Terenure, south Dublin, to assess how we had done.

In hindsight the escapade was both reckless and naive. We had momentarily scared the life out of the most dangerous gangster in Ireland and he would not appreciate that. As an impetuous young reporter I didn't count the inherent risk of annoying such a dangerous hoodlum. It never featured as a concern. It was all about getting the exclusive story – and it was exciting. Over subsequent decades chasing the story got me into plenty of hot water. By the time that I realized that it was a very dangerous profession, and I had risked the safety of my family, I was too involved to go back.

While the plan worked out perfectly we failed to achieve the mission objective and Cahill's anonymity remained intact. The camera could not penetrate the reflection of the autumn clouds on the windscreen of his car. Nature had conspired to help the gang boss. Nevertheless the operation hadn't been a complete waste of time.

As he hung out the van door Liam had captured a striking image that was worthy of the front page. In the picture Cahill was behind the wheel looking straight at the camera. Through the narrow slit in the balaclava his eyes stared directly into the lens. It was a perfect illustration for my feature about the life and crimes of the faceless crime boss. It would sell a lot of newspapers.

My brilliant news editor and mentor Sean Boyne had encouraged me to bring together all the strands of Cahill's story from the information we had about him at the time which came from sources I had built up over the previous few years. They were mostly gardaí who knew him best and also members of the underworld. Both before and after the stakeout whenever I met sources about other stories I always asked them about the General. I collated every piece of information, no matter how insignificant. I also got his criminal record and talked to some of the victims of his heists.

The information already in the public domain thanks to *Today Tonight* was a huge help. Sean Boyne was a superb journalist who had been the lynchpin of the paper since its launch in 1973 and even came up with its iconic name, the *Sunday World*. In his role as news editor he was the one who encouraged me to cover crime.

In the end our efforts came to nothing. The story was spiked because of the climate of fear that Cahill had created. Sean had cleared the feature and sent it on to the lawyers to check it for libel as per newsroom procedure. The first indication that there was a difficulty came after it was sent up to one of the senior editors at the paper. He sent the copy back a number of times, each time demanding that parts be cut. The lawyers we had at the time were extremely cautious and risk averse. They also wanted sections excised, even though the offending material was based on fact and was clearly not libelous. It had also been reported by *Today Tonight* with no issues.

Eventually, what had initially been intended to fill a two-page spread had shrunken to the size of an anodyne page filler that really meant nothing. Even the picture had been dropped. It was all done under the guise that the story was legally dangerous. I later discovered that the senior editor deliberately spooked the already nervous lawyers because he had decided the story would never see the light of day.

We argued that the information was not libellous and was based on Cahill's record. He could not sue because he would have to testify in court and answer questions he didn't want to address. Taking a legal action against the paper would also mean he was taking the media coverage seriously and he would never be seen to do that.

When I was called into the executive's office I hoped that our arguments had won them over. To my astonishment I was severely reprimanded for going after the godfather and potentially drawing his ire down on the newspaper. As I saw it I was being carpeted for doing the job I was paid to do. For a while it appeared that my career as a crime reporter was to be short lived. He ranted on about the fact that 'this Cahill fellah' is very dangerous' and posed a threat to the staff of the *Sunday World*. He said that Cahill could 'have the printing presses burned down' and recited as corroboration the litany of major crimes I had intended sharing with our readers that week. I later discovered that this would not have happened because Cahill knew people who worked in the print hall. He would never deny them their livelihood.

It became apparent that what the senior executive feared most was the prospect of having his tyres slashed. After the Tango Squad operation whenever the General was arrested or searched or generally pissed off by the police he would remind them in a soft Dublin brogue: 'You know I will carry out my usual peaceful protest tonight over this.' The warnings would inevitably be followed by a tyre slashing spree damaging hundreds of random cars in the upmarket neighbourhoods close to Cahill's home in Rathmines.

It was another way for Cahill to embarrass the gardaí and intimidate the public. He thought he could drive a wedge between the force and the law-abiding middle-class community who had to buy new tyres. His warped logic went that the public would exert pressure on politicians to order the authorities to lay off the mobster. It didn't work. However, the same intimidatory tactics had certainly succeeded in scaring off the biggest selling newspaper in the country – and put paid to my exposé.

But the executive's concerns were not completely unfounded as the newspaper had already suffered an appalling attack. Six years earlier, in 1984, Jim Campbell, the fearless editor of the northern edition of the *Sunday World*, had been shot and seriously injured in Belfast by a Loyalist UVF (Ulster Volunteer Force) assassination gang. The attack took place when I was still a journalism student and we were all hugely impressed by Jim's courage. It reaffirmed our idealistic reasons for becoming reporters. The attack was in retaliation for the paper's coverage of the UVF's criminal activities. In Dublin the shooting of Jim Campbell was compartmentalized as a terrorist attack that happened in Northern Ireland in the midst of a brutal conflict, dismissed as, 'That kind of thing didn't happen in the Republic'. It was redolent of the partitionist mindset of the South which was also reflected in the media coverage. The most active terrorist group operating in the Republic was the IRA and they steered clear of shooting journalists in the South for pragmatic and strategic reasons.

The shooting of Jim Campbell did not justify capitulating to terror tactics. Campbell proved that because after the shooting he continued to do his job without fear. I recall once discussing the ill-fated Cahill story with him. The courageous editor wholeheartedly agreed that it should have been published. Spiking the story went against the grain of what journalism was supposed to be about – telling the truth without fear or favour. It was also a shock for me, given the *Sunday World's* impressive record of investigative journalism. Since the 1970s its reporters had exposed rogue builders, corrupt politicians, scam artists and vice bosses – stories that the traditional Irish newspapers looked down their noses at. In the early 1980s when heroin first hit Dublin, undercover reporters bought the drug from pushers on the streets and then exposed them on the front page. The new tabloid was seen as fearless and became the public's go-to newspaper to expose injustices. Reading those stories as a teenager drew me to journalism and ultimately to the *Sunday World*. I wanted to be out on the streets doing the same thing.

The senior editor banned me and my colleagues from targeting the mobster from then on. We could loosely report news events related to him – without his name or moniker or any specifics about him – but there was to be no more in-depth digging or attempts to get his picture. We were to leave the General in peace because we wanted him to leave us in peace. Sean Boyne and most of the editorial team disagreed with the capitulation but there was nothing anyone could do about it.

In my mind at the time it made no sense to kill the story on the General or to ban future articles, especially over a fear of tyre slashing. Crime was a big story that couldn't be ignored. Despite whatever threats such coverage might attract, I believed that it was the media's duty to inform the public of what was going on. As a budding crime journalist it was an ideological *grundnorm* shared with all my peers.

The ban was an important learning curve. That memorable incident was the first time that I experienced the insidious effects of the kind of fear that organized crime instils in society. Fear is one of the most important weapons in the gangster's arsenal. Most law-abiding people in any society are afraid of crime and criminals. It is why citizens often don't go to the police with information or refuse to be witnesses in criminal cases. Fear ensures silence or what the mafia call *omertà*. The General understood the importance of fear in fortifying the wall of silence. It explained why the police never recruited informants from his inner circle and they never nabbed him. Fear kept him out of prison and off the front page of the *Sunday World*. Fear is a recurring theme in the story of crime.

For the next few years I never referred to Cahill by name or nickname in stories that referenced his crimes or his associates. In a trawl of old files for this book my reports went from referring to 'Martin Cahill, the man who denies he is the General' to simply a 'south city crime boss' or '*one* of the city's top gangsters'. We were being constrained and censored because of fear. To say it was frustrating would be putting it mildly.

Cahill would have loved the absurdity of it all. We made sure that he never found out.

CHAPTER THREE

———

PUBLISH AND BE DAMNED

Back in 1990 there was an awful lot that I didn't know about Cahill or indeed organized crime in general, but I was learning fast. I later realized that given the gangster's record the senior executive hadn't necessarily been overly cautious. In my youthful naiveté I stupidly believed that, apart from what happened in Northern Ireland, the media were somehow immune from the danger posed by criminals. I believed there was an unwritten rule in the code of so-called ordinary decent criminals that attacks on the press were off limits. The executive's decision prevented us from finding out if the theory held true.

Apart from the terrorist activities taking place, crime ordinary – non-subversive crime – had not featured in any great depth in the public narrative before Cahill and his mob burst onto the public stage. In the early 1980s his old friends the Dunnes had dominated the news agenda when they were blamed for unleashing the heroin scourge on Dublin. (See Chapter 4.) But within a few short years the Dunnes were a spent force and almost all of the clan was behind bars.

After that the staple of crime reports concerned the explosion in street crime caused by the Dunne family's former customers:

the growing army of desperate junkies looking for money to get a fix. Bag snatches, muggings, burglaries, assaults and chaotic armed robberies by knife- and gun-wielding addicts became a daily hazard. The shootouts between the professional armed gangs and the cops brought the story to a new level.

The broadsheet newspapers didn't have a requirement for reporters to exclusively cover crime. The news organizations of the day – RTÉ, *Irish Times*, *Irish Independent* and *Examiner* newspapers – had designated security correspondents who covered day-to-day crime, policing and military matters. The ongoing Troubles in the North and the terrorist threat to the State dominated the security news agenda. The General was the catalyst that changed all that. The unexpected consequence was that I hold the rather unremarkable distinction of being the country's first by-lined crime reporter.

The ban on writing about Cahill didn't curb my enthusiasm for reporting crime. I continued to cultivate sources from amongst the criminal justice milieu: gardaí, prison officers, lawyers, villains, heroin addicts and victims. I spent a lot of time in the courts, getting to know the faces of the good and bad guys. But during that period crime was not being given the space or prominence that it deserved in the paper. The editorial priority was given to sensational tit 'n' bum yarns because the old newspaper mantra went that sex sells.

Nevertheless I quietly continued to gather information about Cahill and his activities. He was such a colourful character that I was already thinking about a possible book. Over the years, and especially when I began to research the book about his life and death, I sought out sources who knew Cahill best including cops, friends and associates. I also interviewed victims and officials who had crossed swords with him. The objective was to learn more about the dynamics of the criminal underworld and to understand why such a complex character loomed so large in gangland. I wanted to know what made the General tick.

I discovered that it wasn't a case of understanding his *personality* but rather one of trying to understand his *personalities*. I later spoke to criminal psychologists who diagnosed Cahill as a narcissistic sociopath, an anarchist suffering from acute paranoia with multiple personalities lacking remorse or empathy. In fact there was enough material there for a PhD in either criminology or criminal psychology, or both.

Of the criminals whose biographies I have written in the last thirty years – including the likes of Gerry Hutch, Marlo Hyland, John Cunningham, Christy Kinahan and John Gilligan – Cahill remains the most intriguing character. In comparison with the army of dangerous psychopaths who came after him, it is a remarkable distinction that none of them matched his destructive creativity and sublime malignancy.

Cahill's experiences as a child in a brutal reform school helped mould the development of a sociopath. In 1965 at the age of sixteen he was sentenced to two years for burglary in St Conleth's reform school in Daingean, County Offaly. Sexual, physical and psychological abuse was commonplace in the institutions which religious orders ran like veritable gulags for children. In one of the rare in-depth interviews Cahill ever gave he spoke to journalist Michael O'Higgins (now eminent Senior Counsel) and recalled bitterly: 'If anyone corrupted me it was those mad monks down in the bog.' Cahill described how he honed a psychological strategy in the reform school which he used in his dealings with the police.

If you try to harm me, I'll say, 'Can he get me?' And you can't. I'm
not afraid. There's nothing that you can do to get me. I'll go down
the lowest. I'll go down so low that the only way left is back up.
The only thing is, I can't bow down to you. I'd rather be dead, so
I'll make fun of you. If you annoy me, I'll make fun of you. I'll react
but I won't attack. And I'll keep on smiling.

When I began studying criminology and looked into the
backgrounds of major criminals of the day it became apparent that
the industrial and reform schools had played a pivotal role in the
origins of organized crime. A common theme shared in the lives of
many of the first generation of gangland figures was that they had
been incarcerated in the inhuman system. These former inmates
were released with a deep-seated hatred for the rest of society. They
were poorly educated but they had learned one important lesson
from the religious orders – that violence was the most effective tool
in life. They would spend a lifetime fighting back and getting even.

Friendships made in the reform schools by young delinquents
like Cahill became strong bonds of fraternity and loyalty which,
in turn, provided the nucleus of the first gangs to emerge in the
1970s. Amongst them were the notorious Dunne family who
served sentences with Cahill in Daingean reform school. Another
alumnus of the child gulags was John Cunningham who would
later help Christy Kinahan build one of the most powerful crime
cartels in the world.

In 1990 I interviewed Henry Dunne, who had been one of the
family's most talented armed robbers, shortly after he was released
from prison for firearms offences following a shootout with police.
It was Henry who first introduced Cahill and his brothers to
armed robbery. However, he only shared that information after

the General's death when I again interviewed him for the book. It was motivated out of loyalty to his old pal and had nothing to do with fear. After his death Dunne wanted the world to know of Cahill's exceptional talents. Henry recounted how he and his brothers brought Cahill on his inaugural blag on 18 November 1974. The professional Dunnes and their amateur pals the Cahills held up a security van as it collected cash from a supermarket in Rathfarnham, south Dublin. He described the future General as a 'natural' blagger:

> We [Dunnes] were used to the buzz from a good job but Martin was all excited and said he loved it. He was a natural and after that he was doing at least one decent job, every week or so. But the day after a big robbery he still went out breaking into people's houses after pulling a big one. He was strange like that.

The on-the-record interview in 1990 was given the space it deserved in the paper because it didn't pose a risk of retaliation – and the Dunnes were still box office in terms of public interest.

Henry provided a searing insight into the effects of the industrial/reform school system which he blamed for brutalizing him, his brothers and compatriots, and turning them to crime. Other criminals I interviewed over the years provided the same explanation for why they turned out like they did.

Sceptics would say that was an easy cop-out considering that the vast majority of victims of the barbaric system did not become criminals. Henry, however, told me:

> They [Christian brothers] beat and sexually abused us so much they made animals of us. When we came out of there all we wanted to do was hit back at society. We were angry and warped

with no loyalty to anyone except our own. They savaged us even
when we played by the rules. After that we felt 'what's the fucking
point?' The brothers made us the way we became and crime was
the obvious choice. When we came out we just wanted to fuck up
society.

Criminologically there is no doubt that the reform system played
a significant role in the history of organized crime in Ireland.

Whatever his motivation, Cahill became a criminal workaholic.
His whole orientation in life revolved around crime – plotting it,
committing it, getting away with it, talking about it. Outwardly he
came across as soft-spoken, even gentle, with a flat Dublin brogue.
He tended to avoid noisy confrontations and was a believer in actions
speaking louder than words. That was the persona that his victims
initially encountered. If they made the mistake of not listening
to his warnings, Cahill would return like a ghost in the night and
shoot them in the legs without uttering a word. Given the number
of people he attacked during his lifetime it is remarkable that he
never actually added the crime of murder to his inglorious record.

As a professional burglar since childhood Cahill was a night
person who preferred prowling around in the dark which became
a metaphor for his life. Cops and associates told me that winter
was Cahill's favourite season with its endless supply of shadows to
hide in. He certainly never intended winding up in the national
spotlight: it was just that his big robberies, acts of violence and
crimes against the State made it impossible for him to avoid it.
During the 1980s Cahill and his gang robbed art, jewels and cash
worth up to €100 million in today's values.

Long before I took an interest in Cahill his repertoire of
crime included armed robbery, kidnapping, shooting, extortion,

bombing, arson, intimidation and aggravated burglaries where people were robbed at gunpoint in their homes. By the mid-1980s garda intelligence reported that he controlled a gang of thirty hardened villains who were carrying out armed robberies on an industrial scale across the country. The jobs included the seminal 1983 O'Connor's jewellery factory heist in Dublin when Cahill and his gang made off with gold bars, gems, diamonds and gold rings worth over €7 million today. Admiring acolytes gave him his nickname in recognition of the military precision and planning involved in the job.

It wasn't long before the gardaí were also calling him by his new title. The *Today Tonight* documentary made it a household name. When researching my book John Traynor gave me a detailed account of the O'Connor's job. Traynor was an impeccable witness as he had got the inside information about the security at the factory and planned the heist with Cahill. Traynor was also at the General's side when he later pulled off one of the biggest art heists in the world.

In 1986 he had masterminded the theft of the eleven most valuable paintings in the Beit collection of old Dutch Masters. Cahill carried out the daring raid in the mistaken belief that he would have little difficulty offloading them to eccentric billionaires around the world. As the search for the paintings went global Cahill gained celebrity status of sorts in the international law enforcement community. His name featured prominently in investigations by Interpol, the FBI, Scotland Yard, the Turkish secret service and the Dutch and Belgian police.

He had also shown that he was afraid of no one. Not even the most powerful and pernicious terrorist gang in the country, the Provisional IRA. In 1984 the Dublin underworld had teetered on the brink of an all-out war as the General limbered up to take on the Provos after they tried to put the squeeze on him for a slice of the proceeds from the jewel factory job. No other criminal has ever stood up to the Provos.

Traynor had been present with Cahill at a meeting with the Provos in the aftermath of the robbery. When senior IRA men told him they wanted a share of the gold Cahill shouted: 'If you want gold then go out and rob yer own gold like we did. Youse do your strokes and we do ours. Yer not gettin' a fuckin' penny.'

The standoff reached a climax when a four-man IRA gang were arrested after trying to kidnap Cahill's then close associate Martin 'the Viper' Foley. It was a major victory for the General and the police. The IRA had lost an entire active service unit in one fell swoop. After that both sides stood back from the brink and got on with their separate wars. But the Provos would not forget.

Cahill's war against the gardaí and the State exemplified his psychopathy. He went out of his way to show contempt for the police, the law and indeed the rest of society – in fact anyone who lived outside his small, subcultural world where crime was seen as the only honest way of making a living. He called it the 'game' or the 'grudge match'. By talking to cops and his associates I discovered that unlike any other crime boss Cahill harboured a pathological, visceral hatred for the State. As the years passed the obsession grew more irrational and paranoiac. He particularly despised the police. In his mind the police were the root of all evil. It was clear that his experiences of reform school and growing up in poverty had embittered him against society and its norms. His natural bent towards crime inevitably put him in conflict with the police against whom he vented his hostility.

The feeling was entirely mutual. To the gardaí he was their

most wanted and hated adversary. He was also the hardest to catch. When other villains did everything to avoid the cops, Cahill never missed an opportunity to try to humiliate and discredit them, regardless of the inevitable backlash it would provoke. Getting one over on the cops was sometimes his sole motivation.

He equipped his extensive arsenal of pistols, shotguns and machine guns by robbing them from the Garda depot where confiscated weapons were stored. The thefts were only discovered in the early 1980s when analysis of forensic tests on seized weapons showed that they were officially still in the possession of the police. Ballistic tests on the bullet that had injured Garda John Moore in 1990 confirmed that it had been fired by a pistol from the stolen cache.

When the law got too close for comfort Cahill showed an even more sinister side to his 'game' by resorting to acts of terrorism. In January 1982 Cahill blew up the country's top forensic scientist, Dr James Donovan, after planting a bomb under his car. At the time Cahill was facing a trial for armed robbery and the scientist's forensic analysis was central to the case. Miraculously Dr Donovan survived the blast. The courageous scientist was left with horrific leg wounds and a legacy of pain for the rest of his life. I have interviewed Dr Donovan many times over the years. In 2022, on the 40th anniversary of the appalling act of terrorism, the seventy-seven-year-old revealed that Cahill's death eighteen years earlier had given him a small degree of psychological solace:

> The effect is that we felt for twenty years at least that there was still someone waiting out there to finish me off. No one was ever

charged but we knew who was involved. When he [Cahill] died it
was a small source of comfort I suppose.

In his efforts to thwart the same case Cahill had also burned down
a Dublin criminal court and the administrative office of another.
In the end Cahill got off on a technicality. He was never brought
to justice for either the bomb or arson attacks despite a massive
garda investigation.

Over four decades later the attack on Dr James Donovan still
stands out as one of the single worst acts of narco-terrorism ever
seen in Ireland. History tells us that these incidents were warning
shots that organized crime was spiralling out of control. This one
emboldened the gangland anarchist even further.

In August 1987 he had struck a stunning blow to the criminal
justice system by stealing the country's most sensitive crime files
from the office of the Director of Public Prosecutions (DPP). A
month later the gardaí had come tantalisingly close to catching
their nemesis in possession of the Beit paintings after Cahill took
the bait in an elaborate sting operation involving an undercover
Interpol agent posing as an art expert interested in buying
them.

But just as the General walked into the trap with the paintings in
Killakee Woods in the Dublin Mountains it went horribly wrong.
At the last moment the police discovered that their radio network
didn't work. The officer in charge of the garda district covering
the mountains, Superintendent Bill McMunn, later confirmed to
me that he had identified the area around Kilakee as being a black
spot in the garda radio net. The secrecy surrounding the operation
meant that he had not been consulted. If he had, then history
would have perhaps turned out differently. In the confusion that

followed, Cahill and his cronies slipped the net with the paintings. When he later discovered how close he came to being nabbed the General was ecstatic. Typically, instead of keeping his head down he openly taunted his adversaries.

It was shortly after the failed Killakee sting that I was first acquainted with Martin Cahill. On 10 October 1987 the *Sunday World* became the first newspaper to write about a mysterious crime boss called the General in an article penned by John 'Jumbo' Kierans, who went on to work in Fleet Street and later became the legendary editor of the Irish edition of the *Daily Mirror*. Cahill wasn't named in the article which focused on his recent near miss and the theft of the DPP's files.

I began to take an interest in the crime boss after that. A month later the General and his gang carried out a terrifying armed robbery in which two families were taken hostage at gunpoint. It was at this point that a decision was taken to smash the General and his mob once and for all, and the Tango Squad was mobilised.

Cahill's status as 'Public Enemy Number One' was further validated when he was the subject of furious debate in the Dáil, the Irish parliament. RTÉ reporter Brendan O'Brien had confronted Cahill as he was queuing to collect his Unemployment Assistance payment at Werburgh Street labour exchange – a place Cahill and his gang had robbed a number of times. The godfather wouldn't shut up once he had started and at one stage claimed that he was a businessman who was involved in efforts to recover the Beit paintings for an insurance company. Government ministers were asked to explain why a man with a long criminal record was receiving social welfare and living between a high-end suburban home and a corporation one. It was very embarrassing for the Government.

Ireland in the 1980s was a grim place to live. High unemployment, mass emigration and punishing taxes meant that the vast
majority of the population struggled to live just above the bread
line. The voting public found it particularly galling to think
that a notorious criminal could enjoy a millionaire lifestyle and
claim the dole money their taxes paid for. The insouciant General
considered it an added bonus if his criminal success meant causing
embarrassment to the Government in front of the electorate. I was,
like every other member of the public, astonished to learn that the
State was powerless to do anything about the wealth of criminals
who were clearly flouting every law in the book. This issue had a
major impact on my future journalistic work.

The only option open to the Government was to order the
Department of Social Welfare and the Revenue Commissioners
to investigate Cahill's finances and entitlements. A member of
the Progressive Democrats, Mary Harney was the first politician
to articulate the crying need to target the mob's wealth. She told
the Dáil that Cahill should be investigated in the same way Elliot
Ness had pursued Al Capone. She wanted the General evicted
from his local authority house and said that if the law didn't
exist to take action then the laws should be changed to make it
possible to do so.

In those halcyon days for gangsters Ireland was a thieves'
paradise. It wasn't unusual for a criminal to rob a bank and,
when the dust had settled, to return without his mask or shotgun
and lodge the cash in his legitimate bank account. He could
then drive around the corner to the local labour exchange in his
top of the range car and collect his dole money. The laws in the
late 1980s, or lack of them, aided and abetted the development
of organized crime. The legislative inaction also reflected the

priorities of corrupt politicians like the former Taoiseach Charles Haughey, who wanted to protect themselves and the millionaires who bankrolled them.

The various arms of the state or financial institutions could not share information about individuals with the police. And even if they did there were no laws to enable them to do anything with the information. The Government of the day did nothing to address the issue. It would take eight years and another gangland atrocity, the murder of Veronica Guerin, before the legislature was forced to finally take decisive action with the establishment of the Criminal Assets Bureau (CAB). In the meantime the General continued to illustrate his contempt for the law.

When nervous inspectors from the Revenue Commissioners called to interview Cahill at his home in Cowper Downs he was characteristically cordial and charming. He arranged for the interview to take place in the upmarket residence so that it might annoy the official even more. Everything Cahill did was orientated to playing the part of the rebel joker. The mobster diverted attention from his taxes to complain about the problem of vandalism. To illustrate his point he gestured towards the front window. The officials' car was engulfed in flames outside. Revenue didn't bother Cahill again. He was also interviewed by social welfare inspectors but refused to answer any questions.

Over the next few years I reported on the succession of convictions as a result of the Tango Squad's activities as each of the once feared hoodlums came before the non-jury Special Criminal Court which, over thirty years later, still plays a pivotal role in the prosecution of organized crime cases.

Apart from losing his most loyal and capable lieutenants, other trusted associates began to back away from Cahill. They were fed up with the non-stop police harassment and the media spotlight that his performances attracted. But despite the Tango Squad's best efforts their primary target eluded them. Tango One had managed to stay one step ahead and remained free.

The nearest the police came to depriving Cahill of his liberty was a three-month stint in prison for a breach of the peace in June 1988. He served his time in Spike Island prison in Cork Harbour which he jokingly called Treasure Island, saying he was glad of the break. The rest and the sea air would recharge his batteries.

Around the same time I got closer to Cahill than I expected when we exposed the criminal activities of one Wally McGregor, his long-time friend and associate. It was part of an undercover investigation into the lucrative illicit trade in forged identity and motoring documents such as driving licences, passports, insurance documents, vehicle logbooks and stolen credit cards. Before the digital age these illegal documents were vital to the smooth running of organized crime and facilitated a wide variety of activities. We had successfully exposed a number of individuals involved in the trade a year earlier.

I had a bit of experience going undercover since joining the *Sunday World*. On a number of occasions I had posed as a junkie and bought drugs from dealers who were then unmasked. A few years later, posing as a customer with the help of an inside source, I exposed how the Junior Common Room in prestigious Trinity College Dublin had become a hub for ecstasy dealing. I passed on the information and the drugs we had bought to the Drug Squad who launched a raid while I was sitting there with the source. I was frisked by one of the detectives against a wall so that I could discreetly point them towards the dealers who were sitting in a corner of the Common Room. They arrested two men who were supplying the E. Most importantly we had photographers watching the college to snap the action as the cops took the suspects through TCD's iconic front gates. It made for a sensational front page story at the time. The modus operandi was much the same when it came to the trade in illegal documents, although the sellers were more circumspect than the drug dealers.

Based on information that we gathered from underworld and police sources we knew the right people to target. Once a connection was made the whole operation was pretty straight-forward. Watched from a distance by colleagues in case things went wrong and I needed to be rescued, I would pose as a criminal from out of town, either from the country or the North, and bluff the supplier of the documents into believing I was a genuine customer. Once I could show that I had plenty of cash on the hip it was plain sailing. The only other important requirements were holding my nerve and keeping up the façade, no matter what happened. If the transaction was completed the criminal would be secretly photographed and we'd publish the story.

That was how I came to McGregor's door in June 1988. A career criminal in his late fifties from Clondalkin, west Dublin, McGregor was one of the top suppliers of stolen and forged documents in the city. Despite being initially wary I managed to win the confidence of the veteran villain over a cup of tea in his kitchen. My cover story was that I was involved in smuggling along the border and needed insurance documents for a number of stolen cars we were using. As part of my cover I was deliberately vague in conversation to create a suspicion that I might be part of a terrorist group like the IRA.

I gave him the registration numbers and details of the fictitious cars and he told me to return a few days later. I secretly recorded our conversation and remember how he apologized for being so suspicious at first. Ironically he told me that another associate had been exposed by 'fuckin' reporters from the *Sunday World'*. As the General was beginning his holiday on Treasure Island we put his pal Wally on the front page.

Following his holiday on Spike Island, Cahill carried out a string of terrifying aggravated burglaries where the occupants of upmarket houses were held at gunpoint before the gang made off with jewellery and valuable paintings. In a follow-up investigation two of Cahill's last remaining gang members, Harry Melia and Eugene Scanlan, were later jailed for the robberies.

A year after he featured in the *Sunday World* sting, Wally McGregor was arrested in possession of stolen paintings he had been holding for Cahill. When I wrote the story about McGregor's subsequent conviction in December 1990, when he got two years for receiving stolen goods, I could only mention that he was a friend of 'one of the city's top gangsters'.

By then Cahill had orchestrated another sinister act of terrorism against a public servant. Following an investigation on the back of the *Today Tonight* programme, the Department of Social Welfare decided to block his dole in January 1989. The General saw his entitlement to the dole as an inalienable right and appealed the decision. He blamed Brian Purcell, the courageous social welfare inspector who had led the inquiry, and decided to express his displeasure.

Shortly after midnight on 29 May 1989, Brian Purcell was abducted at gunpoint when four armed men burst into his home in north Dublin while his two small children slept upstairs. The gang put a hood over Purcell's head. They then tied up and gagged his pregnant wife Sandra. The terrified civil servant was taken to railway lines in the south of the city where he was kept until Cahill arrived. The General shot the inspector once in each leg before letting him go.

Inevitably the attack caused public and political outrage. The Social Welfare Minister Michael Woods characterized it as a 'new and sinister departure in intimidation'. For the second time Cahill had sent a chilling message to the Irish State. The incident exposed another gaping hole in the State's ability to tackle organized crime, yet nothing was done. It was incredible to watch.

Cahill was not bothered by the fact that he would be the obvious suspect. On the same morning as the shooting an appeal board was due to hear Cahill's application to have the decision overturned. He wanted them to know who they were dealing with. But the board was unmoved and upheld the decision to cut his money back to a mere 50 pence a week.

Each week Cahill would queue up wearing his mask to collect his single coin which he would then throw down the length of the unemployment exchange shouting: 'Youse need this more than I do.' He repeated the spectacle every week without fail. When researching *The General*, I tracked down the social welfare clerk who had the uncomfortable job of handing Cahill his weekly stipend. Just before Christmas 1989 the clerk recalled how Cahill reached over the protective screen and handed him a gift-wrapped package, saying 'this is for you'. The young clerk didn't know whether to accept it or call the bomb squad. Inside was a Schaeffer pen with a note. The clerk never forgot the little rhyme from Ireland's most notorious gangster. It read: 'For all your kindness throughout the year, You've made it worthwhile to come in here.'

Despite a major police investigation neither Cahill nor any of his associates ever faced justice for the appalling attack on Brian Purcell. After his abduction other Department of Social Welfare officials dealing with the Cahill case were placed under police protection.

But even then the General was intent on adding insult to injury. While Brian Purcell was in hospital recovering from his horrific ordeal gangland's joker sent him a 'get well' card which simply read: 'The General prognosis is good.'

Cahill had again struck fear into the heart of society and the public service. From then on staff with the revenue and social welfare departments steered clear of cases involving dangerous criminals. Fear effectively made criminals untouchable. But when Brian Purcell recovered from his ordeal he showed that he wasn't prepared to be scared off by a gangster. He later joined the Criminal Assets Bureau as a senior investigator and went on to become the Secretary General of the Department of Justice. Brian Purcell is one of the unsung heroes of the war against organized crime.

Despite the enormity of the outrage, the extensive media coverage it received and the fact that I was covering the story, not a word about the incident appeared in the following week's edition of the *Sunday World*, Ireland's biggest selling paper at that point. I was told a story about the incident wasn't required. I knew it was because of the Cahill ban. The splash – front page story – was about a woman who had stripped naked in a garda station and then asked the cops to have sex with her! Martin Cahill was winning on several fronts. By getting away with the attack he had set a new dangerous precedent for gangland to follow.

He certainly inspired his long-time criminal associate John Gilligan. In the mid-1990s, the Revenue Commissioners sent Gilligan a tax demand. Despite having no visible means of income the arrogant narcissist had developed a world-class equestrian centre near Enfield in County Kildare which cost millions.

Gilligan wrote the words 'fuck off' on the demand and sent it back. He didn't hear from the Revenue again. He used similar tactics to get an investigation into his daughter Tracey's lone-parent allowance dropped a few years later. A note on Tracey's file recorded how her father, who was described as 'a very dangerous man', had made 'unspecified threats'. No one could blame the civil servants for dropping the inquiry. The climate of fear was Martin Cahill's legacy.

Apart from tyre slashing sprees whenever he was annoyed by the cops, Cahill kept a low profile after the bank robbery in Ranelagh. The next time he featured in a serious crime came one night in January 1993. A businessman called Wolfgang Eulitz was shot in the legs at his home in Donnybrook, south Dublin. I rushed to the scene with Padraig O'Reilly after we heard the incident being reported on the police scanner we had in the car. At the time we used to cruise the city at night in the hope of picking up a major incident. As we arrived the injured man was being placed in an ambulance and was in no mood to talk about his ordeal.

The shooting was the culmination of a long-running campaign of intimidation and arson attacks directed against the innocent victim because Cahill wanted to take over his hot dog business on Leeson Street in Dublin city centre. The 'Leeson Street Strip' was the hub of the capital's nightlife, consisting of a dozen or so pokey, smoke-filled basement clubs charging a fortune for cheap plonk. Selling hot dogs to thirsty drunks was big business. Through my sources I learned that the prime suspects for the shooting were two younger criminals Cahill had recruited since his gang was jailed. They were intensely loyal to their boss. Being part of the General's gang was a badge of honour to young hoods. Cahill referred to them as his 'Rottweilers'.

Around the same time I discovered an even more sinister side
to the hooded bogeyman. I got a call one day from a concerned
grandmother who asked me to come and see her as she had
something urgent to discuss. She wanted to talk about her late
daughter's husband, who also happened to be a very close associate
of the General. I knew of the criminal and his violent reputation. A
few months earlier he had been charged with raping his fourteen-
year-old daughter, the woman's grandchild.

An hour later I was sitting in the front room of her home in
Crumlin, south Dublin. The elderly woman had been looking
after her granddaughter since the incident. A few years earlier her
daughter, the victim's mother, was killed when the vehicle driven
by her husband was involved in a crash. The grandmother had
reported the rape to the gardaí in Crumlin and was determined
that her depraved son-in-law would stand trial for what he had
done. Even though most of her family were active criminals, she
assured me that the code of *omertà* did not apply to those who
rape children. In gangland sex offenders are despised as the lowest
form of life and are housed separately from the rest of the prison
population for their own safety.

When Cahill heard about what happened he was furious.
As a family man who genuinely loved kids he was repulsed by
what his pal had done. But it was also bad for business. Traynor
and garda sources later confirmed that Cahill and the rapist had
been planning to kidnap a businessman and the crime had to be
cancelled. The grandmother also revealed that the General was
most concerned that she had gone to the police.

Five years after Cahill's definition of a 'real criminal' being 'a
man who abuses kids' it was obvious that he had changed his view.
To him anyone, even a child victim of rape and incest, was a tout

(informant) if they agreed to give evidence in court. The plucky grandmother told me how Cahill first approached the terrified girl on the street near her home and offered her money to drop the case. He had also contacted the grandmother who told him to shove it – she said she had no fear of Cahill. I can still recall her saying, 'Sure, what can he do to me, an old woman? I told him and his rapist friend to fuck off, I wasn't afraid of them.' When Cahill was rebuffed he resorted to a sinister campaign of intimidation against the terrified child and her family.

The elderly woman related how in the weeks after the confrontation she and her grandchild would be woken in the night by noises around the house. Prowlers shone flashlights through the windows. The teenager, she said, was terrified. One of the girl's uncles, the woman's son, was a criminal with close links to the INLA, the paramilitary Irish National Liberation Army. He had been a friend of Cahill since childhood and often took part in robberies with him but his greatest loyalty was to his own blood.

When the intimidation escalated he took the child to live with him and his wife in Tallaght, a few miles south of Crumlin, for protection. Cahill approached him and asked what he was going to do about the 'fuckin' tout in your house?' The uncle told him to fuck off and also refused the money Cahill offered to buy silence. In the weeks that followed shadowy figures were seen prowling around the uncle's house late at night to intimidate the victim and her family.

Gardaí sent extra patrols to the area to protect them. Cahill's thugs then daubed slogans on walls around the area calling the uncle and his niece 'touts' and 'rats'. The intimidation amplified the victim's trauma. The victim later told me how she had been so scared that she could not sleep or eat for months. It was an appalling ordeal for a young child to suffer. She was also diagnosed as suffering from post-traumatic stress disorder (PTSD). Eventually the uncle enlisted the help of the INLA who sent word to Cahill: if he continued to harass the child he would be shot. Although the General had shrugged off the threat he ceased his efforts. The young victim eventually testified against her father at his trial in 1994 and he was convicted. I covered the story in great detail but had to omit the connection to the General. I had also interviewed the girl's uncle. In another bitter twist to the story he was shot dead in the same year by one of his INLA associates in an unrelated row.

Around the same time as he was trying to prevent his perverted associate from going to jail Cahill pulled off what was to be the final major crime of his long career. On 2 November 1993 the General's newly formed gang kidnapped the family of Jim Lacey, the CEO of the National Irish Bank. The following day Lacey was instructed to go to the bank's main cash-holding centre in College Green, central Dublin, in the company of gang member Joseph 'Jo Jo' Kavanagh, who drove a van. Cahill had ensured that the vehicle's suspension was reinforced to take the weight of the cash he hoped to get.

As part of Cahill's elaborate plan Kavanagh pretended that he had been forced to participate because his family were also being held hostage by the gang. Lacey was instructed to empty the contents of the safes. In the end the quick-thinking banker duped Kavanagh into thinking there was just cash to the value of around €300,000 in the vaults. The actual figure was almost €9 million. I wrote a number of exclusive stories in the aftermath based on information from the heart of the investigation. I also spoke to a source close to Kavanagh who confirmed that he was part of the kidnap gang. By the time they were published the stories had been eviscerated and only referred to the fact that the kidnapping had been organized by a 'top Dublin crime boss'. The ban was becoming tedious.

The yield from the Lacey kidnap was a major disappointment for Cahill and his advisor John Traynor who had helped to organize it. They planned to invest the proceeds as seed capital to help Traynor and John Gilligan set up a drug trafficking racket. Cahill was amongst twenty suspected criminals arrested and questioned by the gardaí but as always he had ensured there was little evidence with which to charge him. A tyre slashing spree marked the event. The gardaí managed to blow holes in the cover story Cahill and Traynor had concocted for Kavanagh. He was the only member of the gang convicted of being involved in the kidnap and was jailed for twelve years.

———

By the time the Lacey kidnapping took place the *Sunday World* had been haemorrhaging readers for a number of years as the paper failed to keep pace with the changing tastes of the Irish public. The old formula that had once made it the biggest selling newspaper in the country, the inclusion of a scantily-clad woman on the front page, had grown tired and jaded. The aversion to running in-depth investigative stories was a symptom of how the paper had lost its way. It reached its nadir in 1992 when the paper ran the outrageous front-page headline 'Sex With Sheep in Hotel Bedroom' which pushed the 'sex will sell' philosophy to a ludicrous extreme. Rather than titillating the public it caused a national outcry as tens of thousands of newspapers were returned. It left everyone in the newsroom mortified. Like any organization the paper required a reboot. In January 1994 the management changed hands when Michael

Brophy was appointed managing director and Colm MacGinty became editor. Brophy had been editor of the Irish version of *The Star* and MacGinty his deputy. Together they had turned the tabloid into one of the biggest selling daily papers in the country.

The move was a game changer in the *Sunday World's* history and was a career turning point for me and many of my colleagues. From the moment they arrived, Brophy and MacGinty transformed the place, and life suddenly became a lot more interesting. What I admired most about my new bosses was their determination not to be intimidated by vested interests and their willingness to push out the boundaries, especially in the face of risk-averse lawyers whose almost irrational fear of libel actions tended to kill stories before they were even written. For the staff it was the opening of a whole new journalistic world where no issue was off limits.

Brophy and MacGinty understood the mood of the public and what made for agenda-setting campaigning journalism. They brought out the best in people and were always supportive and encouraging, imbuing confidence in the place. Working with them over the following sixteen years or so was exciting, inspiring and a great honour. Soon the drop in circulation stopped and the readership figures gradually began to increase again – in a short time the *Sunday World* had reclaimed its spot at the top of the newsstand pile. It was no longer derided as a down-market tabloid. Under their leadership, in 1995 I became the first tabloid journalist to win the prestigious Irish 'Print Journalist of the Year' award for a series of interviews with Phyllis Hamilton, the secret lover of celebrity priest Fr Michael Cleary.

One of the first changes to the editorial agenda was lifting the ban on writing about the General. Brophy instructed me to write up a long feature that would include all the information I had on Cahill and his gang. I was delighted to oblige. I had plenty of unused material gathered over the years. On 4 April 1994 the headline on the front page said it all: 'Exposed – The General'. Over a four-page pull-out section, it catalogued Martin Cahill's long list of crimes including the inside story on the Lacey kidnapping six months earlier which was still being investigated.

In the meantime I had also managed to acquire the first decent picture of Cahill without his mask. In it he was wearing a wig which he often did when he was at home with the family.

We also published the striking picture that Liam O'Connor had snatched during our mad attempt to unmask the bogeyman nearly four years earlier. Ignoring the inevitable warnings from the lawyers we discarded the old safety line of Cahill denying he was the General. The feature left the reader in no doubt that Cahill *was* the General. We also profiled the individual members of his gang. It was the first time that a newspaper had published such a comprehensive piece, and with exclusive pictures.

It wasn't long before I discovered that the gang boss and his mob were not entirely delighted with the coverage. Three days after the story appeared my local gardaí based in Crumlin contacted me with an urgent message – members of Cahill's gang were hopping mad and threatening to target me in revenge for the article. The alert had come from the Serious Crime Squad at Harcourt Square, central Dublin.

On 7 April an urgent circular was issued by the chief superintendent in the Southern Division which covered the areas where I worked in Terenure and lived in Walkinstown. It read:

Information received on this date from the Detective Inspector
Noel Kane, Central Detective Unit, Harcourt Square, that serious

efforts are being made by a number of major criminals in an
effort to identify the home address of Paul Williams.

This issue relates to an article written in the *Sunday World* on
Sunday 3 April 1994 relating to Martin Cahill and his general
exploits as a criminal.

It is the belief that the enquiries now being made about Paul
Williams is [*sic*] with the intent to retaliate for the content of the
article in the paper.

This matter has to be taken very seriously and Garda patrols
should be directed to pay particular attention:

1. The home of Paul Williams (address in Walkinstown).

2. To the *Sunday World* offices in Terenure where he is
   employed.

Members when patrolling the vicinity of the two locations
should be on the alert for suspicious persons or vehicles and
be sure to check out and to establish credentials. Any incidents
should be reported to this officer post haste.

This was the first time that I was threatened. Realizing that
people want to harm you or your family over doing your job is
daunting and scary to say the least. For me the 'game' had suddenly
changed and I had entered uncharted waters. I had never really
considered the dangers inherent in pissing off bad people. I was
worried for my family's safety and that of my colleagues. At the
time our son Jake was four and my wife Anne was pregnant with
our second child. The former senior editor who reprimanded me
in 1990 had been vindicated to an extent. As I worked out how to
deal with the situation I kept most of the information from Anne
for obvious reasons. But I knew that we could not capitulate to the
thugs. As Michael Brophy always said: if the mob were resorting

to threats it meant that we were exposing the truth that the public had a right to know.

At the time we lived in the garda G district which covers Crumlin, Drimnagh and Walkinstown in south Dublin. This presented an added difficulty as the area was known as the home of organized crime because it was where most of the major villains of the day lived. I used to joke that most of the thugs I was writing about lived within shooting distance of my house. The local garda chiefs reassured us that we would be protected. From then on all garda units in Dublin's Southern Division patrolled around my home roughly every half hour, particularly at night.

I later learned from a number of intelligence sources that members of the gang had initially suggested to Cahill that they launch an arson attack at my home. Cahill ruled it out telling his associates that the family home was out of the question. 'His wife and kids live there,' he said to one of them. I appreciated that. It was then suggested that they burn the printing presses in Terenure. Thankfully there were friends and associates, members of Cahill's pigeon club, who still worked in the print hall so that wasn't a runner either.

The only alternative was to come after me in person to either give me a beating or shoot me in the legs, his preferred type of punishment. In hindsight I don't believe Cahill ever intended doing harm to me. Given his previous record he certainly had the capacity to do it, no matter how many cops were around me. The gangster leading the charge was one of his lieutenants, Martin Foley, the Viper, who had taken a serious grievance over what I had written about him down the years including in the General's feature. I had written about Foley's criminal past, his involvement in the gang and his conviction for smashing the jaw of the Tango Squad detective. I published the first full picture of the Viper for which, it appeared, he had never forgiven me. Foley was a world class whinger who hated publicity even more than his cohorts.

A senior garda visited the Viper at his home to let him know that the police knew what he was up to. Foley was told of the consequences he would face if they did carry out an attack. He backed off but the gangster would go to great lengths to make my life difficult in the years ahead. He tried on numerous occasions to intimidate me and when that failed he came after the *Sunday World* with his lawyers by threatening to sue or seek injunctions.

In the months following the threat armed garda officers escorted me to and from work to make sure that I wasn't harmed. I have always been hugely appreciative of the garda protection I received whenever there was a credible threat to my life over the years that followed. Individual gardaí were hugely supportive because we were dragging criminals into the spotlight. Many of the officers concerned became lifelong family friends as security alerts became a regular occurrence in the years that followed.

The most credible threats were uncovered by the police using secret intelligence sources such as gangland informants and phone taps. The rule of thumb is that when criminals make public threats they don't tend to follow them up. When they plot in secret you need to worry. I believe that I would not be alive today if it weren't for the many times that the police intervened, often without my knowledge, to prevent criminals carrying out attacks.

Checking under the car in the mornings became an almost unconscious routine. I was informed that the risk of attack is highest while driving and had to vary routes and times to avoid becoming predictable. Scanning the rear view mirror or the street ahead for anything suspicious became second nature. Over time I developed a sharp instinct for dangerous situations. All crime journalists share the same self-preservation instincts. As subsequent events proved crime reporting is the only area of domestic journalism that is hazardous to life and limb.

In many ways the threats made me more determined that I would not be silenced from doing my job. The intimidation meant that everyone in the company, especially the journalists, had to be more security conscious. The support and encouragement from Brophy and MacGinty gave the staff the confidence to continue to do the job. They believed strongly that we could not lie down in the face of intimidation.

Security was beefed up around the *Sunday World* premises in Terenure and monitored panic alarms were installed at my home. The garda Command and Control dispatch system registered us as 'very high risk' to prioritize garda responses in the event of an alarm activation. Once when I accidently pressed the alarm two squad cars were at the door within five minutes. It was a bit embarrassing that time – but very reassuring.

As we tried to work out how to respond to the threats a decision was made to keep them under wraps and not to go public. This was new territory for a newspaper in Ireland. But the general situation became a lot more dangerous a few months later when shots were fired at the home of Veronica Guerin. Then the following January a lone gunman shot her in the leg when she answered the door. It later emerged that the attack had been orchestrated by John Traynor even though at the time he was one of her sources. I never trusted Traynor. It was a very worrying development.

Two weeks after the exposé on the General appeared Cahill's henchmen slashed the tyres of twenty-three random cars in his local area. The information at the time suggested that the attacks were to express his annoyance at being stopped and searched by gardaí and were not in response to the *Sunday World* articles.

However, in the months following the story an insignificant reporter was soon the least of Cahill's concerns. In May the UVF attacked a Sinn Féin fundraiser in the Widow Scallans pub in central Dublin. The plan was to plant a massive bomb in the packed function room where over 300 people were in attendance. The UVF shot and killed an IRA member who prevented them gaining entry. They abandoned the device and made their escape. Fortunately the bomb was defused by some of the Provos who were present before it caused what would have been an unprecedented massacre.

The Provos launched an investigation throughout the under-world to discover if Cahill had assisted the UVF. He was their obvious choice because it had already been revealed that he had dealt with the organization in a bid to offload some of the Beit paintings. They also had unfinished business after the O'Connor's robbery. Cahill was not prepared to bend the knee for them.

Republicans even approached me seeking information that implicated Cahill but I had none to offer. The truth was that Cahill had nothing to do with it. When researching *The General*, I discovered that in the wake of the Widow Scallans assault a leading member of the IRA, Fr Paddy Ryan, became a regular visitor to Cahill's home. John Traynor revealed how Ryan assured Cahill that he was not under threat from the Provos. He claimed the notorious former priest wanted to discuss a joint criminal venture. The General was being lulled into a false sense of security.

To make matters worse, at the same time he was also involved in a row with members of the INLA. The organization had morphed into a criminal gang and were muscling in on the burgeoning drug trade. Cahill burned down a corporation flat which had been allocated to an INLA member instead of one of the General's relations. As he grew more volatile Cahill reasoned that if the relative could not live there then no one would.

To top it all, behind his back, his partners in crime, John Gilligan and John Traynor, were plotting to manipulate the situation to suit themselves. While I was researching my book *Evil Empire,* about John Gilligan and the murder of Veronica Guerin, I discovered that Cahill had loaned them the capital to buy the first shipments of hashish and was putting the squeeze on them for money they didn't want to pay. The treacherous pair told the Provos that Cahill was involved in the Widow Scallans attack. Needless to say Traynor never shared any of this information with me when he agreed to co-operate for my book on his dear friend.

Time was running out for the General and the end when it came was as momentous as any of the other big events in his colourful life. The Provos bestowed upon Cahill the dubious honour of being its last victim before announcing the first ceasefire to coincide with the Northern Ireland peace process.

Like our stakeout four years earlier, the IRA were also aware of Cahill's predictable daily domestic routine when he was at his most vulnerable. They knew that he would drive down Oxford Road and turn onto Charleston Road as he moved between Swan Grove and Cowper Downs. The difference this time was that an assassin was waiting for him and not a photographer.

For a number of hours on that sunny afternoon of Thursday 18 August 1994, a Provo hit man from Finglas, North Dublin, waited beside the stop sign at the junction of Oxford Road and Charleston Road – about to make gangland history. Wearing a high-vis jacket he pretended to conduct a traffic survey with a clipboard in his hand. His accomplice on a motorbike drove up and down Oxford Road waiting for Cahill to emerge from the cul de sac, ready to give the hit man the signal.

At 3.20 p.m. the General's reign over Ireland's gangland came to a brutal end when he slowed to stop at the junction. The killer dropped the clipboard and stepped over to the driver's door. He produced a powerful .357 Magnum revolver and fired once at point-blank range, hitting Cahill in the shoulder and head. The blast of the shot forced the General to slump to one side. The car chugged across the road as the hit man ran alongside pumping another three shots into his victim. When the car came to a stop the Provo reached in and fired another round into Cahill's head for good measure.

My memory of that day has not dimmed after thirty years. Within minutes squad cars were speeding to the scene. At the same time, *Sunday World* colleague and fellow Leitrim man Mike McNiffe and I were actually discussing the General with an informant six miles away in Clondalkin. About five minutes after the shooting the phone rang. It was Philip Galvin, one of the detectives who had been protecting me over the past four months. He excitedly shouted: 'Cahill's down… Cahill's dead… For fuck sake they've killed him.' We were both stunned as we sped towards Ranelagh.

The police scanner I always carried in the car confirmed the ground-breaking news. 'Tango One is down… Tango One is down,' the message crackled frantically across the Garda radio network. 'Control, can you repeat that last message?' asked a clearly disbelieving voice over the wailing of a squad car siren. The dispatcher in Command and Control responded: 'The number one man is down… Get everyone down here… All other alarm calls to be put on hold. Priority for Tango One.'

When we arrived at the scene an eerie silence hung over Oxford Road as police began to cordon it off. Traffic was being diverted from the area and the road was closed except for garda vehicles. News of the dramatic hit had spread like wildfire and journalists and photographers were descending on the area for one of the biggest gangland stories in the history of Irish organized crime.

The cops hurriedly spread a tarpaulin over the car to prevent photographers taking shots of the bloodied corpse. The man they had spent so long trying to catch was allowed to die as he had lived, a faceless man. Cahill would have had a good laugh at that. He was never destined to die in his sleep. Being dispatched by a professional hit man was the kind of exit Cahill would have appreciated.

The silence was shattered when Christy, Cahill's twenty-one-year-old, arrived on a bike along with his father's 'Rottweilers'. There were scuffles as they threatened photographers. The emotional young man threw the bike at a garda van, shouting: 'Youse fuckers better not have had anything to do with this… youse fuckers killed him.' Another son, Martin Junior, shouted at photographers to 'get to fuck out of here'. He lunged forward to his father's side but was restrained by uniformed gardaí. 'That's me Da. Is he dead?' A cop who had known the General for many years put his hand on Martin's shoulder. 'I'm sorry, Martin, it is your father and he is dead.'

The body of the arch criminal was wrapped in plastic before being taken away. As the remains were being moved to a hearse the hand he had habitually used to cover his face trailed beneath the covering. It was a poignant sight. Given the stress over the past few months, I really didn't know whether to be happy or sad. One thing that was sure was that this was the biggest story I had yet covered.

———

The weekend after the General's murder was one of the most momentous of my life. On the Saturday morning a source gave us the scoop we wished for: the first proper, full-length picture of the General which was much clearer than anything we'd had before. His maskless and wigless smiling face beamed out of the recently taken photo in an ill-fitting leather jacket and tee-shirt. Strands of hair scattered across his bald pate as he stood proudly beside one of his daughters who was in her First Communion dress. The picture had been taken outside the church in Rathmines where his funeral mass was to take place on the following Monday. The next day Colm MacGinty devoted the full front page to the picture that everyone had wanted to see. The newspaper sold out in hours.

As Mike McNiffe and I sat down to write up the story of the life and death of the General, I got an urgent phone call from home. My wife's waters had broken a month earlier than anticipated. I rushed home and took her to Mount Carmel nursing home.

By the afternoon, when there was still no sign of our eagerly awaited new addition arriving, I nipped off to keep an eye on the funeral home in Crumlin where Cahill's body was reposing for friends and family to visit. It presented a one-off opportunity to photograph the gangland luminaries who had turned up to pay their respects to the godfather. Over a few hours I sat with two photographers as they snapped everyone who came and went.

Amongst them were several of the underworld's biggest players. Over the weeks that followed garda contacts helped me identify the faces in the frames. I compiled whatever information there was on each face including the crimes they had been suspected of and their connections with other criminals.

After that we regularly carried out photographic surveillance at gangland gatherings including funerals and weddings. Over time I built up intelligence files containing background information and individual pictures of the emerging big names in organized crime. Our knowledge grew exponentially as we built a picture of gangland. We were the first newspaper to do that. Apart from the gardaí, the *Sunday World* could boast having the biggest collection of gangland mug shots and intelligence in the country.

When I got back to Mount Carmel there still hadn't been any developments but some of the nurses gave me dirty looks for leaving my wife. Later that night Anne gave birth to a baby girl, our little princess. We called her Irena, which means goddess of peace, to reflect the momentous fact that the peace process was coming into view. Twelve days later the IRA announced its ceasefire. The ghost of Martin Cahill even came into the delivery room.

I'd brought my brick-shaped mobile phone in my pocket under the PPE gear I had to wear in the operating room. It was a force of habit always to have the phone nearby. Moments after our little girl was welcomed into the world the phone rang. I was in a state of elation when I answered. Colm MacGinty was on the other end to say that we had a cracking front page that was going to scoop everyone the next day. I put him on the phone to be the first person to congratulate Anne. It was rather bizarre, especially for Anne and the medical staff. I remember that event clearly because I have never been allowed to forget it!

The hat trick of memorable events on that historic weekend took place the next day when Leitrim played Dublin in the All-Ireland football semi-final in Croke Park. Even though we lost it was still a victory for our proud little county. It was the second time in the history of Leitrim GAA that we had made it to the semi-finals of the senior championship.

When the excitement died down I focused on writing a book about the General. At the time the true crime genre was non-existent in Ireland. The only book written about Irish crime had been published a decade earlier. *Smack – The criminal drugs racket in Ireland* by *Irish Times* journalists Sean Flynn and Padraig Yeates was an instant bestseller when it came out in 1985. It was a ground-breaking and superbly written account of how the drug problem and organized crime took hold. The authors were the first journalists to refer to an unknown crime boss known as the General. As a young crime reporter it was my bible and it, along with the books of UK crime writer Duncan Campbell, provided the inspiration to write my first book.

Unfortunately a few characters who featured in *Smack* sued the publishers, Gill and Macmillan, and it was taken off the shelves. The underworld had succeeded in using the law to scare off the media again. After that publishers were understandably wary about going near true crime. My colleague Eddie Rowley, the *Sunday World* showbiz editor, had written a bestseller with Daniel O'Donnell and knew the ropes. He put me in touch with his publisher Michael O'Brien of the O'Brien Press. Michael's brother Brendan was the reporter behind the 1988 *Today Tonight* RTÉ documentary on Cahill so he had a better understanding than most of the story. Given the aura of intimidation that swirled around the subject matter, coupled with the memory of what happened to *Smack*, O'Brien was at first wary of the proposition. To his great credit he decided to publish the General's biography. In the process the O'Brien Press breathed life into the Irish true crime genre – and my career as an author.

But as I was doing research for the book there was another security alert. On the night of 17 October 1994 a neighbour called the gardaí having spotted two men in a van with its lights switched off driving past my home. Some days later I got a call from an individual I knew who was involved in the Concerned Parents Against Drugs movement which was formed in the early 1980s as working-class communities rose up to eject the drug dealing scourge in their areas. They asked me to meet them. When we met up they said they had information that Martin Foley and Seamus 'Shavo' Hogan had been carrying out surveillance on me at work and at home over the previous three weeks. The gangsters knew the make and registration number of my car. They claimed that the plan was to either kidnap or shoot me.

When I contacted the local gardaí they carried out an investigation which corroborated the information. The reported sighting of the van was further confirmation of the story. An internal report sent by a senior officer to Garda HQ concluded: 'From my dealings with Martin Foley or Seamus 'Shavo' Hogan I am quite satisfied that they are capable of carrying out these threats of vengeance against Paul Williams.'

I was always mystified as to what triggered Foley and Hogan to seek vengeance over what I had written about them. I gave them much more reason to be annoyed when *The General* was published in May 1995. In it I revealed how Cahill had suspected Foley and Hogan of being police informants. I later discovered that Cahill did not trust Foley and believed that he was a tout. That was why he gave him the infamous nickname, the Viper. I dug up the reference which was buried in an interview Cahill did with London-based *GQ* magazine in 1991. I also confirmed it with the journalist Niall McCormack who authored the excellent piece. Cahill claimed that Foley was a police informant and had tried to set him up during the Tango Squad operation. I subsequently made sure to share that with our readers and the Viper became a household name.

The book also told the story of how, in October 1990, other members of the gang sliced off the tops of Hogan's ears with a knife in the exercise yard of Portlaoise Prison. They had all been sentenced to long stretches for armed robberies during the Tango operation. It was a crude and brutal gangland ritual. The intention was to make Hogan's ears resemble those of a rat, the criminals' term for an informant. Hogan had set up another gang member who was caught with guns and he was also blamed for planting a gun in the General's home which was subsequently found by the police. The State never proceeded with the case which indicated that it had indeed been a plant. The fact that Hogan and Foley were stalking me increased my determination to include their stories in the book.

Armed gardaí again stepped up security patrols around our home. The *Sunday World* made an arrangement with a garage so that I could change cars every week as a precaution. The two gangsters were then approached and warned that if they made a move they could easily find themselves facing the ERU. Foley and Hogan pulled back.

Then I discovered that the General's former associates weren't the only ones suddenly interested in me. In early October the anti-terrorist Special Detective Unit (SDU) stopped a senior Provo intelligence officer who was suspected of involvement in the murder of Martin Cahill. He was one of five IRA men convicted in

1983 for the attempted kidnapping of businessman Galen Weston, the owner of the Quinnsworth and Penneys chains in Ireland. The Provos later kidnapped Weston's chief executive, Don Tidey, who was eventually rescued near my home town of Ballinamore, County Leitrim. A young garda, Gary Sheehan, and soldier Private Patrick Kelly were gunned down without mercy by the IRA gang as the kidnappers made their escape.

When detectives searched the senior Provo they found a document containing detailed information about my personal life. It listed my address, telephone number and the type of car I drove. It also included details such as my wife's name, the name of our son and the fact that we'd recently had a daughter. The names of our parents and their political affiliations were even mentioned. In the same batch of documents there were also files on individual gardaí, some of whom had been singled out because they were fond of drink and could possibly be corrupted. Without realizing it I had become subsumed by the crime world – and had a growing entourage of enemies to prove it.

In the meantime I continued researching material and wrote the book. When *The General* hit the bookshelves the police across south Dublin braced themselves for a spate of tyre slashings. It coincided with my first appearance on RTÉ's *The Late Late Show* to discuss the book with the undisputed godfather of Irish broadcasting, the late great Gay Byrne. Despite the alerts there were no incidents reported that night. Thankfully, the book was a huge success and stayed at number one in the book charts for several months. In 1999 when booksellers Easons published the top 100 bestsellers of the past century *The General* was ranked at number fifty-five. But the godfather's immortalization wasn't confined to print – John Boorman adapted the book for the movie of the same name.

Being present on the set of a major movie that was based on my book and being made by one of the most respected names in the business was an amazing once-in-a-lifetime experience. The cast featured Oscar-winner Jon Voight, Brendan Gleeson, Adrian Dunbar, Sean McGinley, Angeline Ball and Maria Doyle Kennedy. Brendan Gleeson's uncanny portrayal of Cahill launched him on the road to becoming a Hollywood A-lister. The movie received widespread critical acclaim. Francis Ford Coppola, renowned for *The Godfather* trilogy, declared that this was the picture he had always wanted to make. Gleeson and Boorman were also hotly tipped for Oscar nominations but it wasn't to be. Gleeson won a host of other awards for his performance. Boorman received the award for best director when the movie premiered at the Cannes Film Festival in 1998.

The highlight of the whole experience for me was receiving the red carpet treatment at the movie's world premiere in the Palais des Film, a magnificent 2,000-seater theatre in Cannes. I sat next to Boorman, Gleeson and the rest of the cast. Everywhere you looked there were wall-to-wall celebrities, some of the biggest movie stars in the world. When the final credits rolled across the screen the theatre erupted in spontaneous applause with a standing ovation. Hollywood superstars Matt Dillon and Morgan Freeman shook our hands. It was easy to get carried away in the excitement and glitzy surrealness of it all.

Later we were chauffeured to Morrison's Irish Pub, just off the Rue d'Antibes where Guinness and champagne flowed freely all night. Colm Meaney, John Hurt, Neil Morrissey and Hugh Leonard were amongst the gaggle of celebs who joined the party. I recall how Brendan Gleeson confided that all of the glamour and superficiality of the movie festivals and premieres was not for him. He was a real down-to-earth Dubliner but it was something he would have to get used to as his career flourished. As for me the flirtation with the luvvie world ended when I got my flight home the next day; back to a version of the real world where I felt much more comfortable.

There were two other movies about Cahill's life and crimes. The first was a 1999 BBC movie called *Vicious Circle* in which Ken Stott played Cahill. A year later *Ordinary Decent Criminal* starring Kevin Spacey and Colin Farrell was released. Cahill even had posthumous walk on parts in two further pictures including *Veronica Guerin,* produced by Joel Schumacher and featuring Cate Blanchett as the eponymous heroine. The other was *When the Sky Falls,* also about the life and death of the journalist who was played by Hollywood star Joan Allen. Cahill literally is Ireland's most famous celluloid anti-hero.

The final chapter in the story of the General came in the summer of 2005 when the Criminal Assets Bureau sold his former home at Cowper Downs. It was an important symbolic gesture from the forces of law and order. Eleven years after his murder the General was finally being made to pay. The man who made sure of that was the then head of the CAB, Detective Chief Superintendent Felix McKenna, a veteran of the old Tango Squad who had been chasing Cahill for years. Felix, who had been attached to the CAB as its second in command under Fachtna Murphy after its establishment in 1996, had become a lifelong friend after we first met when he was on Cahill's trail.

The sale was not without a degree of drama. Even in death Cahill's ghost was having a giggle at the State's expense. McKenna ordered specialist Garda search teams to conduct a thorough search of the house and garden before the property went on the market.

Special scanning equipment was brought in to check for possible hidden cavities in the house. A digger was brought in to excavate the garden at the back. While the search was going on we hired a helicopter to photograph the dig from the air.

After two days nothing was found. I ran the exclusive story in that week's paper. The story of the General had come to a close.

CHAPTER FOUR

SHOOTOUTS AND DEATH ON THE STREETS

Over the years of writing society's roughest draft of history and my interest in criminology I became something of a de facto gangland historian. The evolution of organized crime in Ireland fits into four distinctive phases that are neatly bookended within specific decades: the 1970s saw the emergence of the armed robbery gangs and ended with the first shipments of heroin brought into Ireland by the Dunnes; the 1980s was the decade of armed crime and the growth of the drug trade; the 1990s saw the transition from armed robbery as the country's criminal elite moved into narcotics, which were much more profitable; the fourth, most brutal phase, began in 2000, the era of the Narcos.

Criminal justice history shows how the 1960s were the final years of a halcyon age when there was virtually little or no crime in Ireland. In the latter half of the decade, after Ireland had celebrated the fiftieth anniversary of the 1916 Rising, the Government gave serious consideration to closing down prisons, where the average daily population was 300 inmates. Today it is over 4,000.

The situation dramatically changed in 1970 when armed crime became the stock and trade of a new generation of young criminals and ardent terrorists. The callous murder of Garda Dick Fallon on 3 April 1970 by the country's first armed gang, Saor Eire – a group made up of republicans and thieves who tried to give themselves a political tag – stands out as the beginning of the era of the blagger.

The upsurge in violent crime that followed was the result of a perfect storm. The outbreak of the Troubles in Northern Ireland in 1969 spilled over the border as the Provisional IRA unleashed a campaign of robbing banks, post offices, businesses or anywhere else they could get cash to fund their so-called war. They were also hell-bent on destabilizing the State. In the process a new generation of emerging young villains, who were reckless and dangerous, took their lead from the Provos and became armed robbers. Soon it created a major industry as underworld entrepreneurs branched out to provide logistical support to the gangs – stolen getaway cars, weapons, inside information, safe houses, alibis and even disguises.

The Dunne crime family in Dublin became the first well-organized professional armed robbery outfit. They showed the ropes to the likes of Martin Cahill, their star pupil. Armed gangs proliferated and the number of robberies spiralled across the country. The gardaí, which was hopelessly ill-equipped to tackle the new crime wave, struggled to keep up. It also suited the new gangs that the State was more focused on the threat posed by the IRA. In the seventies robbing banks was easy.

The Dunne brothers, Shamie and Larry, are credited with ushering in the beginning of the next era in serious crime when they brought in heroin. The year 1980 is remembered as the year that the plague of drug addiction first hit the streets of Dublin devastating already marginalized and impoverished communities. Over four decades later drug addiction is no longer confined within socio-economic boundaries.

As the narcotics industry gained a foothold, armed robbery continued to be the primary source of income for the organized crime gangs. Then in 1990, the first year of the third decade of serious crime in Ireland, another bloody milestone irrevocably altered the course of gangland history – and signalled the end of the blagger era. As gardaí suddenly began turning the tables on the gangs, the criminals were forced to come to the realization that selling drugs was a much safer occupation. As an aspiring crime reporter I was a front seat observer of history in the making.

Martin Cahill experienced his epiphany and decided to retire while trying to outrun a much fitter cop following an armed robbery. Four days later a major undercover investigation into another gang of blaggers was hurtling towards a bloody conclusion. It came on 12 January 1990 when a secret garda weapons and tactics division, the Emergency Response Unit (ERU), literally blasted its way into the headlines in one of the most violent confrontations yet seen between Irish cops and robbers.

The ERU was formed in recognition that the changing face of crime and terrorism required an elite squad that specialized in armed confrontations. The hand-picked officers were issued with the latest firepower and trained with similar units in Europe such as the GSG9 in Germany. Around the same time the Irish Defence Forces also established the commando unit, the Army Ranger Wing, which also trained the ERU.

The unit's public debut involved the interception of one of the most dangerous armed gangs operating in the country at the time. The showdown took place during a robbery at the Bank of Ireland at Emily Square in Athy, County Kildare.

Thomas Tynan, Austin Higgins, Brendan Walsh, P. J. Loughran and William Gardiner were a potent, deadly mixture of criminals and republican paramilitaries. Most of them had previously worked with the General's gang but had gone out on their own when Cahill became an underworld celebrity and was targeted by the Tango Squad. They are remembered in gangland folklore as the 'Athy Gang'. During 1989 they were responsible for thirty-two of the forty-nine armed robberies from banks in Ireland, and got away with the equivalent of over €1 million in today's values.

I later unravelled the extraordinary background to the untold story while doing research for my second true crime book, *Gangland*. A number of sources gave me an insight into how the dramatic showdown unfolded. The confrontation was the culmination of a long investigation by the Serious Crime Squad, codenamed Operation Gemini, and led by Detective Inspector Tony Hickey, one of the country's most outstanding officers who would later head up the investigation of Veronica Guerin's murder. Hickey and the squad, which included Felix McKenna, had already enjoyed considerable success putting most of the General's gang behind bars.

Loughran and Gardiner, who were both IRA members and experienced armed robbers, were the leaders of the Athy Gang. Loughran from Dungannon, County Tyrone, moved to Coolock in north Dublin, to escape the authorities in Northern Ireland who wanted him for terrorist offences there. Gardiner from Cabra was also an active member of the IRA. Their illegal exploits proved that there was a nexus between the 'patriotic' Provos and the criminals they claimed to despise. Loughran and Gardiner had worked with Martin Cahill's brother John Cahill and his crew for nearly two years. That partnership ended when Cahill and two others were caught following a security van job in September 1988. Gardiner, Loughran and another associate, Dutchy Holland had escaped.

Paddy 'Dutchy' Holland was the hit man who shot Veronica on the orders of John Gilligan several years later. After that the Provos teamed up with other members of the same criminal gene pool including Brendan 'Wetty' Walsh and Thomas Tynan both of whom had been members of the General's gang. The fifth member of the soon to be infamous mob was twenty-six-year-old Austin Higgins from Donaghmede, north Dublin. He was unusual in that he came from a respectable middle-class family but had become enamoured by the perception that crime was glamorous.

Gardiner and Loughran, using their IRA training, organized the gang as a cellular model of an Active Service Unit. Secrecy and meticulous planning were the hallmarks of their modus operandi, as was targeting rural banks within a 120-mile radius south of Dublin. The chances of running into armed gardaí in sleepy country towns was substantially less than in the capital and rural cops were not geared to the same level of rapid response as their city colleagues.

Within a few months the Serious Crime Squad had identified the members of the gang and began watching them. The Gemini team used surveillance equipment that included eavesdropping devices which were placed in the cars the gang were using. It was one of the first times that such technology was used by the cops in an investigation. The information that the recordings gleaned could be used for intelligence purposes but not as evidence. That only came into effect in legislation twenty years later.

From what they heard the IRA men in particular were clear that they would shoot their way out if confronted by police – they had no scruples about killing or injuring cops. The Gemini team realized that they would require serious firepower when they confronted the gang. They called in the as yet untested ERU as back up. The breakthrough came when the hidden bugs recorded Loughran and Gardiner planning the job in Athy.

On a frigidly cold Friday afternoon eleven members of the ERU were deployed in the local fire station and a nearby yard, while another fifteen members of the Serious Crime Squad were positioned in an outer cordon. At 12.20 p.m. a detective watching the bank raised the alarm as the gang drove into Emily Square in a stolen BMW and parked outside the front door. Loughran stayed behind the wheel while the other four walked quickly in single file through the front door. They wore long coats, false beards and wigs. As they got to the door they took out their guns. They pushed the porter Noel Reddy back inside and ordered staff and customers, including young children, to get down. Three gangsters vaulted the counter and emptied the tills. They had done the exact same operation in the bank just four months earlier.

As soon as they heard the signal two teams of ERU officers, in high-powered cars, sped into the square. One car blocked the getaway car from the rear while the other blocked it at the front. Loughran frantically tried to shunt his way out from between the ERU cars by driving backwards and forwards. The roar of the car engine and the screeches of spinning tyres added to the confusion. The armed detectives fired a total of twenty shots at the wheels of the getaway car to immobilize it. When Loughran was ordered to put his hands up, he lifted a gun to shoot back. Two officers opened fire on him at the same time hitting him in the neck and head. The leader of the Athy Gang slumped sideways in his seat critically injured.

The rest of the gang heard the gunfire from inside the bank and began to panic. Higgins grabbed a bank official, John Condon, holding his neck in an arm lock. William Gardiner grabbed a customer and Walsh pulled the porter off the ground. Tynan lurked among the huddled group of frightened robbers and terrified hostages.

When the group got to the door the armed cops shouted at the gunmen to drop the weapons. Higgins moved his gun to the back of the official's head. He screamed: 'I'll blow his fucking head off if you don't move back.' As the robber moved his finger to the trigger the ERU opened fire.

The shooting was over in seconds. As silence descended and the cloud of cordite dissipated in the frigid afternoon air, Higgins lay mortally wounded. He had been shot in the head and died a few hours later. Tynan and the hostage John Condon were also lying seriously injured. Three ERU members and a pedestrian, who had been standing on the street 100 yards away, also suffered minor wounds from the ricochets of shotgun pellets. Walsh and Gardiner had retreated into the bank with their hostages but eventually surrendered.

Loughran was crippled as a result of his wounds and was not deemed fit to stand trial. Tynan recovered from his injuries and later joined Walsh and Gardiner in Portlaoise Prison. The survivors of the Athy gang each received twelve years for their escapade. The innocent bank official was left partially disabled from his wounds.

I didn't know any of the details above as I raced with a staff photographer to Athy that afternoon. I remember the excitement on the journey as the first reports of the incident were being reported on the radio news bulletins. They said that there had been a shootout in front of the bank involving gardaí and raiders. A number of people had been injured and arrests had been made. We didn't have mobile phones then so the radio was our only source of information.

By the time we arrived in Athy, along with the rest of the media posse from Dublin, the dying, the injured and the rest of the gang had been taken away in ambulances and squad cars. An eerie, unforgettable silence hung over the square as forensic experts gathered evidence and small groups of detectives in bullet-proof vests huddled in hushed conversation. There wasn't even the hint of a breeze to break the silence; it was as if Mother Nature had also been shocked by the incident. The local people who came to look on were stunned by what had happened.

At the front of the bank the squad cars and the getaway car, which were wedged together in a tangled mess, provided the evidence of the violent drama that had unfolded. The side of the getaway car was peppered with holes, its windows were shattered and the tyres had been blown out in the fusillade of police bullets. Bits of bloodied bandages used to patch up the dying and the injured lay scattered on the ground around the car wreck. Scenes of crime tape clung limply between lamp-posts to keep the public out. It was a startling sight for a young reporter at the scene of their first shootout.

In the days before camera phones we were fortunate to learn that the incident had been photographed by a local man who had watched the drama unfold from a building overlooking the square. The sensational images gave a frame-by-frame record of the shoot out and helped us piece together the dramatic events of a few hours earlier.

They showed armed cops crouching in doorways and behind cars training their weapons on the robbers as they surrendered. The pictures even captured the cloud of gun smoke as the ERU opened fire. In another frame detectives could be seen crouching over Higgins as they attempted to administer first aid – showing his head covered in blood. Through the shattered glass of the driver's window Loughran could be seen slumped in his seat.

It was the first and only time in my recollection that a shootout between cops and robbers was photographed as it happened on an Irish street. The pictures were so dramatic that the incident attracted international media attention. They provided a stark illustration of the gritty reality of the battle between the forces of law and disorder. No amount of words could tell the story in such stark detail. The Irish public had never seen the likes of it before, except in TV dramas.

The first operation by the ERU was a spectacular success and made for big news. It sent out an unequivocal message that chilled the collective spine of the criminal underworld. The gardaí had a deadly new weapon in their arsenal and had top quality intelligence. The Athy Gang was considered to be the best in the business but even they had been infiltrated and had walked into a trap. The aftermath of the incident, however, was not without controversy.

The following week Jim Cusack, the Security Correspondent of the *Irish Times*, broke the story that the ERU did all the shooting in Athy. The gang, whose weapons were cocked and ready to use, hadn't fired a single shot. A subsequent internal review of the shootout found that one of the weapons used by the unit, a Winchester pump action shotgun, had been responsible for the collateral injuries suffered by the gardaí and the member of the public. The weapon was deemed unsuitable for use in a built-up area. Tynan, Higgins and the bank official had been hit by bullets fired from the garda handguns. A review of firearms tactics was undertaken and a new system of communications was also introduced for such situations. It was a learning curve for the ERU.

The gardaí who had risked their lives to take on a dangerous and reckless gang received overwhelming public support. There was no sympathy for the gangsters – they were asking for trouble. The public perception held that it was the gangsters who were ultimately responsible for all the injuries suffered that day. Even the family of the injured bank official expressed support for the gardaí.

About a month after the incident I learned another salient lesson about the human tragedy wrought by violent crime. While our natural emotional reaction is to have sympathy for the innocent victims of crime, there is another side to the story behind the dramatic headlines that the public, and indeed the media, often forget. Even the most ruthless gangsters often leave behind grief-stricken loved ones. In many ways the families of reckless criminals who get killed in confrontations with the police or murdered by rival gangsters, are also victims of the senseless collateral damage created by organized crime.

Austin Higgins left behind a twenty-three-year-old pregnant widow with two little boys under the age of four. When I interviewed Patricia Higgins she was understandably heartbroken and still in shock from the enormity of the tragedy that had befallen her. There were no trappings of ill-gotten wealth in the couple's modest council home. Aside from her grief she was also facing the overwhelming task of being left with nothing and having to rear three children on her own. She only knew her husband as a loving partner and not as the dangerous desperado that died in Athy. Patricia Higgins said she didn't know that he was an armed robber. Their four-year-old son kept asking when his daddy was coming home.

Patricia said that on the morning of the ill-fated robbery Austin left the house as he usually did and said, 'see you later'. He never told her where he was going. She told me:

> When my kids get older I am going to tell them what happened
> to their father. I don't want them to fall into the same trap. I don't
> want them mixed up in crime. I'm scared having the baby on my
> own. No matter what Austin ever did I will always love him... it'll
> never be the same without him.

The dead man's mother, Patty, also expressed her grief, anger and confusion when I interviewed her. 'Sometimes I get really mad... he was such a fool to get mixed up in that mess,' Patty Higgins said, as tears streamed down her cheeks. She had reared her boy well in a good home where everyone worked and no one had ever been associated with crime of any kind. Like so many young criminals, Austin was lured in by the promise of easy money and excitement.

In many ways the sorrow of the Higgins family was compounded by the fact that the public had no sympathy for a dead gangster who was the author of his own destiny. Why should they care about people who instil fear and cause mayhem? I would interview the families of other criminals over the years who were to experience similar grief as the battle between the armed gangs and the police continued.

A few months later on 1 May a seven-member IRA gang raided the Allied Irish Bank in Enniscorthy, County Wexford. But the Provo mob spent too much time in the bank. As they left four local armed gardaí were outside, armed and waiting for them. When they ordered the gang to drop their weapons the Provos opened fire. In the ensuing shootout one member of the gang was shot and seriously injured. The rest of them were arrested. A local photographer captured an award-winning picture of the injured raider lying on the ground, with his head covered in blood. The front pages proclaimed another stunning victory for the good guys.

The wounded raider recovered from his injuries and joined the rest of the gang behind bars.

That July I was sent to cover the scene of yet another armed confrontation following a bank robbery and a high-speed chase in Dublin. Notorious blaggers Thomas Wilson and William 'Blinky' Doyle had been shot dead in a shootout with the ERU. Wilson was a former IRA member from Northern Ireland who had been in and out of prison for armed robberies on both sides of the border most of his life. He had joined the crime gang led by former INLA psychopath Tommy 'Zombie' Savage and his partner Mickey Weldon. Savage and Weldon went on to become major international drug dealers. The Zombie has the dubious distinction of carrying out the first recorded drug-related gangland killing in Ireland.

Wilson befriended Dublin armed robber Blinky Doyle when they met in Mountjoy Prison. By the summer of 1990 they topped the garda most wanted list after they'd carried out five armed bank robberies between 6 and 26 June. But their reign of terror came to an end in the aftermath of a bank robbery in Leixlip, County Kildare, on 6 July. As the heavily armed pair made their escape back to Dublin they were spotted by an ERU patrol near the Phoenix Park and a car chase ensued.

Over the next 15 minutes the two desperados reached reckless speeds of up to 100 miles per hour as they tried to shake off the squad cars closing in on them. Wilson fired several shots through the side window at the pursuing squad cars. At one stage the hoodlums drove on the wrong side of the Finglas dual carriageway facing the oncoming morning rush hour traffic. Garda sources later told me it was one of the most reckless and dangerous chases ever witnessed by the police in Dublin.

The robbers then sped into a warren of narrow residential side streets in Fairview. The getaway car collided with a parked car and spun around, facing the convoy of squad cars which had stopped behind it. Doyle drove at the police and mounted the pavement to get past the first car, while Thomas Wilson fired more shots. One of the detectives fired back. The car careered another fifty feet down the street before ramming into the side of another squad car, trapping the four unarmed officers inside.

One of the raiders could be seen lifting a weapon to open fire on the cops. Two members of the ERU, one of whom was armed with an Uzi submachine gun, fired a burst into the getaway car. Doyle was hit by five bullets while Wilson was hit in the head. They both died instantly. It had been another fatal day for criminals and another spectacular win for the police.

It was my second time to witness the scene of gangland carnage. It was both shocking and fascinating at the same time, like watching the aftermath of a drama on TV. The same eerie silence hung in the air just as it had done in Athy. I was to discover that it is the same at the scene of every shooting. Violent gunfire begets stunned silence. The bodies had been removed but the wreckage remained to tell the story. The getaway car was pock-marked with bullet holes and the windows were blown into shreds. Blood was spattered around the inside of the car and on the street. Such scenes were suddenly becoming a regular sight on Irish streets.

In three armed robberies over six months, three criminals had been shot dead, three had been seriously injured and another seven arrested. The underworld was paying a heavy price. The fact that an elite garda unit was turning the tables on the crime gangs was a big story. The public was fascinated by the shadowy super cops. I later wrote features about the kinds of weapons the ERU used and the training they did. I subsequently even got exclusive access and pictures as they practised storming a house. More than once over the following years the ERU mounted operations to prevent attacks on me and my family. I got to know a lot of the guys in the unit and was even honoured to be a guest at one of their weddings.

The ERU's involvement was the turning point. After the events of 1990 the number of armed robberies in Ireland by organized gangs dwindled. Although we didn't realize it at the time we were witnessing history in the making. Within a few years the blaggers would decommission their masks and guns to become drug traffickers. It made sense for economic and health reasons. A single deal on a few kilos of hash or heroin could yield more cash than ten or even twenty heists.

The underworld transition from heists to drugs started on E1, the wing of Portlaoise maximum security prison where the armed robbers were serving long sentences. The string of successes by the various garda units between 1988 and 1991 had filled the wing with villains who thought they would never be caught. The rest of the fortified prison complex was occupied by republican terrorists. The gang members had learned the hard way that armed crime was no longer a viable proposition. In the 1990s the future direction of organized crime was mapped out behind the slammer's grim stone walls which were patrolled by heavily armed soldiers.

It was here that John Gilligan, who was serving time for warehouse robberies, formed the nucleus of his drug gang including Dutchy Holland, Paul Ward and Brian Meehan amongst others. From Drimnagh, south Dublin, George Mitchell, Factory John's former associate, jailed for robbing a truck load of cattle drench, also came to the same conclusion that drugs were the way forward.

On the outside their associates were already getting involved in narcotics. Contacts and alliances were being made that would ultimately mould the gangland we know and dread today. Irish society was also undergoing dramatic change as the economy was growing into the Celtic Tiger era. Initially the gangs moved into the cannabis business. There was a growing demand for hashish and people had more money to spend on it. Criminals involved in the trade would say that cannabis was more tolerable in society than heroin. Heroin dealers were perceived as one of the lowest forms of criminal life. But that quickly changed as demands for other narcotics grew.

The move into the drug trade changed the gangland landscape beyond recognition. It undermined the old ethics of so-called ordinary decent criminals which had ensured a degree of sanity and pragmatism when it came to disputes. The prodigious profits generated through the sale of heroin, hashish, cocaine and ecstasy created a new generation of underworld entrepreneurs claiming their slice of a trade which by 2024 was worth billions per annum. In the process it made people rich beyond their wildest dreams and very greedy. The flip side of greed is treachery and betrayal where violence, intimidation and murder become the corporate tools of choice. It led to a new gangland phenomenon – the contract murder. In the 30 years since the demise of the General gangland has claimed over 300 lives.

In 1992 I travelled to London to interview Dave 'Myler' Brogan, a former friend and associate of Gerry Hutch, the Monk. He had moved away because he feared that the Hutch family were going to kill him in a row over property bought with the laundered proceeds of armed hold-ups. Brogan was one of the first armed robbers who made the move into narcotics during the first phase of Ireland's narcotics trade in the 1970s. In the early 1980s Brogan established major international supply routes for cannabis into Ireland through his contacts with producers in Lebanon's Bekaa Valley and international dealers in Holland. He was one of the first to realize the value of the hash business – and the chaos that it brought to gangland. He lamented:

> When drugs came everything changed. There was no loyalty and people who had once been friends started turning guns on each other because one thought the other had ripped him off. Fuck it, it just wasn't worth the hassle any more. The money is easy in drugs but then I got out of it because of the sort of reptiles I found myself mixing with.

Within a few years of his release from prison in 1991 George Mitchell had become a formidable figure in the underworld. He built a major international drug trafficking operation and had a large gang of hardened criminals under his command. The gang was also still involved in armed heists and Mitchell imported illegal firearms which he gave as 'tribute' to the IRA so that they wouldn't interfere in his business. I began to hear about the ascent of George Mitchell from garda and underworld contacts around that time and started researching his background.

In 1995 Mitchell gave us an excuse to write about him when he came close to a gang war with the Monk. Hutch's family was involved in a feud with heroin dealer Derek 'Maradona' Dunne who lived with Mitchell's daughter in the north inner-city. Mitchell warned that there would be a conflagration if his daughter or grandchild were caught in the crossfire. Around the same time the godfather sent hit man Mickey Boyle to kill one of London's biggest mobsters, Tony Brindle. Brindle was involved in a feud with Mitchell's London suppliers, the Daleys. The plot was discovered by the gardaí who tipped off the Met in London. Armed police were lying in wait for Boyle and shot and seriously injured the assassin but not before he managed to wound Brindle.

After that I wrote a number of stories about Mitchell relating to the Hutch feud and the London hit. I developed a source who was familiar with the gang and gave me information about his drug operation and gun smuggling racket which were corroborated through garda sources. But we couldn't yet name Mitchell and his picture carried the obligatory black stripe across the eyes. It would eventually come off as I dug deeper into his activities. In the meantime we had to create a nickname for him. John Traynor had been another helpful source of information. He called Mitchell a 'filthy cunt' which was the Coach's line for everyone he disliked. He hated Mitchell. He told me that Mitchell was obese and waddled like a penguin which Traynor mimicked with his arms. That was how the international gangster got his infamous sobriquet. The name stuck and it was even used in garda intelligence documents about Mitchell. But I found out the hard way that George didn't like it.

One morning in November 1995 I discovered by accident that I was under threat from the Penguin. On the way to work I spotted a car in my rear view mirror that seemed to be deliberately keeping pace with me. Later I saw the same car again, this time a few cars behind. When I called the detectives in Crumlin I was told the suspicious car belonged to the surveillance section of the Central Detective Unit (CDU). The operation came to light when a local patrol car pulled in a red van near my home which, it turned out, was a surveillance vehicle with armed officers on board.

On that occasion CDU had received intelligence that the Penguin was planning to have me attacked but there was no information about what form it would take. The plan was that the armed officers would intercept the gang in the act. I was to be kept in the dark which was a little unsettling. Around that time a garda friend gave me a Kevlar bullet-proof vest to wear under my clothes as a precaution. It was bloody uncomfortable to wear and it tended to make my stomach sick. In the meantime the police let Mitchell know that they knew what he was up to and the threat subsided.

I put the vest back in the wardrobe. I was going to need it again.

CHAPTER FIVE

———

THE PSYCHO

William 'Jock' Corbally always wanted to make a name for himself as a major player in gangland. Like many villains I have known over the decades, Jock aspired to pulling off the one big stroke that would set him up for life. The likeable rogue and petty thief, regarded by criminals and cops alike as 'harmless', spent more time dreaming of pulling off the elusive 'big job' than actually doing anything about it. The problem was that his ambitions far exceeded his abilities.

The hapless wannabe mobster didn't possess either the ruthlessness or acumen to make his mark. Jock was also cursed with bad luck which meant he tended to end up behind bars whenever he tried anything. In a bitter twist of fate, however, Jock Corbally did make his mark in the blood-spattered pages of gangland history. He is remembered as the victim of one of the most depraved and gruesome murders ever recorded in the underworld.

Jock, from Ballygall Parade in Finglas, on the west side of Dublin, was a source of mine when he vanished without trace in February 1996. He was forty-four years old.

Shortly afterwards rumours began to circulate that he had been abducted, tortured and murdered. The word was that his body was then dumped in an unmarked grave and covered in lime to ensure it would never be found. The prime suspect was Jock's neighbour and former friend, a drug dealer called Peter Joseph 'PJ' Judge, who held the distinction of being one of the most savage monsters gangland ever produced. Even when compared with some of the barbarians who have emerged in recent decades, he stands out as being one of the most feared godfathers in organized crime.

When I first heard a rumour of Jock's disappearance I began to investigate what happened to him. Over the following months I found myself in extremely dangerous territory as I set about unravelling the mystery around Jock's murder and exposing Judge to the world. I went on to bestow on Judge the fitting sobriquet the Psycho. He decided then that I would suffer a similar fate as my erstwhile informant.

———

To the unsuspecting observer Peter Joseph 'PJ' Judge was a small, unremarkable, average-looking man with a taste for designer clothes. He spoke with a calm voice and had a warm, charming smile which women found attractive. He helped old ladies across the road and was a devoted, loving son to his widowed mother. But behind the façade of benign respectability lurked an individual who was the polar opposite to the persona he presented to the world.

He was one of the first gangsters in Ireland to make the transition from armed robbery to the drug trade at the start of the 1990s. Judge controlled his extensive drug trafficking network through the exclusive use of fear and extreme violence. He was a classic psychopath who took pleasure dispensing pain and death to those who crossed him or those he *thought* had crossed him. By comparison he made Martin Cahill almost look normal.

While researching the mobster's background I spoke to a detective who had spent most of his career in Finglas and witnessed Judge's rise to notoriety. He left no doubt that the nickname the Psycho was deserved:

> I have known practically every major criminal in Dublin for over thirty years and I have never met one like Judge. There was a behavioural kink in the bastard. He was the worst, most evil fuck I ever came across. He committed two of the most brutal murders I have investigated and he even tried to murder guards.

In the 1990s garda intelligence reports described Judge as 'a vicious and extremely dangerous criminal and contract killer'.

The same view was held by Judge's peers. A criminal who once worked with him agreed with the veteran cop – but only after Judge's demise:

> He scared the shit out of everyone. There was something about that fucker that just wasn't right. He talked like butter wouldn't melt in his mouth but could cut your heart out and smile into your face at the same time. Most criminals kill because it's just part of the business but Judge loved it.

Born in 1955, Judge was the youngest of four – he had two sisters and a brother – and grew up in the family home at Ballygall Crescent in Finglas. Jock Corbally, who was four years older, grew up around the corner. They were once friends and even took part in crimes together.

From the age of ten PJ Judge was already set on his chosen path in life as he regularly got into trouble with the local police. Kids who grew up with him described a small scruffy kid with a bad stammer which gave him an inferiority complex. His peers recalled how PJ always seemed to have to prove that he was tougher than the other kids in the neighbourhood.

His criminal career started in much the same way as every gangster at the time: robbing cars and breaking into shops and houses. Judge was a particularly skilled driver and one of Dublin's first joyriders, revelling in getting involved in high-speed chases with the police.

Judge's criminal CV began in 1967 at the age of twelve – the same year he dropped out of school – when he was convicted in the Children's Court for larceny, assault and burglary. In each case the District Court Judge gave him the benefit of the doubt and applied the Probation of Offenders Act (POA). The Act is intended as a slap on the wrist to a first-time offender and is designed to give them a chance to mend their ways and incentivize their return to a law-abiding life. Every gangster in Ireland has the letters POA recorded alongside their first convictions. The evidence suggests that it is probably the most ineffective legislation in the criminal justice system and points to the depressingly predictable fact that once a young delinquent embarks on a life of crime there is rarely any going back.

It wasn't long before the darker side of his character began to emerge. When he was thirteen PJ Judge befriended a group of kids from another neighbourhood. His new friends convinced the insecure small, fair-haired kid that he should dye his hair a darker colour. Anxious to fit in with the kids from the upmarket estate PJ allowed them to do the honours. When he returned to Ballygall Crescent his friends laughed and told him that they had made a fool of him.

That evening he and one of his pals from Ballygall Crescent broke into a gunsmiths on Glasnevin Avenue, Finglas, and stole shotguns and ammunition. Around 4 a.m. the following morning Judge took out his rage on the kids who had made him look like a fool when he fired a number of shots into their upmarket home. PJ Judge was later arrested and sentenced to two years in the notorious St Conleth's reform school in Daingean, County Offaly, for the attack. Given the level of sexual, psychological and physical violence that was endemic in the religious-run hellholes Judge, like Martin Cahill, the Dunnes and many others, learned that violence was an effective tool in life. He emerged more dangerous than when he went in.

When he was released he went back to the same gun dealers and stole more weapons. He later shot and seriously injured another teenager who had been picking on him. In November 1972 he was convicted and sentenced to six months for assault. The conviction was later overturned on appeal. By the age of seventeen other kids described him as a 'head case'. Judge had a growing criminal record to match as he progressed from petty thief to armed robber. The local gardaí realized that the teenage thug was a serious problem in the making. 'From the first shooting incident we knew he was going to be a wrong one. He was a natural born killer,' recalled another former detective.

Judge led a burglary gang of four other local kids. He was a natural organizer and ran the gang like a business. Soon they were one of the most prolific and violent of the new generation of gangs to emerge in the early 1970s. In one of the robberies an elderly man died as a result of his terrifying experience. The gang began hitting jewellers, warehouses and rural banks, earning a fortune.

Unlike the other gang members who spent their stolen cash on a good time, Judge was more prudent. He did not drink very much or take drugs. He lodged the loot in various bank accounts under different names, reinvesting some of the loot to buy guns for his arsenal.

One of his then associates later told me:

> Judge was the man in charge and no one messed with him because they knew what he was capable of. But he was a good planner and there was good money in his robberies, although there were times he didn't pay everyone their fair share.

Judge hated the gardaí with the same passion as he loved crime and fast cars. From the time he was a teenager he refused to speak while being questioned about crimes and never admitted to anything. In one joy riding incident he rammed a garda motorcyclist off his bike. As he went to reverse over the injured officer a passer-by pulled him out of the way in the nick of time.

During a hold-up at a post office in Ballyfermot, south Dublin, in 1979 he shot and seriously injured the postmaster. This time the gardaí were hot on his heels and he was arrested. The van used in the heist was registered to Jock Corbally but he hadn't been involved. When he was quizzed by gardaí he told them that he had loaned it to Judge to move furniture. The Psycho was charged with the robbery and possession of firearms with intent to endanger life. The incident deepened his dangerous grudge against Jock.

While out on bail for that offence Judge was caught again robbing a bank at Annesly Bridge in central Dublin. During the raid he was confronted by an unarmed garda. Judge aimed his gun at the policeman and pulled the trigger. The gun jammed and the Psycho was nabbed again. Judge had run out of road.

In April 1980 he was sentenced to ten years imprisonment for the post office robbery. He subsequently received another ten-year stretch for the bank robbery. He served nine years in prison for the two offences.

On his release in 1989 he was one of the first armed robbers to move into the drug trade – an obvious career choice. The Psycho began selling large quantities of cannabis and the money came rolling in. Then he branched out into heroin, ecstasy and amphetamines.

The universal criminal move into drugs changed the ethos of gangland. The prodigious profits led to greed which in turn brought treachery, betrayal and violence. The transition resulted in a steady increase in the new phenomenon of gangland killings and turf wars. PJ Judge had little difficulty adapting to the new scene.

Within two years he controlled one of the biggest drug trafficking networks in Ireland. He supplied a number of young up-and-coming drug dealers from Finglas, Ballymun, Ballyfermot, Crumlin, Clondalkin and the inner-city. He controlled 'patches' right across the capital and was doing business with drug gangs in Limerick and Cork. I learned how, as the money piled up, a criminal associate who ran a milk round was given the job of organizing cash-counting centres where the money from the Psycho's network of drug pushers was collected and totalled. From there it passed through a myriad of bank accounts under false names both in Ireland and offshore. It was also laundered through a number of front companies, including a taxi firm.

From the get-go Judge was hands-on in the business. It was not unusual for him to be spotted driving around at 4 a.m. supervising his pushers as they moved his product around the city. He also operated a zero tolerance approach to anyone who tried to rip him off or who wasn't paying up in time. If money or drugs were lost or seized from any of his lieutenants Judge punished them by doubling the value of what was lost. If the debt wasn't paid then the errant pusher was severely beaten or even shot. Judge was guaranteed total loyalty and secrecy from his people because they were absolutely terrified of him.

As his business grew, the Psycho had overcome his stammer, and jettisoned the scruffy look for a clean cut image and designer clothes. Judge always drove flashy cars. He had a string of girlfriends including a number of prostitutes who worked for him when he branched out into brothel keeping. The fact that he was also bisexual added to the complexity of his character. Judge went to great lengths to hide this predilection. Being a gay gangster in the macho crime world of the 1990s had to be kept secret. And such was his ferocious reputation that none of gangland's other hard men would dare to speak openly about it.

As I began digging into his background I discovered that it was well known in gangland circles that he regularly sexually exploited young vulnerable male and female addicts – some of them children in their teens – who depended on him for their drugs and money. He was known to sadistically beat some of his male and female lovers, for no apparent reason.

One young guy who was in his late teens told me how the Psycho beat and raped him. 'I never said anything to anyone because he told me he would kill me if I ever opened my mouth and I knew he would,' he said.

On another occasion he gave a girlfriend such a beating that she ran into the Bridewell garda station for protection. Judge burst in after her demanding that the terrified woman leave with him. The police told him to get out or he would be charged. The girlfriend, however, was too scared to prefer charges and later moved out of town to avoid bumping into her psychotic former boyfriend.

Another girlfriend whom I subsequently interviewed recalled how he took pleasure hurting her. The young woman from a respectable middle-class background fell for Judge's charm but it wasn't long before his dark side emerged. She said:

> He would beat me and seemed to like it. Once he broke my fingers in a rage and refused to let me see a doctor. I had to sit there, sobbing and in pain, trying to bandage my fingers together. PJ wouldn't let me get a doctor. He kept looking at me and laughing. On another occasion he left me for dead and I was forced to leave the country for over six months. I was like a down-and-out and wore disguises in case PJ or any of his friends found out where I was. I was so frightened of him – I was absolutely terrified. My father reported the assault to the gardaí to get him off my back but he didn't seem a bit worried about them.

Judge might not have been worried about the gardaí but they were beginning to take a serious interest in him as intelligence sources revealed that he had moved into drugs in a major way. The surveillance units attached to the Serious Crime and Drug squads regularly attempted to keep track of the Psycho's movements around the city. But it was an extremely difficult task because Judge had trained himself in counter-surveillance techniques. Although some of his drug shipments were seized Judge always ensured he was a safe distance away. His pushers were so scared of him that they preferred to go to prison, whatever the length of the sentence, instead of testifying against him in court.

In 1993 Judge copper-fastened his fearsome reputation when he murdered a small-time fraud merchant called Michael Godfrey. The fifty-five-year-old sealed his fate when he agreed to do business with PJ Judge in 1989. Their first stroke together was a money counterfeiting scam. Godfrey had a contact in England who produced good quality Irish currency which Judge bought and passed off through his lackeys in Dublin. The racket came to an abrupt end when Godfrey was arrested in the UK with a consignment of dud £20 notes. The con man was convicted and jailed for thirty months.

After his release Godfrey and the Psycho decided to set up a front company to import large quantities of cannabis thus cutting out the middlemen. They travelled to Amsterdam and did a deal for 30 kilos of hash for which Judge paid the equivalent of €74,000. In February 1993 the dope was shipped to an industrial unit the pair had rented in Glasnevin. But the scam came unstuck when Judge checked on the merchandise and refused to accept it on the grounds that it was not the hash he had sampled in Amsterdam.

He flew into a blood-curdling temper and ordered Godfrey to get the money back. Instead of returning the hash Godfrey sold it for almost double the original price to a young drug dealer called Peter 'Fatso' Mitchell from the north inner-city. Mitchell was the best pal of Brian the 'Tosser' Meehan. The pair went on to become key members of John Gilligan's crime gang. Meehan, who was in prison with Gilligan at the time, was later sentenced to life for the murder of Veronica Guerin. When Judge got wind of the deal he decided to exact revenge.

On the night of 31 March 1993, Judge went looking for Fatso Mitchell armed with a pistol. When he couldn't find him he shot one of Fatso's associates in the leg. The drug dealer was hospitalized but refused to co-operate with the police. Three days later, Judge sent two of his henchmen to abduct Michael Godfrey. They took him to an area of waste ground on the outer edges of Finglas called Scribblestown Lane where the Psycho was waiting.

According to sources who were there that night Judge caught his erstwhile partner by the throat and beat him. He ordered one of the henchmen to execute his former partner. The bullet only injured Godfrey who began pleading for his life. Judge grabbed the gun, cocked it and fired another shot into the back of Godfrey's head. He calmly walked away without speaking, got into his car and drove off. The gardaí knew Judge was the killer and he was one of a number of people arrested and questioned. There was no evidence to charge him.

Members of his gang who were interviewed told gardaí off the record that Judge terrified them. The brutal gangland murder, one of three that took place in 1993, scared a lot of people in the criminal underworld. It suited Judge that it was well known he was responsible – it would keep people in line and too afraid to talk to the cops.

———

People who knew Judge best revealed how there were three types of people that caused the narcissistic Psycho to spiral into a murderous rage: those who ripped him off as Godfrey found out; those who made him feel inadequate; and those who made him lose face. Tragically, William Jock Corbally managed to do all three at once.

Jock was very different to Judge. Despite his posturing, he was neither violent nor dangerous. Handsome and charismatic, he was the quintessential 'ladies' man'. But his luck with women was not reflected in his criminal life. By his forties, Corbally had accumulated a total of twenty-three convictions mostly for larceny and theft. Some of his earlier crimes were committed with Judge. The same detective who earlier described Judge said of Corbally:

> He was a harmless lad, there was no badness in him. Whenever
> he did anything he was caught. We [gardaí] were always telling
> him to give up this crime lark, it simply didn't suit him.

I was told that Judge's resentment towards Corbally could be traced back to when he was released from Daingean in the late 1960s. Jock was seen by the other teenage crooks in the area as the main man on the block. Judge was intensely jealous of his rival. When the former friends had a punch up in the street Corbally came out the winner which humiliated the Psycho. Even though they later patched up their differences, Judge never forgot or forgave his defenestration.

Around the same time that Judge began moving into narcotics in the late 1980s, Jock was jailed for two years for possession of cannabis with intent to supply. When Jock was released in 1991 Judge was running things. Corbally began selling small quantities of cannabis for Judge in the Ballymun and Finglas areas but the arrangement didn't last long. Judge accused Corbally of ripping him off and threatened to sort Jock out. Jock's brothers later told me how Judge broke up a car Jock was being driven in and let it be known that Corbally was going to get what was coming to him.

The situation worsened when Jock discovered that while he was in prison Judge had been using Corbally's two teenage sons to sell hashish for him. The boys were a chip off the old block. Unfortunately the hapless pair had sold a small portion of the hashish Judge gave them and took the rest for themselves. When the Psycho had found out he'd gone to one of Corbally's brothers and warned of dire consequences if the money was not paid up. Jock was furious when he heard this. He didn't want his sons getting mixed up with Judge. They met and he promised Judge he would pay back the balance of the money. The Psycho said he now wanted double the money but Jock didn't have the cash.

In April 1991 the situation came to a head when Judge confronted Jock and his sixteen-year-old son Graham on the street. He said he would spare them if they left the country. A row ensued during which Jock hit Judge across the head with an iron bar. The Psycho was later hospitalized and received thirty stitches. Jock had effectively signed his own death warrant.

Six weeks later Graham Corbally disappeared for two days and his father thought the worst. He reported his son missing to the police who treated this particular missing person case very seriously. They were aware of the conflict between Corbally and Judge and of the Psycho's propensity for extreme violence. A few days later however the emergency was called off when Graham turned up unharmed. His disappearance had nothing to do with Judge – he had gone to ground of his own volition.

In late 1992 Corbally was given a reprieve of sorts thanks to the team of detectives who arrested him behind the wheel of a truckload of beef stolen from the Larry Goodman empire. He was jailed for five years at the Dublin Circuit Criminal Court.

What Jock lacked in criminal acumen he made up for with chutzpah. In early 1995 he phoned me at the *Sunday World* and said that he would like to meet. He said he had plenty of information about what was happening in gangland and wanted to share. He had been in contact with me on and off over the few years before his latest conviction. Jock would ring in from time to time with a tip off about some crime or other in the hope of getting a few quid for his efforts. The information that he shared tended to be low level and insignificant.

I agreed to meet him that February in the old Circuit Criminal Court building in central Dublin where his sentence was up for review.

I watched him assuring the judge that if he was released he would stay away from crime and go straight. He was so convincing that I, like the compassionate Judge Michael Moriarty, believed him. But half an hour later over a cup of coffee he was bragging loquaciously about his next big job. Jock was clearly a Walter Mitty character and it was obvious that he was no Mr Big. But he was an instantly likeable character. Why else was he telling a crime reporter what he was planning to do next?

His next stroke was certainly grandiose in scale and ambition. He was talking about pulling off a counterfeit money scam with the notorious Jamaican Yardies gang in London. At the time the Yardies were one of the most violent drug trafficking gangs in the UK and had been involved in gang wars in Manchester and London.

'We hope to move £25 million worth of dud sterling notes around the country,' he confided enthusiastically.

He actually wanted me to do a story about it which was extremely bizarre to say the least. He even gave me the date when he claimed to have flown to meet representatives of the gang in London. Jock wanted to be referred to in the article as the 'Professor'. It didn't take a psychic to read into Jock's naïve plan. He wanted the story published to convince other potential partners-in-crime that he had finally found the scam that would set him up for life. The born chancer probably also thought the story depicting him as a hard man with fearsome connections would scare off enemies like Judge. Sure, why else would the *Sunday World* be writing about him? It was all fantasy but I published a short piece on the supposed

Yardie scam because it made for an interesting read – and let Jock have his bit of fun.

From talking with Jock it was obvious that he desperately wanted to go straight and become a businessman, rubbing shoulders with what he described as 'the respectable people'. His hero was the much younger Gerry Hutch, the Monk, who had claimed Martin Cahill's title as the mastermind of the biggest armed heists in the history of the State. Around the same time Hutch pulled off his biggest heist yet, the robbery of €5.5 million (today's value) when his gang hit the Brinks Allied cash-holding depot. It was well known that the Monk had invested his stolen loot in property and Jock wanted to get in on the action. He told me he was friends with Hutch, which I later confirmed, but that was as far as the relationship went with the wily Monk. Everyone considered Jock a likeable messer. He confided: 'All I need is to pull one big job and then I'm going straight. I want to invest some with the Monk down in Sherriff Street. I don't intend stroking for the rest of my life.'

In the meantime Jock was back living in Ballygall with his mother Maureen, a gentle, deeply religious woman who was hugely respected in the local community. She always prayed that her wayward son would give up crime and go straight.

Thanks to Jock's reputation for bad luck and loose talk most of his old criminal buddies didn't want to work with him anymore. It wasn't helped by the fact that everyone knew that Judge was also on his case and no one wanted to fuck with him.

I used to hear from Jock from time to time after that. The information he offered had to be always taken with a pinch of salt but I genuinely liked talking to him. However I do recall him suggesting that I keep an eye out for a major drug dealer who was also very violent. He said his name was PJ Judge. I had already heard about Judge through garda sources investigating the murder of Michael Godfrey. It was Jock's last tip off.

In the summer of 1995 Judge spotted Jock one day in Ballygall Parade while out walking with his third child, a five-year-old son from another relationship. Jock had kept out of the Psycho's way up to then.

Judge flew into a blind rage when he spotted his nemesis. Jock symbolized all that was wrong in the world in the Psycho's twisted mind. He jumped out of his car with a hammer in his hand and lunged at Jock in front of the terrified child. The 'Professor' was a very capable street fighter. He disarmed his attacker and gave him a few punches.

A member of the Corbally family later told me about the incident. The Psycho stood snarling and spitting on the pavement. 'You're a fuckin' dead man,' he hissed. Then Judge suddenly composed himself, smirked and drove off for tea with his mother.

Jock had succeeded in humiliating the Psycho yet again. Corbally's family said that he was terrified. He had to leave town but couldn't until he had enough money. Jock had plenty of reasons to be afraid. In June 1995 Judge found himself at the centre of another gangland murder investigation.

Thirty-one-year-old David Weafer from Finglas, a former member of Factory John Gilligan's gang, had become one of the Psycho's dealers. Following a row over the proceeds of a drug deal Judge threatened to kill Weafer if he didn't pay up. The terrified gangster knew that the Psycho would carry out the threat so he decided to kill him first. Garda sources revealed that Weafer had waited to shoot Judge outside his mother's home but the killer hadn't turned up. A week later Weafer was blasted to death as he answered the front door. In the following edition of the *Sunday*

World I wrote about Weafer's background and the belief that he had locked horns with a dangerous drug dealer. The article was accompanied by a stark picture from the scene showing just two blood-stained bare feet, pointing upwards at the front door.

———

In February 1996 William Jock Corbally vanished without trace. Shortly after, rumours began to trickle through the gangland grapevine that he had been murdered by PJ Judge and his body buried in an unmarked grave. Jock's family reported him missing and gardaí, who had also heard the same rumours and were aware of the problems with Judge, commenced a major investigation. The few details circulating about the murder shocked even hardened criminals. There was a lot of sympathy for the family, who were well regarded, particularly Jock's mother, Maureen.

A garda contact rang me and mentioned Jock's disappearance and the theory about what had happened to him. I was shocked. He was the first gangland victim who I had come to know personally. But he wouldn't be the last. I was already aware of PJ Judge but didn't know much about him, other than now he was a suspect in three gang-related murders.

In Garda Headquarters the focus of the investigation was finding Jock's body. Deputy Commissioner Noel Conroy had known and arrested Judge when he was a detective based in Finglas. He knew Judge had to be stopped. He also knew Jock Corbally and had huge sympathy for the family who were seen as decent people. It was decided that every effort would be made to put the Psycho out of business. A special investigation team was set up and units throughout the Dublin Metropolitan Area were put on alert to stop and search Judge whenever they spotted him. The heat was coming down hot and heavy.

I began talking to gardaí who were close to the investigation and were happy to share background information about the Psycho. They knew that it was important that the public got to hear about Judge's dirty work. In my experience the reason gardaí speak to the media off the record has always been to expose criminals and their rackets. At the same time garda sources were warning us about how John Gilligan was building a crime empire but nothing could be done about his millionaire lifestyle. Focusing a public spotlight on the lawbreakers helps get the gardaí the resources they need to do their jobs. In this case they were pushing an open door.

I also reached out to Jock's brothers, Derek and Eddie, who had been conducting their own investigation. They had been out day and night searching ditches in fields where they thought they might find their brother's grave. They knew that Jock was never coming back alive.

The brothers helped open doors by convincing sources that I could be trusted. Apart from the police, everyone I spoke to was terrified of Judge. I spoke to some of the Psycho's victims who only co-operated on conditions of strict anonymity. I also spoke to criminals who were genuinely upset for the Corbally family and wanted to see Judge exposed. It was one those rare occasions when diverse interests converge for the common good.

Over the following months I put the different bits and pieces of information together and unravelled the mystery of what happened to Jock. A dark and sinister picture began to take shape in my notes. I started to compile a dossier on the disappearance. The story was truly shocking.

In January 1996 Judge got the opportunity that he had been eagerly awaiting – to permanently close Jock's eyes. The wannabe super criminal handed himself up on a plate.

Declan 'Decie' Griffin from Coolock in north Dublin was involved in the heroin business with the Psycho. The twenty-five-year-old thug was a treacherous individual who was also a garda informant, when it suited his interests. Griffin recruited Jock to courier a kilo of heroin from Amsterdam back to Dublin. Offered the equivalent of €1,300 to do the run Jock could not help himself. But Corbally had no idea that Griffin was in business with Judge.

When he returned to Dublin Jock came up with a hare-brained plan to make easy money. He arranged for an associate to hide the heroin near Sutton Dart station after he'd purloined a quarter kilo for himself. Corbally then tipped off the gardaí detailing where the stash was hidden. Reports that gardaí had seized 784 grams of almost pure heroin, worth the equivalent of over €630,000 on the streets, were all over the media. Griffin realized he – and Judge – had been ripped off.

On 28 February Griffin called Jock with the offer of another trip to Holland. He assured Jock that the seizure was nothing more than bad luck. Griffin said that he needed help digging up the money for the drugs which was hidden in a field. They arranged to meet in Chapelizod, near the Phoenix Park in Dublin's city centre. Jock's family and friends later recalled that he was 'very excited' that evening, saying he was going to make another 'earner' although he didn't specify what it was. Griffin picked him up at a phone box outside the Mullingar pub in Chapelizod.

It was a dark and particularly cold evening. The pair made small talk as Jock was driven the ten miles or so to his death. Griffin had been instructed by Judge to drive to a field at the rear of the Green

Isle Hotel near the Air Corps base in Baldonnel, on the western edge of the city. When the car pulled up in the field I was told that Jock was horrified when Judge suddenly looked into the open passenger door and said: 'Jock, we want to have a word with you.'

Also waiting in the field was twenty-two-year-old Mark Dwyer from Cabra, north Dublin, who was one of Judge's trusted enforcers. Dwyer, who was small and prematurely bald, shared Judge's passion for violence. A third member of the gang, a former member of the INLA from Belfast who acted as the gang's bagman, was also present. The sources revealed that the Psycho had picked the location because no one would hear his victim's screams.

I was told that Jock tried to beat them off but they dragged him from the car to the side of the field. Griffin later confided to gardaí that Dwyer and Judge beat Corbally with iron bars and a pick-axe handle as he screamed in agony and begged for mercy. But the more he screamed, the more frenzied Judge became and he accused Jock of being an informant: 'Mountjoy is full of fellows because of you.' Blood oozed from welts and cuts and broken limbs as Jock tried desperately to fend off the flurry of blows and kicks.

According to Griffin, Judge stopped the frenzied attack to check that his victim was still alive. After waiting for so many years he didn't want Jock to die too quickly. Judge then stabbed his former friend a number of times around the body as he lay groaning facedown. The Psycho didn't push the knife in too far because he wanted Jock to suffer more. Then he turned him over and smashed Jock's pearly white teeth with an iron bar.

Griffin later confirmed to me: 'Jock had always prided himself on his nice teeth. They were part of his good looks. Judge really enjoyed smashing them. It was a bonus for him.'

After a while Judge and Dwyer took a break because they were so exhausted. Jock was lying on his stomach whimpering. His body could take no more and he fell silent. Judge, Dwyer and the third man dumped Jock into the boot of a second car.

The Psycho told Griffin to drive Dwyer back to Dublin before he drove off alone in the direction of County Kildare. It was believed that Judge had dug a grave near Straffan, north Kildare, where he regularly hid his drugs. It was later claimed that before covering his enemy's body in lime and dirt, Judge cut Jock's throat for good measure. It was not known if Jock was dead or alive when he was dumped into his grave.

Later that evening Mark Dwyer arrived at a friend's flat in north Dublin. His clothes and shoes were covered in blood. He told the people in the flat what had happened and seemed to be in high spirits about the gruesome affair. The witnesses said that Dwyer got a call from the Psycho.

'Is the baby asleep?' asked Dwyer.

'The baby has been tucked in and is sound asleep,' Judge is said to have replied.

The gardaí got plenty of information about the incident as the weeks and months dragged on. Decie Griffin typically tried to play both sides. He gave information to the police and to me but ensured he played down his own role. As a police informant he could not be charged on the basis of any information he shared. In any event there was the added difficulty that there wasn't a body to prove a murder had taken place.

A number of other individuals who had spoken with Dwyer also secretly reported what they knew to the gardaí. But such was the Psycho's reputation the cops knew that no one would stand up in court against him.

In the *Sunday World,* in consultation with Colm MacGinty, we decided to go big on the Jock Corbally murder. Over the months we had built an extensive dossier with pictures of the monster and his victim. I had been firmly advised by Jock's brothers and the police not to approach Judge for a comment. I was told he would go berserk and it would not end well. In any event I didn't need to talk to Judge – the information we had spoke for itself.

We kept the investigation under wraps for obvious reasons and took the approach of effectively creeping up on Judge. Just before we were about to publish the major exposé a senior detective contacted Colm to advise against it. He warned that the Psycho was likely to have me murdered. I was getting used to receiving death threats and had long made up my mind that I wasn't backing down. Colm had reservations but ultimately we made the decision to print and be damned. We were determined to expose PJ Judge to the world. Having brought so much fear and heartache into the lives of innocent people it was the least the bastard deserved. There was no room for impartiality dealing with a monster.

On 12 May the front page had the dramatic headline 'Executioner'. We gave him the nickname the Psycho and told the story of Judge and the murder of Jock Corbally over four pages. It included pictures of him with thin black stripes across his eyes. Even though we didn't name Judge for legal reasons everyone in gangland knew who he was. We even gave the readers a big hint and sent a message to Judge that it would not be long before we would be taking away the black stripes. The last line of the front page stated: 'Today we uncover the sordid world of the Psycho, the gangster who considers himself Judge, Jury and Executioner.'

The story revealed the extent of his drug dealing empire and his propensity for violence. We even made sure to reveal that he was bisexual to add to his humiliation amongst his peers. I was proud of what we had produced. Exposing monsters like Judge was what the *Sunday World* was all about. As a precaution I timed the publication to coincide with a three-week family holiday in Spain. Gardaí had told me it was probably safer to be out of the country.

When the newspaper hit the streets it came as shocking bolt out of the blue to Judge. His gang members said he went berserk. He called a meeting of all his henchmen and began an internal witch hunt to find out who had been talking. Within twenty-four hours of the story appearing gardaí received intelligence that he had placed a contract on my head. He gave orders that I was to be abducted and tortured to discover the source of the story. Like Judge's other victims, I was then to be dispatched with a bullet in the back of the head.

When I returned from holidays I was met by senior gardaí who officially informed me that there was a threat to my life from PJ Judge. Gardaí increased patrols around my home yet again. I retrieved the Kevlar bullet-proof vest from the wardrobe at home and began wearing it again, just as a precaution.

There were plenty of developments to take my mind off the problem with the Psycho. On 7 June an IRA gang murdered Detective Garda Jerry McCabe and left his partner, Ben O'Sullivan, critically injured. The attack took place when the Provos attempted to rob a post office delivery truck in the village of Adare, County Limerick. One of the terrorists had opened fire on the two detectives with a lethal AK-47 rifle. The officers were given no warning or time to react. The crime shocked the nation and put Sinn Féin's electoral ambitions back by years.

But then nineteen days later on 26 June 1996, Ireland was rocked by another atrocity when journalist Veronica Guerin was murdered on the orders of John Gilligan. A garda friend called to tell me the horrifying news and I was one of the first journalists to arrive at the scene. I will never forget the sight of our colleague lying in the driver's seat of her car, her clothes drenched in blood, dead.

That was the moment that a gut-wrenching reality suddenly struck home that crime reporting was no longer a game. Even though Veronica had been shot and injured before I didn't actually believe that the criminals would step across the line and fire fatal shots. I was convulsed with fear and shock. My mouth went dry, my legs felt like jelly and I started throwing up.

A lot of lives changed forever that afternoon. The Psycho's old friend John Gilligan had set a deadly new precedent for him to follow.

In the months and years ahead the Guerin investigation became the centre of my attention. We were determined that the story would remain front and centre of the news agenda for as long as it took. It was our way of honouring a brave colleague who had paid the ultimate price. The garda investigation was led by Assistant Commissioner Tony Hickey. It was the single biggest offensive ever seen against organized crime at that time. New legislation was passed to create the powerful Criminal Assets Bureau to go after and seize the assets of the crime bosses. PJ Judge was one of the new unit's top priorities. Over the following months the police seized cash equivalent to €250,000 today from the Psycho's coffers.

Practically every week we had revelations from the murder investigation and the activities of Gilligan and his mob. Criminals began to call the *Sunday World*, the 'Sunday Veronica'. We photographed hitherto unknown gangsters Meehan, Mitchell and Holland in the streets and I gave them nicknames like the

Tosser, Fatso and Dutchy. We pursued them across Europe when they went to ground. Shortly after the murder I exposed the relationship between Gilligan and the INLA, and revealed how the republican thugs had been acting as Gilligan's private army.

The INLA issued a media statement from Belfast, which Garda Headquarters interpreted as a serious threat, condemning me for the story. In July I interviewed John Traynor in Portugal about Veronica's murder. The Coach later admitted that Gilligan had 'ordered him' to set me up so that he could silence me through blackmail. The day that I flew back to Dublin gardaí searched my car for a suspected booby-trap device and armed patrols increased at our home.

One of the INLA leaders, a lowlife thug called Declan 'Wacker' Duffy, then approached me one Sunday afternoon in August as I left a cinema in Tallaght with my kids. He told me to 'stop writing lies about us or else…' I was alarmed by the approach which caught me unawares but knew that he and his two associates would not try something in such a public place. I felt my gut tighten as he looked at the children as they sat in a *Postman Pat* kiddies ride. I was also angry and told him to fuck off. Then I called the gardaí who rushed to the scene. Anne and the kids were taken home in a squad car and I went with special branch officers to make a statement in the local station as they launched an investigation. Duffy was subsequently arrested by the anti-terrorist Special Detective Unit and he backed off. But I never forgot him and in the years ahead ensured that he was a regular face on the front page.

I also hadn't forgotten about Jock Corbally. Through the summer and into the autumn of 1996 I continued to write about Judge and the disappearance of Jock Corbally which ratcheted up the pressure on him. The story was gaining traction and he was becoming a pariah in the underworld. In the meantime Judge was linked to a fourth gangland murder.

On 5 September I spent the day with the award-winning investigative journalist Chris Moore from UTV. Chris was making a documentary about the murder of Veronica and the broader issue of gangland violence in the Republic which included the murder of Jock Corbally. I arranged for Eddie Corbally to pose as a source and to be filmed with me in the field where Jock had been taken. He explained what happened that night, with the agreement that his image and voice had to be heavily disguised before broadcast. Later that evening I was socializing with friends drinking in Frank Ryan's pub where an eclectic group including journalists, cops and others gathered every week for what we called the Thursday Club.

Around 9.30 p.m. some of the cops who were based in the nearby Bridewell station got a call and rushed out. A few minutes earlier a man called Michael Brady had been shot dead in a gangland style execution around the corner. A pillion passenger on a motorbike shot him four times in the head and chest. Brady was the brother-in-law of twenty-seven-year-old Martin 'Marlo' Hyland, one of Judge's most trusted lieutenants in the drug trade. Hyland was a dangerous criminal who was involved in Judge's plot to have me killed. He later became one of the most powerful gang bosses in Ireland – before Eamon 'the Don' Dunne put an end to his reign.

Marlo's sister Ellen was Judge's permanent girlfriend at the time. Despite his reputation for using violence on his lovers there was no record of him ever assaulting the woman.

Michael Brady had been released from prison a few months earlier having served a life sentence for the murder of his wife Julie, Marlo's sister. Brady beat and raped his wife in a drunken rage before strangling her. It didn't take anyone long to work out the motive for Brady's execution.

Photographer Padraig O'Reilly and I left the pub and ran to the scene. When we got there, police cars were still arriving and a sergeant I knew suggested that I have a look at the corpse to see if I recognized him. I didn't.

Brady sat lifeless in the driver's seat of his car. His mouth was open, his eyes closed and his head lay back on the head rest. If it hadn't been for the bullet hole in his forehead he looked like he was asleep. The sight sent a chill through my body. For the second time in a few short months I was witnessing firsthand the carnage created by Ireland's growing problem with gun crime. Brady's lifeless body loomed over the front pages the next morning.

In the follow-up investigation gardaí believed that Judge had helped Marlo organize the execution. I wrote a story the following Sunday which pointed the finger at Judge and Hyland, although neither of them was named for legal reasons.

That afternoon Hyland bought up all the newspapers in a local shop and gave them out to customers in his local pub where he was celebrating. A female associate phoned and told me: 'Marlo wants you to know he was delighted with the coverage of the shooting.'

I responded by telling her that Marlo could show his gratitude by telling me about Judge's contract on my head.

A few weeks later the Psycho made another attempt to have me abducted and murdered. A garda intelligence source later revealed that one of his associates pointed out that this was not a good idea in light of the Guerin murder and ongoing crackdown. Judge said he did not care.

I got a call one afternoon to say that Michael 'Styky' Cahill, the General's younger junkie brother, wanted to meet me. He had escaped from a prison van after threatening warders with a blood-filled syringe. I was told Micheal wanted to give himself up but I had to bring him in. The caller claimed that the cops wouldn't beat Cahill up if I was there. I stupidly fell for the story.

It was a Friday night when Liam O'Connor and I arrived at a dingy nightclub in Clondalkin called the Blue Banana. We had taken the bait. The two of us were on full alert and held bottles of beer as rudimentary weapons in the event that we got into trouble.

A guy strolled over to me and said he was the one on the phone earlier. He said to follow him over to a back door beside the toilets where Cahill was waiting. As we followed cautiously I got a sudden sense that there was something wrong. I remember asking myself what in fuck was I doing. As I walked past one table, in my peripheral vision, I saw four guys getting up at once. Liam also spotted them. At the last moment we turned and moved briskly to the front door and got out of the place.

The following Monday I got a call from a very irate garda friend, Detective Sergeant Joe O'Hara who was also one of the local gardaí keeping an eye on us. He had just been phoned by an officer in the Crime and Security section in HQ. He yelled:

> You were in the Blue Banana the other night you stupid bollix...
> you almost walked into a trap with PJ Judge. How in fuck could
> you be that careless, are you fucking mad?

He was absolutely right. Garda intelligence had been informed that Judge had up to six gang members waiting to drag us out the back door of the club and into a waiting van. The Psycho was waiting at a location where he planned to torture me to find out who had been talking to me. Then he was going to kill me and most likely Liam as well.

The Psycho had also come up with an even more sinister plot. I subsequently learned that Judge had discussed with an associate the prospect of getting a gang member to rape me and record it on camera. In the days before WhatsApp and TikTok he planned to circulate the VHS video tapes around the Dublin underworld. It was mind-blowing madness from a depraved and evil brain. I had been swallowed up in a dark and demented world. When I realized just how close I had come to the edge I was disgusted and angry that I had dropped my guard so easily and put Liam in danger to boot. My enthusiasm to bring Cahill's brother back to prison had almost cost our lives. It was another steep learning curve. I never made a mistake like that again.

Shortly afterwards the UTV documentary aired and drove Judge mad again. The show blurred the image of the source, Eddie Corbally, and we used the voice of a Dublin actor to ensure that the informant wasn't recognized. I was later told that Judge played a recording of the interview over and over again to try and identify the tout. Judge suspected that it was Mark Dwyer.

Over the following weeks Judge became dangerously paranoid and volatile, scaring his associates. He began asking his terrified lackeys awkward questions which showed he suspected them of talking to the media and the cops. Decie Griffin later told me:

> He [Judge] was the type of mad fucker who, if he even suspected you of talking about him, he was liable to have you taken up to Scribblestown [area of waste ground near Finglas] and put a bullet in your head. He was crazy and totally unpredictable.

On Jock's forty-fifth birthday I published a heart-rending interview with his mother Maureen which isolated Judge further from the rest of gangland. We brought the grieving mother to the field where her son had been killed to lay flowers. At one stage she dropped to her knees and cried, as she prayed for her boy's soul:

> I just can't believe that this happened. It was inhuman what they did to my boy. William was always my baby; he was very close to me. That man [Judge] has put me through a living hell. Now he is torturing me by not allowing me the right to give my son a Christian burial. I can't stop wondering about what happened to him... did he suffer much or did he call out for his mammy when they were killing him. The thought that his body was just dumped somewhere and left to the elements absolutely breaks my heart. He never did anything in his life to justify something like that.

Maureen revealed how the night Jock disappeared she had a dream that he was beaten by men and his face was covered in blood.

Around that time a member of the gang, Martin Dunne, approached the Corbally family and the gardaí to warn that Judge was again planning to kidnap and murder me. Dunne also told them of Judge's twisted idea of having me raped. This time the plot involved me being ambushed on Whitehall Road in Terenure on the way home from work. He had vans and a snatch team organized and Dunne even admitted to cops that he had been hired to take part in the job. The National Surveillance Unit and the Emergency Response Unit were deployed to watch the gang and also to shadow me. I only heard about it after the fact. In the meantime the Psycho was running out of road.

Judge's denouement finally came at 12.30 a.m. on Sunday 8 December 1996. He was just about to drive away from the Royal Oak Pub in Finglas with Ellen Hyland when a figure emerged from the shadows. The hit man produced a handgun and shot Judge twice in the head. The Executioner had been eliminated.

Marlo Hyland was the prime suspect for organizing the most dramatic gangland hit since the assassination of Martin Cahill. In the gangland succession stakes he took over the reins of the Psycho's empire to become the new godfather.

One of Jock's brothers phoned me about it minutes after the shooting. I didn't ask how he knew so quickly. I phoned Colm MacGinty to share the momentous news and wondered if we could stop the presses and put it on the front page. The edition on 8 December was the biggest paper of the year as it was stuffed with Christmas ads. MacGinty checked with the print hall. If we stopped the press we could get the exclusive story into the final 50,000 copies of the run. Colm, me and two of the sub-editors who had been roused from their sleep headed back to the paper. On his way across the city centre, one of our executives who had enjoyed a few pints earlier that evening was stopped at a garda drink-driving checkpoint. There was nothing wrong with his driving. Before the garda could say 'Breathalizer', our intrepid colleague announced who he was and that he was rushing to the *Sunday World* to put the murder of the Psycho on page one. 'Drive on, sir, and mind yourself,' he was told.

The new front page headline was 'Psycho is shot dead'. It was accompanied by his picture which no longer required black strips. The first paragraph of the story read: 'Peter Joseph Judge, the feared gangland boss nicknamed the Psycho, joined the ranks of Ireland's criminal dead in the early hours of this morning.'

It was fitting that we should break the story first. A lot of people were thankful to hear the news. I was certainly relieved to think that I would no longer need to look over my shoulder for him. But Judge took the secret of where he buried Jock to the grave with him. His remains have never been found. Maureen Corbally subsequently died from a broken heart.

Three days after Judge's funeral Mark Dwyer was the victim of a gruesome murder that was chillingly similar to Jock's demise. 'Cotton Eye' Joe Delaney, a former partner of Judge's, used a jemmy nail bar, an iron bar, pick-axe handle and a number of knives as he tortured Dwyer over several hours. He suspected Jock Corbally's co-killer of ripping off a shipment of ecstasy. Dwyer was then taken away to Scribblestown Lane where he was shot in the back of the head with a sawn-off shotgun. Superstitious gangsters believe the Corbally murder brought down a curse on his killers.

The final chapter of the Jock Corbally story came on Saturday, 5 April 2003, when Decie Griffin was shot dead in a pub in Inchicore, south-west Dublin, by assassin Shay Wildes. Griffin was involved in a tit-for-tat feud with dissident republican and drug trafficker Stephen 'Dougie' Moran, a member of the notorious McCarthy/Dundon clan in Limerick. Gardaí had already foiled two previous assassination attempts on Griffin.

Griffin handed Wildes an envelope containing the upfront payment of €5,000 for a hit on Moran. The hit man put the money in his pocket and then shot Griffin in the head before casually walking out of the stunned pub. Wildes had received a better offer from the intended target. Fear and intimidation later ensured that the hit man was acquitted of the brazen murder. Gangland's grim reaper caught up with Moran a decade later when the Kinahan cartel had him murdered. I wrote Griffin's requiem in the *Sunday World* the following day.

I covered another chilling postscript to the Psycho story. In 2004 his gang member and police informant Martin Dunne was sentenced to fourteen years for carrying out a horrifying contract rape on a young mother of one. The then forty-six-year-old thug was paid by the victim's estranged husband to carry out the attack in the hope that the woman would give up the family home where she lived.

For the Corbally family it was something close to justice that Jock's killers had perished violently. His brothers continued their unsuccessful search for his remains for several years.

———

CHAPTER SIX

THE BATTLE FOR GALLANSTOWN

On 23 November 2023 Dublin city centre was set ablaze when one of the most violent riots in the capital's history erupted. Hordes of rampaging, feral thugs turned O'Connell Street, the nation's premiere boulevard, into a smoke-engulfed war zone. They vandalized property, looted shops, set fire to squad cars, buses and a Luas tram in their wanton orgy of nihilistic destruction. The mob, which reached an estimated 500 at its peak, launched ferocious attacks on the gardaí who for a while seemed to be overwhelmed by the suddenness and intensity of the conflagration. It happened on the eve of the Black Friday sales. The jamboree of anti-social behaviour will be remembered as the Black Thursday riots.

The spark was a frenzied knife attack on three young children and their care assistant outside a primary school in Parnell Square, central Dublin, that afternoon. A five-year-old girl was critically injured and the care assistant was seriously injured as she used her body to shield the children from the psychotic attacker. In the hours that followed far-right racists used social media to foment public anger by highlighting the fact that the horrific incident was committed by an immigrant who had been living in Ireland for several years.

It didn't take much encouragement to rally the army of opportunistic, anti-social yobs who have been intimidating, assaulting and robbing law-abiding citizens in O'Connell Street for years. The horrific stabbing of innocent kids was just an excuse for some recreational mayhem and to run amok. The vast majority of the rioters were young, disaffected teenagers. The Garda Commissioner Drew Harris later described them as 'a complete lunatic hooligan faction driven by far-right ideology'.

The 'patriotic' rioters were interested in just two things: looting shops for new clothes and runners; and attacking the gardaí. As the smouldering wreckage and burnt-out carcasses of vehicles were cleared from the streets the following morning the cost of the riot was being estimated at over €20 million. During the Black Thursday free-for-all the shelves in the shops in and around O'Connell Street had been stripped bare. In the wake of the destruction, however, it emerged that the stock on the shelves of the landmark Eason's bookshop – at ground zero of the riots – had gone untouched.

It was miraculous that none of the police on duty that night, who bore the brunt of the violence, had been killed or critically injured. Over sixty officers were assaulted, three of whom were seriously injured.

It was the second major riot to engulf the heart of the capital in the recent history of the Irish Republic. The last one took place seventeen years earlier, in February 2006, when the fathers and uncles of the Black Thursday delinquents attached themselves to another cause under the republican flag in an excuse to attack the police and steal runners and track suits. On that occasion the spark was the foolhardy decision to allow the Love Ulster march by Northern Unionists to take place in the capital. At the time the move was seen as a gesture of reconciliation but the thugs and the dissident republicans put paid to that.

The Dublin riots, including a more recent anti-immigrant one in Coolock in July 2024, were fuelled by a toxic combination of nationalism and thuggery. Apart from the social media call to arms there was nothing organized or planned about the upheaval. It was opportunistic chaos. The same, however, cannot be said of another riot that erupted in the sprawling working class suburb of Ballyfermot on Halloween night 1995. In the history of public order disturbances on the streets of Dublin it ranks in third place.

The conflagration in 1995 holds the distinction that it was planned and choreographed by a gang of young drug traffickers for the sole purpose of killing and maiming gardaí. It wasn't an explosion of pent-up frustration due to socio-economic deprivation or a lack of jobs. The architects of the mayhem had very lucrative jobs and were defending their right to work. The Ballyfermot riot amounted to an act of war against the State by an organized crime gang in a bid to stop the police disrupting one of the biggest heroin dealing operations in the country at the time. I was there to record the terrifying event that night, along with Padraig O'Reilly. We witnessed what became known as the Battle for Gallanstown.

———

The members of the Ballyfermot gang were Derek 'Dee Dee' O'Driscoll, Seanie Comerford, Mark Desmond, and brothers Paul and Kenneth Corbally (no relation to William Jock Corbally). The thugs were the first embodiment of veteran heroin dealer Larry Dunne's chilling prophecy as he started his prison term for drug dealing, 'If you think we were bad just wait till you see what's coming next.' The only true words Larry Dunne ever spoke in public became the epithet for the evolution of organized crime.

The gang began their criminal careers as joyriders and ram-raiders. Their notorious exploits earned them the name the M50 gang in the media because they indulged in high-speed nocturnal jousts with the police on the first stretches of the new M50 motorway which had opened in 1992. Within a short space of time their names would become synonymous with the new, violent gang culture that dominates Ireland today.

By 1995 the gang was running one of the biggest heroin distribution network in Ireland. PJ Judge, the Psycho, was their main supplier. The heroin trade was still concentrated in Dublin and junkies travelled from other Irish cities and major towns to buy their gear. The M50 mob turned the streets of a new corporation estate on the edge of Ballyfermot called Gallanstown Lawns into a thriving heroin marketplace.

The grim estate became a hub for the city's drug gangs and their customers. The fearful residents of the area had effectively become prisoners in their homes as parents tried to shield their children from the mayhem outside. I once watched as a never-ending stream of taxis carrying addicts to meet their dealers entered and left the area in broad daylight. The scenes were like those depicted in the US TV drama *The Wire*.

Local people expressed how terrified they were but told us they could never be seen talking to a cop or a reporter as their home would be burned down.

The local gardaí from the L district, covering the sprawling working-class areas of Clondalkin, Ronanstown and Ballyfermot, and the Garda National Drug Unit had decided to do something about it over the previous year. They systemically targeted the gang and its dealers. Over time scores of drug pushers were busted and brought before the courts. In October the cops struck a major blow against the gang with the seizure of a heroin shipment worth over €500,000 today. The offensive was taking its toll on the business.

The brash M50 thugs were having none of it and decided to teach the police a lesson. In the build-up to Halloween O'Driscoll and his crew put out the word that they were going to do battle with the cops. The buzz was in the air for weeks. The threatened showdown for Tuesday 31 October was even advertised. Slogans were daubed on the walls around Ballyfermot.

The thugs were making no secret of what they had planned. Local officers who were seen as being particularly active had been openly threatened by the thugs. They were told that they were going to be targeted on Halloween night. Two houses on the estate where the occupants were accused of being police informants were to be burned. The criminal anarchists put a lot of planning into the operation which they didn't share with anyone. It later transpired that the gang's younger delinquents made hundreds of petrol bombs from milk bottles and sixteen stolen cars were hidden off-side to joust with the police in the forthcoming 'games'. Planks were collected and nails hammered through them, to puncture the tyres of the police vehicles. The planks were painted black to make them practically invisible at night. The plan was to lure the police into a trap and pelt them with petrol bombs with the clear intention of killing or maiming officers.

I heard about the threatened riot through the grapevine a week beforehand. Gardaí were talking about it and local people phoned in to make sure we knew what was happening. Gallanstown was to be the centre of the action. I took a drive up to the area one day and saw the graffiti advertising the fun and games. One read: 'Let the games begin.' Another slogan named a particular local garda warning that he 'is going to get it'. Photographer Padraig O'Reilly and I decided to take a spin around the area on Halloween evening just in case it did kick off. But we were sceptical that anything would happen because, as natural cowards and bully boys, criminals tend to bluster a lot. And with so much advance notice pinpointing the night that the 'games' would kick off, the cops would be out in force. It turned out that that was what the gang wanted. There was no point in coming out to fight if you had no one to fight with.

After taking my kids trick or treating that evening Padraig and I headed for Gallanstown. Halloween is traditionally a busy night for the emergency services in every major western city. For some reason the pagan festival sparks anti-social behaviour and an urge to create mischief. But as we got closer to Ballyfermot the scanner tuned into the local garda radio frequencies seemed uncannily quiet.

The only clue it gave that there was definitely something major happening was when a Command and Control dispatcher asked each unit to confirm their presence in the area. In the Garda L district the prefixed radio call sign 'Lima Alpha' was assigned to each individual patrol car or van. In a normal shift there would be no more than two or three patrol vehicles on the streets of Ballyfermot. As we listened it became apparent that the gardaí were preparing for a battle. Fifteen individual Lima Alpha call signs reported in, in quick succession.

It was around 8 p.m. when we arrived in the area. The place was eerily silent. There was no sign of children out trick or treating. Parents who still had control of their kids had shuffled them indoors at least an hour earlier. The smoke from the scores of Halloween bonfires hung over the streets like a ghostly mist, creating penumbrae around the yellow streetlights.

As we drove through the empty streets we spotted police vans and squad cars parked discreetly in the shadows, waiting. Out of sight and under the cloak of darkness people stood poised for action – the tension and sense of apprehension was palpable. It was unmistakable. No one was bluffing that night.

Meanwhile, in the comfort of a local pub in Ballyfermot, the architects of the violence that was about to be unleashed sat drinking pints. My sources later confirmed how the gang listened to a scanner radio placed on the counter with mobile phones in hand. This was the gangster's operational command centre. When they heard the police units calling in the order was given to 'let the game begin'.

At the same time the first of the stolen cars, a BMW five series, emerged to challenge the police. It had been driven at speed across west Dublin, screeching through the streets, making its way to Gallanstown. It transpired that the driver was in constant touch by mobile phone with O'Driscoll and Comerford and the other bar stool generals. Their network of spotters lurking in the shadows sent back intelligence about where the cops were parked and what areas to avoid. The information was then relayed to the drivers.

At 8.27 p.m. the violence suddenly exploded around us. We found ourselves driving in a convoy of police vans and cars down Gallanstown Drive when, about fifty yards ahead of us, a hail of stones and petrol bombs flew from the shadows. We stopped the car and watched, as the Garda scanner suddenly screeched into life.

'Lima Alpha Six to control we're being bombed... we need assistance now... they're throwing petrol bombs at us.'

The frantic voice crackled over the Garda airwaves as the ten officers in the packed police van stared in terror at the yellow flames curling around their vehicle.

We could see Lima Alpha Six on the road ahead of us. The blue garda van with wire meshing across the windscreen took the brunt of the first attack. Stones and rocks rained down as petrol bombs exploded around the vehicle. We later discovered that the driver had just returned to work after being injured from when his squad car was rammed on a previous occasion.

'This is Lima Alpha One Five... we are on our way to assist. We'll be with you in a minute,' replied the crew of a high-powered garda jeep. It had been specially drafted in for the job.

The jeep was unusual in the garda fleet as it had protective grills attached to the windows and front windscreen. Despite a steady upsurge in attacks on garda vehicles through the early 1990s garda management had refused to introduce purpose-built vehicles for use in confrontational situations such as riots. The skewed, delusional thinking of the time was that the use of specially adapted vehicles would amount to an acknowledgement that there was a major problem with anti-social behaviour. The politicians didn't want the issue highlighted for fear that they might have to do something about it. The people who suffered the brunt of the institutionalized indifference were the cops sitting in the vans and squad cars around us being rammed, bombed and stoned by an angry mob.

As Lima Alpha One Five raced to assist their colleagues it was hit.

'Lima Alpha One Five to control we are coming under attack. We've received a direct hit from a petrol bomb. There's petrol everywhere. We're pulling back... we're pulling back.'

A milk bottle petrol bomb had smashed the glass in the passenger door behind the protective grill. Miraculously, it failed to ignite as the petrol soaked the officers inside. One spark and they would have been burned to death. As the jeep reversed out of the battle zone we could hear a chorus of cheers from the crowd lurking in the shadows.

We now found ourselves at the centre of the action which focused on Gallanstown Lawns and Cherry Orchard Avenue. We instinctively got out of the car to see more. Beside us dozens of officers wearing helmets sprang out from police vans.

'Keep yer fucking head down... it's too dangerous here, get out,' a sergeant shouted, as we stood watching the mayhem engulfing the area. We stayed put, transfixed by the dystopian drama unfolding before our eyes, until O'Reilly began photographing the action.

The group of gardaí surrounded a house where a petrol bomber had been seen retreating inside. The door was smashed in and the thug arrested. Officers emerged with crates of petrol bombs and an array of weapons. At the same time another fusillade of stones and bricks were directed at them from the shadows on the other side of the road.

We raised our hands over our heads for protection. I didn't really mind if the car was damaged – it was a well-insured company car and I was doing the job. About ten officers with batons drawn charged into the darkness to find the source of the missiles.

'Stick together, stick together... don't get cut off; they'll murder you,' an inspector shouted at his men.

Adrenaline and excitement had clouded out other emotions. Everything was happening so fast. It was only later when I got home and the rush subsided that I realized how close we had come to being injured. We were standing in the middle of a war zone.

Amid the cacophony of screams, shouts and cheers, another stolen BMW came barrelling through the whirling mist. I still remember the rush of air as it passed within a few feet of us at high speed as we stood in the road. It expertly rammed into the side rear of the Garda van, Lima Alpha Six, which was in the process of withdrawing after the petrol bomb attack.

The car continued on without losing speed as the darkness around Gallanstown Lawn echoed with whoops and yelling. A squad car emerged and pursued the stolen car.

We watched in stunned silence as a passenger in the BMW threw a lighted petrol bomb, hitting the squad car windscreen. It was momentarily engulfed in flames as the bomb exploded on the front bonnet. Incredibly the fire didn't take hold and the officers inside were uninjured. The BMW disappeared into the fog.

A moment later the scanner crackled a terse message to all units: 'Everyone pull back... the bastards are trying to kill someone.' We reckoned that it was also a cue for us to withdraw as well.

The battered and bruised cops and garda vehicles withdrew to regroup at Ballyfermot garda station, a five-minute drive away from Gallanstown Lawns. The station had been placed under heavy guard in case it too was attacked on the orders of the thugs in the nearby pub. As reinforcements arrived and the gardaí regrouped a force of seventy officers assembled for the counter-offensive.

At the station I briefly met Sergeant Pat Flynn, a neighbour from home in tranquil County Leitrim. It felt like Leitrim was on a different planet to Ballyfermot that night. Pat was the officer in charge of Lima Alpha One Five and his clothes were still saturated in petrol. He and his crew had come back to change clothes and then they were going back to continue the battle for Gallanstown Lawns.

The officer-in-charge of Ballyfermot at the time was Superintendent Mick Carolan, a soft-spoken man who had spent most of his career working in the district. He was well respected by the locals as a fair cop and a man who made peace not war.

When he heard we were hanging around outside he invited us in. He was glad that reporters were there. He wanted the public to know what was happening to his officers that night. Superintendent Carolan had prepared for the violence but there was no realistic way that the disturbances could have been prevented in advance. It would have meant forcibly clearing the streets and alienating all the locals.

Now the game was on and the rules had changed. We listened as he called his officers together. The main locker room where he stood and the corridor outside were packed to capacity with uniforms. He had to shout so everyone could hear his firm voice:

> What we've seen up there tonight is a total disregard for law and order. But enough is enough. We are not putting up with this any longer. We're going back up there and we will restore law and order because there are innocent people there who need our protection. I want you to be cool and calm up there but if force is needed then use it. OK? Let's go.

There was a traffic jam of police vehicles outside the station as the large convoy headed back to retake Gallanstown from the grip of a drug gang. We had no intention of missing this.

As we followed behind, the scanner in the car reported that a young child had been hit in the face with a petrol bomb in Gallanstown. An ambulance was on the way but would need assistance. We later discovered that the petrol bomb was being thrown at a passing squad car by the four-year-old's father when it prematurely ignited. The child suffered horrific life-changing injuries. The parent later tried to claim in media interviews that it had been the fault of the police.

As the convoy got near Gallanstown Lawns the petrol bombs and stones began flying again. The mob would not allow an ambulance in to take the child to hospital. We watched as about thirty officers in riot gear charged into Gallanstown Lawns, beating a path through the rioters. They covered the paramedics as they collected the badly injured child. The following day some of the drug gang's lackeys claimed that the police had blocked the ambulance and were the instigators of the violence. As journalists at the scene we were able to debunk the lies and report the truth of what happened. From what I could see the cops had heroically risked their safety to save the child.

As the battle continued to wage another wave of cops baton-charged their way into the cul de sac where the child had been rescued from a small knoll overlooking it. The rioters were beginning to retreat. As the line of cops charged across the knoll O'Reilly's camera flash illuminated the dimly-lit area. A group of pumped-up cops thought he was one of the rioters and turned and chased him down the grassy mound in my direction. As he darted past I stood with my eyes closed and my press card held up in the air, shouting something like, 'We're press… we're press'. At the last moment the pack stopped in front of me. I was later told how close we both came to having our heads knocked off!

They shouted at us to 'get to fuck out of here' and 'you're going to get fuckin' killed here' as more stones and bottles smashed on the road around us. We decided that maybe they were right. It was time to call it a day. We had been extremely lucky not to have at least required a few stitches after the evening of madness. Amazingly, apart from the child who suffered horrific burns, the casualties were otherwise light that night. We had witnessed in real time how it could have been a whole lot worse.

By 10.30 p.m. the gardaí were firmly back in control of Gallanstown. The streets were again silent and deserted. The police cars and vans patrolled through the debris created over a few short hours. As we drove along one street we spoke to a group of local people who were standing around talking about the night's drama.

'I hope you tell what really happened here tonight,' one of them urged.

'These bastards are getting all the people of this area a bad name which we don't deserve,' another man angrily declared. 'The vast majority of the people living here are good people and trying to rear their kids decent… these thugs are ruining our children's lives.'

Gardaí mounted a massive investigation in the aftermath of the riot in 1995 which led to dozens of convictions, although the masterminds remained free. The fact that O'Driscoll and co had not physically taken part meant that they could not even be arrested. As society's first responders to dysfunction the police worked closely with the community to address their problems. There has never been a repeat of the kind of disturbances seen during the Battle for Gallanstown Lawns.

Within a few years of the riot Dee Dee O'Driscoll, Seanie Comerford, Mark Desmond and the Corbally brothers were running an international heroin racket worth millions. They were also classed as being amongst the most dangerous criminals in the business. In 1998 I had the pleasure of exclusively reporting that Comerford and his associates had been busted. Under the headline 'Heroin King Bust' I told the story of how Comerford had been caught in a joint heroin smuggling surveillance operation between the Garda National Drug Unit and the UK's Greater Manchester Police.

Comerford was caught in possession of £5 million worth of the drug. In a period of just four months it was estimated that the bilateral mob had shipped £40 million worth of heroin to Ireland. Comerford was subsequently convicted and jailed. When he was released from prison he went back into the heroin business with his old pals Paul and Kenneth Corbally.

Dee Dee O'Driscoll, despite being hit with a large tax bill by the CAB, continues to be one of the biggest drug traffickers in Dublin's west side. By 2024 he was regarded as a major player in organized crime.

The other members of the old M50 gang have been less fortunate. In 2000 I gave Mark Desmond the nickname the Canal Butcher after he executed two younger associates – nineteen-year-old Darren Casey and twenty-year-old Patrick Murray – on the banks of the Grand Canal in County Kildare. Desmond, like PJ Judge, was a monster and stood out from the rest of the rabble. After the double murder Desmond went on the run to London from where he contacted me and said if I came to meet him he would, like all criminals, clear his name. I arranged to meet him in Leicester Square in late January. He never turned up.

Desmond murdered at least four people and terrorized and tortured scores more during his reign. Also known as the Guinea Pig, this brutal, atavistic creature raped male and female victims – usually strung out junkies who he treated as dirt on the sole of his designer trainers. Others he drove to suicide. I interviewed his victims and their families over the years. Desmond was subsequently charged with the Canal murders but the case was dropped after vital witnesses pulled out on the grounds that they were terrified of the monster. He was eventually convicted of possession of firearms. In the end he got what he deserved. Living up to the gangland paradigm that the life of a dangerous criminal is 'nasty, brutish and short' Desmond died as he had lived. A hit man shot him dead in the street on 2 December 2016. The hit came from the Kinahan cartel after Desmond threatened to kill one of their dealers.

Desmond was pre-deceased by Seanie Comerford, who died from a brain tumour in 2012, and by the Corbally brothers. They were violent bully boys with uncontrollable tempers to match. Like Comerford, when the heat from the gardaí got too much, the brothers moved to Manchester where together they became major suppliers of heroin to the Irish market.

In 2010 they became embroiled in a bitter feud with their former partner Dee Dee O'Driscoll. They had escaped a number of assassination bids and had also made a few failed attempts to kill O'Driscoll. Killing scumbags isn't quite as easy as it is made out to be in TV dramas like *Love/Hate* or *Kin*. On 28 June that year a three-member hit team gunned down the former armed robbers when their car was ambushed in Clondalkin in west Dublin.

Looking back through the prism of reporting on the decades of misery and despair the M50 gang caused, humanity was better off without them.

CHAPTER SEVEN

THE PLAGUE, THE GODFATHER AND THE JUNKIE

The sculpture of gilded bronze in the shape of an eight-foot flame housed in a limestone structure stands like a war memorial. Simply called 'Home' it is a poignant reminder of the many hundreds of young lives wiped out since the heroin tsunami struck the streets of Dublin's inner-city communities over forty years ago. It is also a public acknowledgement of the unending heartbreak and grief of their surviving loved ones.

When the flame was smelted relatives of the dead dropped cherished little mementoes into the molten metal – Confirmation and Communion medals and little toys from a distant childhood innocence before heroin arrived. At its base are the poignant words dedicating the memorial to 'Loved ones carried off by the plague'. The solemn monument at the junction of Sean McDermott Street and Buckingham Street in the north inner city was unveiled in 2000 by the then Irish President, Mary McAleese.

Two decades earlier the site of the memorial was the epicentre of the city's heroin trade and one of the open marketplaces run by Shamie and Larry Dunne, the gangland brothers from Crumlin, south Dublin, who first introduced smack to their home town.

In the 1980s demand for the drug spread like a bush fire as it thrived on the ingrained misery of high unemployment and a lack of opportunity in a section of society that had been left to its own devices and conveniently forgotten by the Establishment.

The epidemic brought devastation and despair and led to an unprecedented upsurge in addiction, crime, disease and death, creating a human wasteland strewn with the debris of destroyed lives. It broke down the old bonds of social solidarity that had held together the most deprived inner-city neighbourhoods during the worst of times in centuries past.

Families were torn apart as young addicts stole anything of value they could find in the home to raise cash to buy drugs. They also targeted relations and neighbours. Regularly violence was used and sometimes people died. The plague spared no one. As it spread door-to-door soon practically everyone had a relative who was an addict.

And then the aftershock of the heroin explosion came in the form of hepatitis and HIV/AIDS from the sharing of dirty blood-filled needles. While there was a chance of surviving addiction, until the 1990s, AIDS was a death sentence.

Heroin created a depressingly predictable pattern of life that endures to this day. An addict's time was punctuated between garda stations and the courts and periods in prison. The victim's torment only ended when they died. When I joined the *Sunday World* in 1987 heroin was firmly embedded in the life of the working-class estates across Dublin. From the start I was regularly assigned to cover heroin-related stories. I'd also posed as a junkie to buy heroin and expose dealers. At the time the *Sunday World* had a proud tradition of being the only newspaper reporting on the crimes, misery and death plaguing working-class communities. A large proportion of our readers came from working-class communities. In many ways the paper was the only voice for people trying to convince an indifferent society that they needed help to quell the problem.

We reported on the ongoing tragedy that as younger kids grew up they too were sucked into the living hell of despair. And then the young addicts began having children. Hundreds of babies were already on a loser from the moment of birth – inheriting HIV and a craving for heroin from their mothers. As they grew up the kids followed their addict parents into the vortex. The contagion of addiction quickly fanned out to infect the suburban working-class sprawls on the edges of Dublin. It then spread to Limerick and Cork. Within a decade we were reporting how the drug was available in several provincial towns,

Innocent kids joined a growing army of zombie-like addicts roaming the streets – half-dead, mindless creatures whose sole purpose of existence was how to get the next fix. When a junkie wasn't stoned they were out desperately seeking the money to buy the gear to get stoned. An addict needed the equivalent of an average industrial week's wages every day to feed their habit which meant stealing and robbing every day of the year. The epidemic generated a new category of criminal activity as strung-out heroin slaves became responsible for an average of 600 robberies in Dublin each year. In response to the crisis the garda mobilized a specialist armed quick-response team called the Cobra unit to patrol the streets.

Burglaries, muggings and 'jump-over' robberies from local homes, shops, banks, post offices and businesses became a part of everyday life. Armed with a syringe, knife or gun, some addicts might do two or three 'jump-overs' in a typical day. When HIV/AIDS arrived the junkies found that they had a readymade weapon which was as terrifying and dangerous as a loaded gun – a syringe filled with their own blood. As the situation grew worse gardaí, who were regularly bitten by addicts, began to be vaccinated against the related disease of hepatitis.

The all-consuming addiction stripped the addicts of dignity and decency. Young women and men sold their bodies for sex on street corners. There were even some cases recorded where they were prepared to sell their own children to paedophiles. Drug addicts became the new vulnerable underclass who were both victims and victimisers.

They were viewed by society as nothing more than human detritus and by the underworld as the lowest rung of the gangland ladder; glorified cannon fodder who were there to be used and abused. Junkies could be manipulated and coerced into doing a gangster's dirty work, even murder, in return for the price of a 'fix'. Heroin changed the criminal landscape forever.

Every day we got calls in the *Sunday World* newsroom from addicts, the victims of addicts or the loved ones of addicts who said they had a story to tell. They would complain about being beaten up or threatened by dealers or anti-drug vigilantes. It was always easier to pick on the junkies than their more powerful bosses. Heartbroken parents wanted to highlight their plight as they tried to save their children from doom. Business owners in the city centre complained that being robbed by desperate addicts had become a daily occurrence. Garda representative associations were also highlighting the increased levels of violence their members were facing. The same concerns are still being expressed in the public narrative almost four decades later.

We spent a lot of time in some of the worst hit areas of the city reporting on the open drug dealing on the streets or on the aftermath of a robbery or assault. Parents would tell of discovering to their horror that one of their children had become an addict without them noticing. The first time many of them realized there was a problem was when the gardaí rang to say their teenager had been arrested for involvement in a mugging or a theft. Others wept as they described being forced to throw a kid out on the street because they had stolen everything in the house to buy drugs. It was a human catastrophe – and coming from the cloistered world of Leitrim it was a culture shock. I learned a lot about life covering crime.

One of the more depressing aspects of my job was interviewing the heartbroken parents of kids who had died as a result of their all-consuming addiction through overdoses, AIDS or violence. Often they wanted to highlight the lack of help they got from the State when they tried to pull their addicted children back from the edge of the abyss. Mothers told stories of how their once beautiful babies had been lured into the vortex of despair, in the hope that by doing so it would help other parents avoid the overwhelming grief they had experienced.

As we sat and listened to grieving parents over cups of tea, the addicts' stories were brought to life by the cherubic faces beaming out from pictures proudly displayed on mantlepieces. The happy faces poignantly illustrated how the hopes, dreams and potential of the once smiling, innocent children were wiped away by the plague.

On countless occasions we used those pictures to illustrate and contextualize the needless loss and pain. We were trying to humanize the victim for the reader. Our interviewees had experienced every parent's worst nightmare. In some cases the parents had also been left to rear their orphaned grandchildren and were forced to live their later years desperately trying to prevent history repeating itself. I was chronicling a social catastrophe.

Visiting the homes of drug addicts who had children was always distressing. Once during the late 1980s, as a young reporter, I interviewed a teenage couple, both of whom were heroin addicts. They wanted to highlight the fact that the guy had been beaten up by vigilantes who came and smashed in their door in the middle of the night. They had been ordered to leave the corporation flat in Ballymun with their children which meant that they would be homeless on top of everything else.

I watched as they both helped inject each other in the kitchen while their three very young children, including a newborn baby, were left to their own devices in the sparsely furnished living room. They told me that the baby had been born with an addiction to heroin and HIV. I remember the sense of absolute hopelessness and despair in that flat. I don't know what happened to them after that. There were so many similar cases that the faces and stories blurred into one.

I had received my initial education about the workings of the drug business from the seminal true crime book *Smack*, by Padraig Yeates and Sean Flynn. The rest I learned through on-the-job experience. The book chronicled in engrossing detail the genesis of the criminal drug rackets in Ireland and particularly the arrival of heroin via the Dunne family. My first assignment as a junior reporter in 1987 was covering a protest by the Concerned Parents Against Drugs group at the home of one of the brothers, Vianney Dunne, in central Dublin's historic Liberties. The protesters used a barrel as a makeshift brazier to burn timber to stave off the bitter winter breeze. Dunne eventually moved away from the area and began selling his heroin someplace else.

A month later, Shamie Dunne, the founding father of the epidemic, got a lucky break when a charge of possessing heroin worth over €1 million today was thrown out of court on a technicality. The following day Shamie jumped on a plane to London and began a self-imposed exile to escape his tormentors in the Drug Squad who had already busted most of his family. He didn't want to wait around for fear that they might resuscitate the case.

When I interviewed him in July 1991, the fifty-one-year-old former armed robber turned hated drug lord was feeling immensely sorry for himself. After four years in hiding Dunne was unwilling to acknowledge the devastation that he had left back in Ireland. For Shamie Dunne it was nothing personal, it was just business. To illustrate the point the illiterate drug dealer pointed out the upside-down health warning on the pack of cigarettes he was smoking:

> Look at that. They [Government] say that these are bad for you
> but the people who sell them aren't criminals. More people
> die from lung cancer than drugs, so what's the difference? It's
> alright because respectable people are making money from it. It
> [heroin] is a commodity and if people want to take it that's their
> problem. There was heroin around before we became involved.

We were standing on the balcony of his council flat on the twentieth floor of a west London high-rise block while he was delivering a master class in rationalization, obfuscation and cognitive dissonance. He wasn't a godfather and he hadn't caused the misery back home. The Dunne family were as much victims as anyone else. They had been scapegoated by society, especially the police, and forced into crime. He said the media had peddled the lies fed to them by the police. It was all a big conspiracy. The family mantra went that it was always someone else's fault.

On a clear day Shamie could see the rooftop of Wormwood
Scrubs prison from the balcony. But that was as close as the drug
entrepreneur wanted to get to it or any prison. He had started
his criminal career in earnest in London and had done time in
the Scrubs as a younger man. It was through his connections in
London that he sourced the heroin the family sold in Dublin.
As we gazed out across the rain-sodden city he called home, he
took a long drag from his cigarette, flicked it into the night air
and mused:

> Y'know if I was up to anything over here the Old Bill would have
> me in the Scrubs like a shot. I've done me time for all the crimes
> that they caught me for. Now I'd wish they'd leave me to fuck
> alone.

It was the first time that Shamie Dunne had ever agreed to do an
interview. In the past his older brother Christy 'Bronco' Dunne
had acted as the family's eloquent spokesman whenever the clan
was under the public spotlight for its drug activities. Christy took
the blame for leading his younger siblings into crime but claimed
he did so because they were forced into it. His mantra was that the
cops were all corrupt and he was always innocent. Seven months
earlier Christy had given me an interview claiming that he was
being stitched up by the Serious Crime Squad for holding the
family of a Cabra postmaster hostage while he handed over cash.
Christy complained bitterly that he was the victim of a miscarriage
of justice. A week later a jury convicted him and he was jailed for
eleven years. Fifty years after the family first changed the face of
crime in Ireland Bronco still trots out the same argument.

A year before I met Shamie I also scooped an exclusive interview
with his younger brother Henry after he was released from a ten-

year sentence for an armed robbery and shooting at cops. Henry was involved in the armed robbery side of the family business and he articulated his reasons for getting involved in crime. (See Chapter 3.)

Shamie became the third Dunne brother to occupy space in my notebook. He broke his golden rule of never speaking to the press when he invited me to come to London to put the record straight. A few years before he would have probably thrown me after the butt of his cigarette if I turned up unannounced on his doorstep. 'I have no love of the *Sunday World* but I thought it was time to put my side of the story across,' he said.

The reason for the interview was because Shamie was again being victimized – this time by the politicians and media back home.

A month earlier Independent TD Tony Gregory had used parliamentary privilege to publicly name Shamie Dunne as one of the biggest suppliers of heroin from the UK into Dublin. He had good information that Dunne, who had an extensive network of contacts within UK crime circles, was the boss of the operation which was based in Manchester.

I got to know Tony very well over the years and admired his commitment and zeal. He represented the people of the north inner-city and was elected on the back of his work fighting against the drug scourge and highlighting the State's general neglect of his constituency. For many years Tony was one of the only public representatives campaigning against the drug lords. By using parliamentary privilege Gregory knew that the media could faithfully report the accusations without fear of being sued by Dunne, although that would have been unlikely given the criminal's reputation as a social parasite. I did a follow up interview with Tony so that he could double down on his claims.

It was after the interview was published that Shamie phoned me and said he wanted to talk – but only on his terms. When I got to London he would be in contact to arrange a meet. I gave him the number of my sister Caroline's apartment in the city where I would be staying. Happily it was also in west London. At the time I omitted to tell her that Shamie Dunne had her number. I thought there was no point in stressing her unnecessarily over something so trivial! I was a young reporter chasing a major scoop and Shamie was playing ball.

I waited patiently by the phone for two days and was about to go home when Shamie's representative called to check that I was there. The gangster was being very cautious. Several more cloak and dagger calls were made over the following day before I eventually met the associate in a seedy west London pub. He guided me to 'Mr Dunne's' home in a high-rise block nearby. 'I just wanted to ensure that you were alone,' Dunne smiled as he welcomed me in. He offered me a seat and a scotch, both of which I cautiously accepted.

I recall being somewhat surprised when he fixed a sherry for himself – it was hardly the tipple of choice for someone with such a hard man image. The apartment where he lived with his English wife Valerie was modest but comfortable and had none of the trappings of a millionaire drug dealer. I wondered if it had been specially choreographed for the interview.

'Look, I've even got the Beit paintings stashed in me flat,' he joked about the hunt for the collection of priceless paintings famously purloined by his former fellow gang member, Martin Cahill.

When I asked him about Tony Gregory's claims, Dunne insisted that he had left his drug dealing days behind him and claimed that he was making a crust as a used car salesman. The image of Dunne as a version of Boycie or Arthur Daley knocking out dodgy motors seemed to better fit his image than sipping sherry.

Most of the quotes from the interview screamed self-pity and persecution:

> I couldn't take no more of that country... the establishment just wouldn't leave me alone and vigilantes were after me too. Me name was on a bullet in that town. I had to get out before the vigilantes got me first. The cops put me and my family down for so many security van robberies and bank robberies and the bulk of the city's heroin trade but I don't know how we could have managed to do the amount of stuff they claimed we did. I'm not sayin' that we are innocent of everything but we're certainly not guilty of everything either.

Dunne denied Gregory's claims that he was supplying heroin to Dublin. It was more evidence of the conspiracy against him:

> The funniest thing of all is that he called me a heroin godfather. Godfather of what? A small council flat and a half pint of bitter in a local boozer is hardly the lifestyle of a godfather... Just as I thought I had left all that shit behind me the Irish establishment comes along and throws the whole lot in my face again.

I felt there was no point reminding him that Tony Gregory was anything but an establishment figure.

Shamie didn't deny that members of his family were involved in the heroin trade but disputed the share of the drug market they once had, claiming:

> I don't think it would have been ten per cent of the market.
>
> Whatever I may have done in the past is behind me now and I am
> not supplying drugs to anyone anywhere.

It was hard to know if Dunne was telling the truth but we know that he faded into obscurity after that memorable interview and certainly never featured again in any major drug investigation. Back in Dublin one of Shamie Dunne's original clients provided a much starker picture of his legacy.

———

James 'Jem' Dixon and his family were among the first generation to fall for the plague. The Dixons were first cousins of the wife of the Monk, Gerry Hutch. In order to feed their voracious habits they became notorious pushers, openly plying their trade on the streets of Dublin's north inner city. In the early 1980s when I was still at school I read a story about his brother Michael, nicknamed 'Snake', when he was exposed on the front page of the *Sunday World*. He had sold heroin to two undercover reporters in the middle of the day outside the GPO in O'Connell Street – the building synonymous with the fight for a free, better Ireland. It was one of the things that first attracted me to the paper. The story caused a temporary public outcry about a problem which was being ignored by the authorities – as long as it stayed within its own socially isolated geographical boundaries.

By the time we met in the summer of 1994 Jem Dixon's family had long since been surpassed by a new generation of drug pushers trying to feed their habits. He was one of the last remaining members of the family still clinging to life. Jem had agreed to be

interviewed for a feature I was researching about the heroin scourge
fourteen years after it had first taken hold. His harrowing story was
paradigmatic of the experiences of thousands of others who were
engulfed by the tidal wave of addiction. It laid bare the raw, harsh
realities of the plague unleashed by the likes of whining Shamie
and other underworld luminaries such as Christy Kinahan, now
one of the world's most wanted drug barons. Kinahan cut his teeth
moving large shipments of heroin into Dublin in the mid-1980s.
Even after the passage of three decades the shocking image of Jem
Dixon's crumpled, dilapidated appearance remains etched in my
memory.

Jem symbolized a doomed generation of people sucked into
the twilight world of the living undead. When I arrived in his
little corporation flat in the north inner city I was shocked by his
appearance. His lifeless eyes stared blankly from dark caverns in a
withered, jaundiced face cracked with pain. His pale skin looked
like Clingfilm stretched across a bundle of bones. A mutilated
stump was all that remained of his right leg and the index finger
of his left hand was missing. The decaying shell of a once tall, fit
man sat slumped in an armchair in a corner of his inner-city flat
waiting for death. He was only forty-one but looked a century
older. Dixon was dying from AIDS.

Like most of his peers Jem Dixon became involved in petty
crime at a very young age for which he was punished with sentences
in the industrial and reform schools. Like so many of his peers,
the harrowing experiences ensured that he never even considered
rehabilitation. He was a twenty-seven-year-old thief when he first
tried smack in 1980. By then the rest of his siblings were already
becoming hopeless junkies. He ruefully recalled the first hit that
sent him spiralling towards disaster:

My brother Noel was injecting himself along with a mate upstairs
in a house in Matt Talbot Court and I said 'give us a try at that to
see what it does'. I was hooked almost immediately and have been
using ever since then. I felt like I hadn't a worry in the world when
I took it. I was robbing at the time I took the heroin so I had plenty
of money to buy stuff for a while. None of us knew fuck all about
what smack could do to us and we shared needles with no worries
about HIV. Even then we didn't know much about what could
happen to us when we got the virus. I knew of one bloke up in
Mountjoy who got a syringe full of blood from another bloke who
had it. He injected it into himself so that he would be diagnosed
[HIV positive] and then put in the segregation unit and probably
get early release... the poor gobshite is now dying as well.

Jem related the grim chronology of how heroin broke his body
and his spirit. To make matters worse he used a dirty needle on
the wrong blood vein and gangrene set in. Surgeons cut twenty
inches off his right leg. Then he injected himself with a dirty needle
in the hand and doctors had to amputate his left index finger. He
showed me how every part of his arms, leg and groin were marked
with black and blue sores where practically every vein had broken
down from continuously injecting himself.

When I met Jem he was taking the medically prescribed heroin
substitute physeptone to feed his maniacal craving. But even then,
despite all he had been through, he was still injecting the odd fix
of heroin through a vein he managed to find in the stump of his
leg. By then heroin and AIDS had already wiped out his family.

Jem rattled off their names and the years that they perished. In
1986, his brother Snake's wife died of an overdose while she cradled
her two-month-old baby in her arms. In 1991 a brother-in-law

died from 'the virus', what the singer Prince referred to as 'the big disease with a little name'. The following year his sister Ellen and Snake, both addicts in their early thirties, also succumbed to AIDS. A month later another brother Noel followed his siblings to the cemetery, after having his head smashed open with a hammer in a row over a heroin deal. He reflected:

> Most of my family and friends are dead... I've been to about thirty funerals and I know that I'll be going to me own soon. If I see forty-five then I'll be doing damn good, but I don't really care because since the day I was born life has been a pure disaster for me.

Compared to Shamie Dunne, Jem was justified in feeling self-pity.

The only motive Jem Dixon had for doing the interview was to try to educate kids about the dangers of heroin. It was like he wanted to make amends for the past by helping prevent anyone else becoming slaves to the plague. A picture of his shocking appearance, which accompanied the news feature, was enough to get the point across.

> I have fuck all sympathy for some of the youngsters who are on the gear today because they know what damage it can do and all about AIDS. But there is nothing for youngsters to do in these places (inner city) except rob or steal. They get into serious drugs because they are constantly looking for a way out of the depression of the place. Things are going to get a lot worse in this town because there is little hope and no work for anyone... in a way I'm glad I don't have much longer left.

In December 1995 Jem Dixon joined the rest of his family in the graveyard. His words have proved to be prophetic. Whenever I pass the Home monument I think of him.

CHAPTER EIGHT

———

EXPOSING THE WESTIES

When Larry Dunne famously warned 'wait till you see what's coming next' as he was being led away to prison for selling heroin in October 1983, he could never have imagined in his wildest nightmares Shane Coates and Stephen Sugg. Of all the many gangsters I have written about and exposed over the decades the pair I nicknamed the Westies stand out. One of the many victims that I spoke to when I began investigating Sugg and Coates summed up the vicelike hold they had over enslaved addicts:

> Anyone who owes them as much as a pound is liable to be seriously injured or murdered. They are animals. They haven't been caught because everyone is too scared to talk. Most of their victims are just junkies anyway, like me, and they feel that no one gives a shite about them. These boys can do what they like.

Coates and Sugg, from Blanchardstown in west Dublin, were best friends from childhood and started their careers as teenage joyriders and ram raiders. They escalated to armed robberies and, in between several stints in prison, began dabbling in the drug trade.

From the beginning former neighbours, criminal associates and police I talked to recalled how the pair had a natural predisposition to violence. Even as teenagers they had notorious reputations and were feared by other young criminals. One officer who knew them told me:

> You could see then that they were both very close and Sugg was greatly influenced by Coates. They had very little fear of anyone and they were very violent. There was a strange chemistry between them that brought out pure evil when they were together.

When their former boss PJ Judge, the Psycho, was murdered in December 1996 and the Gilligan gang were smashed, they were among the new generation who quickly stepped in to fill the void. Between 1997 and 2003 the Westies controlled one of the biggest heroin distribution networks in Ireland through the exclusive use of extreme violence and fear, particularly on their home patch of Blanchardstown. Described by the police as being 'armed and extremely dangerous' they murdered, injured and tortured their way to gangland dominance. They were real life monsters.

Coates, who was born in 1972 and five years older than Sugg, was the dominant element in the criminal partnership and was seen as being the most violent of the pair. In the days before we named Coates in the *Sunday World* we gave him the sobriquet the 'New Psycho'. The Westies adopted the same business template as their predecessor. Like Judge they operated a strict no credit policy and terrorized and exploited the unfortunate junkies and street dealers who worked for them.

A drug addict owing them as much as €50 was severely beaten or even mutilated. If a street pusher was suspected of stealing heroin or money for himself he got the same treatment. And anyone suspected of talking to the police got even worse. The Westies had no fear of being caught or charged because they knew no one would testify against them. In a short time the pair were responsible for an astonishing catalogue of brutal attacks on competitors, drug dealers and addicts, who were either encroaching on their turf or owed them money.

In one case they attacked a thirty-eight-year-old drug addict, a mother of nine children. During the incident they used lighted cigarettes to burn the woman's breasts because she owed them about €500 for heroin they had supplied. Another female addict had her long hair chopped off, and her home and car were also smashed up. They threw a young junkie from a fifth-floor balcony in the high-rise Ballymun corporation flat complex because he owed them less than €50 worth of smack. Somehow the victim survived the fall and limped away.

Victims told me that friends were forced to betray each other at the behest of the Westies for fear that they might be attacked instead. Another pusher had jump leads attached to his nipples while being tortured and several were slashed with Stanley blades. In one horrific incident Sugg and Coates burned down the home of the innocent parents of an eighteen-year-old drug addict they suspected of ripping them off.

In January 1999 their deadly reputations were confirmed when they shot dead Pascal Boland, a former associate, because he had decided to set up his own heroin dealing operation.

A young couple, both heroin addicts, had witnessed the Boland murder and were able to identify Sugg and Coates as the killers. Over the following months they were attacked and severely beaten by the Westies. They developed amnesia after that. When detectives arrested one gang member suspected of participating in the Boland murder he was asked was he afraid of them and replied: 'Yeah everybody is. They're mental. They beat you and they'd kill you. They've no fear of anybody. They think they're bullet proof.'

The Westies also injured a number of people in separate, unrelated shooting incidents. They shot two bouncers who had thrown them out of a nightclub and then shot a guy who Sugg did not approve of dating his sister.

Derek 'Smiley' McGuinness from Corduff Park in Blanchards-town had a particularly gruesome story to tell. By the time we met he was twenty-eight years old and had been a chronic heroin user for half of his miserable life. The father of three was a habitual criminal who carried out robberies and sold heroin to feed his habit. For two years he had been selling batches of gear for the Westies until they accused him of owing them the equivalent of €600. They haunted McGuinness for months looking for the money while he did his best to stay out of their way.

He told me why he owed the money:

> It was for heroin I used myself instead of selling for them. The
> stuff they sold was so badly cut that you couldn't get a hit off
> it anyway. But I would have paid that money to them only for
> the fact that on my son's Confirmation Day they drove up and
> attacked me outside the church. On a point of principle after that
> I told them to fuck off because I could have paid them the money.

When I asked Smiley McGuinness how he had planned to get the money he candidly replied: 'I was going to steal it, how else do you think I was going to get it?'

The unfortunate junkie had agreed to give me an interview after being released from hospital. His face had been stitched back together after Sugg and Coates demonstrated why no one should ever dare tell them to fuck off.

Around the time of the Boland murder I had begun to hear on the grapevine about the exploits of the two gangsters. Gardaí in Blanchardstown, who were involved in a massive investigation to break the Westies, had suggested I should take a close look at how the new kids on the block operated in their unprecedented reign of savagery and terror.

In October 1999 the Westies ordered two of their flunkies, Andrew Allen and Herman 'the Vermin' White to grab Smiley and teach him a lesson in gangland etiquette. Allen and White, who were both twenty-one, also sold drugs and did the Westies' dirty work to feed their own heroin habits. They were terrified of the two mobsters. On the afternoon of 20 October Smiley McGuinness was walking through Corduff Park when he bumped into Allen and White.

He told me he knew the two men and had no reason to be afraid of them. But suddenly White produced an iron bar and hit McGuinness hard across the head and face, knocking him to the ground in the process. He continued hitting McGuinness in the face with the bar as he lay on the ground, smashing his nose and his teeth. At the same time Allen phoned the New Psycho, delighted to be in a position to please his deranged boss.

'We have Smiley here. Do you want to come up and deal with him now?' he asked the monster on the other end of the line. But Coates could not make it to the park so Allen had another idea for his boss's entertainment. 'Here, listen to this,' said Allen, as he placed the phone on the ground beside McGuinness' head. Then the two thugs began kicking and beating Smiley with the iron bar.

Coates wanted to hear McGuinness scream for mercy. In the meantime Stephen Sugg arrived in the park armed with a Stanley knife and joined in the torture. He slashed McGuinness' ear, the back of his head and the full length of his left jaw. Sugg sliced his victim's left hand and then they walked away leaving McGuinness in a bloodied heap on the ground.

Miraculously McGuinness somehow managed to make his way home where his girlfriend called an ambulance. The drug addict lost nine pints of blood from his wounds and spent several days in intensive care. Both sides of his jaw were broken, all his teeth were smashed and he received over sixty stitches for the knife wounds.

'The doctors told me that my jaw was so badly broken that it was literally held together by the skin. They nearly killed me,' Smiley told me. As I was looking at the stomach-churning, grotesque injuries I knew Smiley wasn't exaggerating. McGuinness wanted to speak out publicly because he'd had enough of the brutality. He was fed up with being scared. He had given the gardaí in Blanchardstown a major breakthrough when he identified his attackers, including Sugg, and gave them a full statement about the attack.

McGuinness further illustrated his determination by agreeing to be identified in the story I was compiling. He posed for pictures so the world could see the Westies' handiwork in all its gruesome detail. That gave us the opportunity to expose Sugg and Coates to public attention for the first time by publishing an investigation into their catalogue of violent crimes which filled over two pages. I reported how a special garda unit set up to target the gang had compiled a list of forty serious attacks the Westies had carried out in just over a year. The feature revealed how they had used guns, baseball bats, knives, broken bottles, batons, iron bars, jump leads and even vice grips on their victims. The vice grips they used to squeeze male genitalia. At the time we didn't name the pair but ran their pictures with the mandatory black strips over their eyes.

I labelled them the Westies because of the gangland connotations from the US and also because their base was in west Dublin. The names, the New Psycho and the Westies quickly stuck. Gangland had two more bogeymen.

In the months that followed I continued to write about their monstrous exploits. The stories gave rise to a steady stream of information and new leads as terrified victims and parents of victims picked up the phone. In another major exposé we published exclusive pictures on the front page featuring the pernicious partners posing with knives and wearing balaclavas, having a laugh with friends. We got the pictures from a source who wanted them exposed. The police were also receiving plenty of information but the problem was that none of their victims were prepared to make statements. We had been warned that there was no point in attempting to talk to either of the Westies on the street. I was told they would cut me up in pieces. Instead, we crept up on them from a safe distance.

While researching the Westies' operation I realized why they were so incredibly greedy – they were making an eye-watering fortune from peddling misery. From information gathered from a number of their street dealers and bagmen in 1999 gardaí conservatively estimated that in 1998, the first year of their operation, the gang had turned over nearly €2 million in today's values. The operating model the Westies used is the same used by every heroin and cocaine dealing gang. The figures have been converted into today's values for a perspective on the kind of profits involved. All that has changed is the prices charged on the streets. This is how it worked.

In 1998 and 1999 Sugg and Coates paid an average of €1,000 for an ounce of heroin. A bagman who later spoke to me confided how he would cut up the ounce of heroin by diluting it down with other substances, including glucose and curry powder, to maximize profits. Each ounce usually made eighteen batches and each batch in turn contained fifteen 'Qs'. Each 'Q' provided a single fix, which an addict either injected or smoked. A typical addict needs up to five 'Qs' per day to feed their habit depending on the purity of the smack.

At the time a 'Q' sold for €34. After paying the bagman €250 for his work the Westies turned a profit of €8,000 on their original €1,000 investment. The bagman concerned was cutting up an average of four ounces per week which meant a cumulative profit of €32,000 per week or over €120,000 per month. In a year the profits rose to around €1.5 million. But this was a small part of the overall operation. At the height of their powers the Westies had six or seven people cutting heroin for them. Some of them were cutting an ounce every day. Business was booming as they were flooding the place with heroin. At the same time demand was increasing.

The initial story I did about Smiley McGuinness and the Westies' catalogue of crime prompted a major public reaction. The decent people of Blanchardstown and their victims wanted the thugs out of their lives. In late 1999 and early 2000 I was at a number of public meetings organized by community groups in the area which were also attended by the police.

Coates and Sugg actually turned up at one of the meetings in an act of bravado designed to intimidate those attending. Even though the gardaí were present I felt the cold chill of fear they brought into the hall as the angry voices in the crowd fell silent. The speakers didn't want a visit in the middle of the night or their homes burned to the ground. The monsters had effectively imprisoned an entire community and were parading their untouchability. The flash, brash gang bosses wanted the world to see that they had no fear of anyone. Even though I was well accustomed to the effects of gangsters on the lives of ordinary people it still made me both depressed and profoundly angry.

Another story I covered about the violent escapades of Coates and Sugg concerned a horrific attack on a thirty-four-year-old woman who had been having an ongoing row with one of Coates' relatives. The woman was abducted and beaten by three men using baseball bats. She suffered smashed kneecaps, broken legs and ribs, and extensive internal bleeding. Armed gardaí protected the woman while she was being treated in intensive care. Later she informally identified her attackers as Sugg and Coates but was too terrified to make a complaint. She told officers she feared that she and her family would be murdered. The gardaí had no choice but to drop the investigation.

Cops seldom speak publicly about their targets but in an interview I had with the officer in charge of the Western Division of the Dublin Metropolitan Region (DMR) Chief Superintendent John McLoughlin was uncharacteristically blunt. The Westies were public enemy number one and he wanted the people's help in putting a stop to them. He told me:

> They've been involved in stabbings, slashings and shootings.
> They put vice grips on a fella's thumb. They're unbelievable,
> they're evil. I would love to see them on a [charge] sheet with
> garda evidence. We've got to nail them.

The narcissistic psychopaths were not in any way offended or worried about their growing reputations or the attention of the police. They revelled in the notoriety. Like all villains they were building a wall of silence on foundations of fear.

In the meantime the gardaí had compiled a number of cases against Sugg and Coates. They were charged with shooting and injuring a man who had identified the pair to the police. Members of the man's family had also witnessed the shooting and given statements. The investigators were confident that if convicted the Westies would be jailed for at least ten years. However, when the case came to trial the victim and the witnesses suddenly developed amnesia.

Despite his initial enthusiasm Smiley McGuinness was also struck by memory loss and refused to testify against Sugg for scarring him for life. McGuinness did not suffer any memory loss about Andrew Allen and Herman 'the Vermin' White, however, who were both convicted and jailed. Their defence counsel told the court that both men had been forced into the attack on McGuinness because of their relationship with a 'major drug dealer'.

Through the successful application of fear Coates and Sugg were free to continue running their drug empire. But the police were gradually gaining the upper hand. By 2001 they had seized over €1 million worth of the gang's heroin and firearms and had successfully busted and convicted several gang members. The CAB was also on their tail. Emboldened by their previous scrapes with the law the Westies decided to hit back by plotting to attack a member of the investigation team.

In the beginning of 2001 Coates and Sugg began targeting Detective Inspector John Mulligan, one of the senior officers leading the operation against the two thugs. The distinguished officer, who was based at Blanchardstown station, was secretly followed to his home, his health club and to a number of social events. In the early hours of the morning in late March a uniformed

1: Martin 'The General' Cahill

2: Talking to Frances Cahill, the wife of Martin, at her front door

3: Martin Cahill's body is removed from the scene where he was gunned down

SUNDAY WORLD

GARTH FEVER
CATHY KELLY DISCOVERS WHY THE GIRLS WEEP AND HOLLER
PAGES 2 & 3

THE WORLD OF
PADDY MURRAY
SEE PAGE 6

Vol. 22   No. 1   April 3rd, 1994   90p (incl. VAT)   C

IRELAND'S No. 1

EXPOSED THE GENERAL

Adam and Naomi are so egg-cited

SUPERMODEL Naomi Campbell flew into New York this week on an Easter shopping splurge for her wedding to U2's Adam Clayton.

The catwalk queen refused to confirm whether the on-off wedding will go ahead as planned in Straffan, Co. Kildare, later this month as she teamed up with Adam in the Big Apple.

But leggy wonder Naomi certainly isn't keeping all her eggs — Easter or otherwise — in the one basket.

She's just been paid £100,000 for her novel "Swan," which will hit the bookshelves here in September.

And Naomi recently completed her debut album in London which is being hailed by Sony music executives as "brilliant" — in the mould of Diana Ross.

A single from the album is due out in June by which time Naomi will have scoffed all her chocolate eggs. But will she be counting her chickens?

THIS is Martin Cahill the 45-year-old family man who denies he is the notorious crime lord, The General.

This is the first time a photograph of the unemployed father-of-five has ever been published.

Mr Cahill, who has never been seen in public without his characteristic anorak and balaclava, has consistently denied he is The General or that he even knows him.

The enigmatic character who has two houses in Rathmines, Dublin — a luxury £90,000 home and a Corporation house — has been under regular Garda surveillance for the past 20 years.

Meanwhile, the Garda Serious Crime Squad are stepping up their efforts to trap The General himself, the

EXCLUSIVE
By Crime Reporter PAUL WILLIAMS
INVESTIGATION
Pages 15, 16, 17 & 18

most dangerous gang boss in the country.

The General has masterminded some of the biggest robberies in the history of the State, and presides over a crime empire estimated to have current assets of over £20 million.

Gardai believe he is responsible for shootings, bombings, torture, armed robberies and protection rackets.

Martin Cahill first hit the headlines when he was one of the men targeted in a high-profile Garda surveillance operation six years ago.

Mr Cahill, who has been imprisoned for house breaking, receiving stolen goods and larceny of a car, became renowned for his theatrical antics outside Dublin courts, where he appeared on minor offences.

On one occasion, a masked Mr Cahill stripped off his clothes revealing Mickey Mouse underwear. On another occasion he emerged from court wearing a bird's nest on his head.

When asked was he the crime figure The General during one of the few interviews he ever gave, Mr Cahill declared: "I will admit to nothing under the alias of The General, Mickey Mouse or anybody else. If the gardai have evidence to connect me with robberies they should charge me."

Gardai admit they have Mr Cahill under surveillance on a regular basis. In response Mr Cahill has told reporters: "It's all a game between me and the Gardai. I never go on holiday but they always ask me to, so that they can have a holiday."

MARTIN CAHILL: The man who denies he is The General.

SHEARER GLORY AS ROVERS STUFF REDS: Pages 70 & 71

4: Martin 'The General' Cahill is first exposed on the front page of the *Sunday World*

5: With John Traynor in Portugal in 1996 where he was in hiding after Veronica Guerin's murder

6: The dramatic shoot-out between gardai and the notorious Athy gang

7: PJ 'The Psycho' Judge, who tried to have me murdered

8: William 'Jock' Corbally

9: With my colleague Liam O'Connor at Veronica Guerin's murder scene

10: Gerry 'The Monk' Hutch whose life I have chronicled for over four decades   *Pic: Mark Condren*

11: Eamon 'the Don' Dunne

12: George 'The Penguin' Mitchell

13: Eamon Kelly

14: Martin 'Marlo' Hyland

15: Martin 'The Viper' Foley

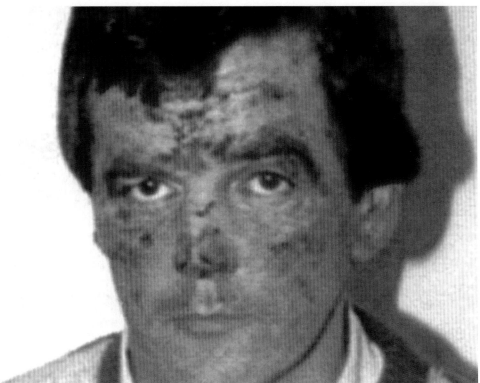

16: Seamus 'Shavo' Hogan

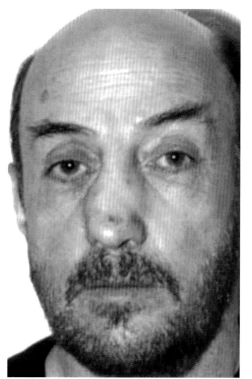

17: Patrick 'Dutchy' Holland

18: Giovanni Di Stefano

19: Confronting John Gilligan's wife, Geraldine, following Veronica Guerin's murder

20: The picture of me with my daughter which annoyed John Gilligan

21: Gilligan pumping iron as he serves time in prison

22: Shane Coates and Stephen Sugg were leaders of the notorious Westies

23: The Westies pose in balaclavas

24: Shane Coates

25: John Daly, who phoned *Liveline* to abuse me

26: Alan 'Fatpuss' Bradley, who also spoke to Joe Duffy

27: Confronting notorious rapist Larry Murphy

28: Murphy with convicted rapist and murderer Rory O'Connor in Amsterdam

29: Larry Murphy refused to talk to me

30: Interviewing the FBI's top criminal profiler, Special Agent Bill Hagmaier

31: A night out in New York with my friend and FBI legend John O'Neill, who died in 9/11

32: Outside my home after the hoax bomb was placed under my car and, below, the front pages published at the time

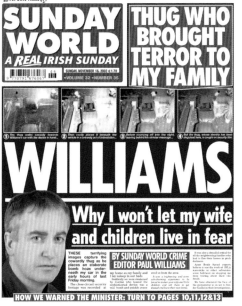

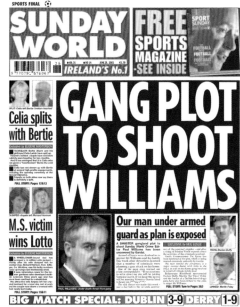

PAUL WILLIAMS NABS PUBLIC ENEMY No. 1

DAPPER DON

We track Europe's cocaine crime boss

SEE YOU IN COURT: Paul Williams greets Christy Kinahan
PIC EXCLUSIVE: Padraig O'Reilly

THIS is Dapper Don Christy Kinahan, one of Europe's most-wanted drug traffickers.

The international crime godfather from Dublin's inner city likes to pass himself off as a suave businessman and shun the limelight.

So he was furious when the *Sunday World* tracked him down on a Belgian street this week.

We can reveal that Kinahan and his associates have been targeted by Europol as one of the biggest cocaine trafficking cartels on the continent.

But it turned out to be a bad week for the Dapper Don, who was slapped with a four-year sentence for money laundering at a court in Antwerp on Tuesday.

ON THE TRAIL OF MISTER BIG: FULL STORY ON PAGES 10&11

33: Confronting Christy 'The Dapper Don' Kinahan on the streets of Antwerp in 2009 and, above, the front page of the *Sunday World*

garda patrol from Rathfarnham station stopped Sugg, Coates and another associate in a car not far from the officer's home where he lived with his wife and children.

Some time earlier a concerned neighbour had spotted the men acting suspiciously at the back of DI Mulligan's home. The disturbing discovery sparked a major investigation and senior officers said they were treating the development 'very seriously'. The officer and his family were given armed protection for several months. The Westies had upped the stakes in their war with the police.

A week after the incident Coates was brought to Blanchardstown garda station on suspicion of drunk driving. Coates was anxious to let the uniformed officers know whom they had arrested. It was the first encounter the two young gardaí had with the hoodlum. The drink test proved negative and as Coates was leaving the station he asked the officers if they knew of his reputation.

The two cops who had been recently posted to the area knew nothing of his criminal pedigree. He smirked and told them: 'You'll get to know me all right... I am an evil bastard.'

Thankfully no harm ever came to DI Mulligan or his family and he went on to have a successful career spearheading several high-profile criminal investigations including a stint as the head of the Garda National Drug Unit. He retired with the rank of Detective Superintendent. Following the alert and the ensuing publicity the Westies had enough intelligence to back off while the police were coming down hard on them. In any event they had other matters on their minds.

———

One man who agreed wholeheartedly with Coates's description of himself as an evil bastard was Jeffrey Mitchell. From Crumlin in south Dublin, Mitchell was an armed robber and drug dealer who had a reputation that equalled the Westies.

Mitchell became their business partner after his release from prison in 1999 at the age of twenty-seven, after serving a sentence for armed robbery. But in gangland, relationships and allegiances are as changeable as the Irish weather. The partnership between Mitchell and the Westies turned dangerously sour when the mobsters fell out over money. One of Mitchell's street dealers, twenty-two-year-old drug addict Neil Hanlon, lost a consignment of heroin he had been holding for the former blagger. Mitchell had bought the drugs on credit from the Westies who demanded payment regardless – as part of their deadly no credit policy. Mitchell didn't have the money and when he refused to pay Sugg and Coates decided their business partner had to die.

In June 2001 the two gangsters burst into Mitchell's home armed with handguns and opened fire on him but he managed to escape untouched. In a fit of frustration the thugs shot Mitchell's dog. A few months later they raided a flat which Mitchell had been using as a safe house to count drug money. He had left the flat ten minutes earlier. It saved his life.

Sugg and Coates beat and tortured the couple who had allowed Mitchell to use the flat. Following the latest near miss Mitchell accused Neil Hanlon of telling the Westies about his hidey-hole. On the evening of 29 September 2001 Neil Hanlon left his family home at Downpatrick Road in Crumlin. The troubled drug addict, who had made several attempts to kick his habit, was never seen alive again.

In February 2002 gardaí found his remains in a shallow grave in a park in Crumlin. I later discovered through sources that the medical examination showed that the tragic young man had been mutilated at the time of his death. Information was received that Hanlon had been drugged and then murdered by Jeffrey Mitchell, with the help of another associate, twenty-two-year-old David McCreevy. A few months after Hanlon's disappearance McCreevy was arrested with €200,000 worth of Mitchell's heroin. He was charged with drug offences.

On 3 February 2002, McCreevy was shot dead outside his home in Tallaght by a gunman who was the pillion passenger on a motorbike. The word on the street was that Jeffrey Mitchell carried out the killing because he suspected McCreevy might do a deal with the cops to finger him for the drugs and the Hanlon murder. That was how I found myself sitting across a table from the killer a day later.

Jeffrey Mitchell had a pal who had a contact in the *Sunday World* printing works at the time. We already knew about him because the gardaí had warned us about his associations. There was also another employee of the company our sources had identified as knowing some major gangsters socially. He was not involved in criminality in any way, but there was always a risk that he could be blackmailed or compromised. That was one of the reasons why we kept our investigations under wraps and known only to Colm MacGinty and a small circle. The day after the McCreevy murder, Saturday 4 February, I had written a story nominating Mitchell as the prime suspect and outlining the motive for the attack.

But we didn't name him and the picture we used was pixelated so that Mitchell couldn't be identified for legal reasons. When the page was laid out it was sent to the case room. At that stage in the pre-print process the picture wasn't obscured and could be seen on a screen in the room where the images were transferred to a printing plate. Mitchell, who apparently had anticipated we would be writing about him, had asked his pal to keep an eye out for what we were going to publish. It was a stroke of luck for us.

Sometime later in the afternoon Mitchell rang the newsroom asking to speak to me. 'I believe that you're writing about me and about me mate's murder,' he announced along with his name. I suggested that he come in to talk and he agreed.

About thirty minutes later he was at the front gate of the *Sunday World* in Terenure and was being covertly photographed for the new front page that he was about to hand us.

At the time a young journalist called Daragh Keany had joined the paper a month earlier. Daragh was enthusiastic and anxious to learn the ropes. His jovial sunny personality steered him towards fun stories and showbiz news which is the area he still covers with aplomb as the *Sunday World* features editor today.

As I was putting notes together for the meeting with Mitchell I suggested that Daragh come with me to the conference room. He still remembers with dread how I asked him if he wanted to meet a real life gangland killer in the flesh. I told him that not many people could enjoy such a rare privilege. I could also do with a second body in the room just in case Mitchell was mad enough to kick off. In any event two armed detectives had quietly arrived in the building as part of the paper's security protocols that had evolved over the years due to the various death threats.

When we sat down at the table Mitchell was clearly on edge and whining that I was putting him in the frame. I wondered aloud how he could possibly know such information when the presses hadn't started to roll yet.

'I'm been blamed for all this in the papers but the guards have told me I am not a suspect,' he began. I told him that our information was that he was the prime suspect and how could the guards eliminate him from their enquiries less than twenty-four hours after the murder, even if he was innocent.

'I sold drugs and robbed banks but I don't go around shooting people. I don't order hits on cops or screws or ordinary people.' Like the vast majority of villains in the world Mitchell was claiming to be the victim of a set up – a conspiracy of lies. The feared thug whined:

> He [McCreevy] was a harmless little cunt. He got involved in the heroin just out of the blue. He was one of me best mates. He even bought me a puppy dog three days ago. I have never even killed a dog or an animal. I am not a violent person. I am not the big gangster that you say I am. I swear to God, man.

I put to him that the word on the grapevine was that the murder of McCreevy was connected to the drug seizure and fears that he had become an informant. Mitchell refused to admit that the seized drugs actually belonged to him:

> If I admitted that then I could be charged. Dave was not doing anything since his arrest and he wasn't talking to the police. When I heard that he had been killed I cried for four hours last night.

When he was pressed about his involvement in the heroin trade Mitchell admitted that he had previously been a heroin dealer. As per the manual of criminal psychology he began rationalizing and distancing himself from the crime:

I was a drug dealer. I was selling smack but it's getting too heavy,
it's too dangerous with people shootin' and killin' each other.
It was alright for the buzz but now it's getting out of hand. The
papers say that I made millions but that's a load of bollix. I lost
everything that I made from the drugs. I got too big. Heroin is the
dirtiest business of all. I haven't had anything but bad luck and
this [McCreevy's murder] is the worst thing to have happened in
me life.

When I asked why he sold heroin which caused such devastation to human lives there was a flash of arrogance when he replied: 'If I didn't sell it then someone else would be selling it. I take heroin meself. It's great when you're depressed.' Mitchell said that he gave up heroin after the attempts on his life in 2001.

As the interview continued he seemed to be getting angrier. That segued nicely to his relationship with the Westies and the fact that they had twice tried to kill him. Mitchell first denied that he even knew Sugg or Coates. 'I have never ever met either of them in me life. I don't know them that's the gospel truth.' But then the gospel truth changed when he admitted that he did actually know them and that they had been responsible for the attempted hits. 'Someone was paid to do it [the hit]. It probably was them,' he said.

But then Mitchell flip-flopped again and said that he knew who had tried to murder him and that it wasn't the Westies. 'I know who did it and he has legged it out of the country since then. If they [Westies] did it I would have killed them,' Mitchell claimed.

As the interview came to a close I turned to the subject of Neil Hanlon's disappearance. I told him he was the prime suspect for the murder of the vulnerable junkie which of course he knew. At that he flew into a rage.

'Ah, yer not fuckin' puttin' me down for that as well ya cunt…
yer a warped cunt you are… no fuckin' wonder cunts want to shoot
ya,' the killer began to shout. He slammed his fists down on the
table and stared at me. But I too sometimes have a short fuse and
wasn't taking his bullshit.

In a rush of blood I slammed my fists down on the table
and stared back at Mitchell who was now a few inches away
and shouted, 'I may be a warped cunt but I'm not a murdering,
drug dealing cunt like you.' A silence descended. I never lost
eye contact with him. Showing fear is a mistake when dealing
with a bully.

I glanced over at Daragh and could see the blood drain out of
his face like a cartoon character. He says he has never forgotten
that moment and still describes how he had been 'shitting' himself
when the row kicked off. Daragh later recalled:

> I sat as far away as I could at the table and watched how Williams
> grilled him, and then when Mitchell blew up I was stunned how
> he stood up to Mitchell and showed him no fear. I wondered
> what I was doing there and was shitting myself. It crossed my
> mind that Mitchell might produce a weapon.

At least I had helped Daragh decide one area of journalism he had
no intention of getting involved in.

The words with Mitchell were a timely ending to the interview
which had lasted about 40 minutes. I told Mitchell that as much
as I would love to spend longer discussing the vicissitudes of his
life I had an editor screaming for copy. I didn't tell him that he
had just changed the front page. The story had to be written up
and sent to the presses which had already started to roll with the
first version of the anonymized Mitchell story. Mitchell pulled his

neck in and left. We had a cracking scoop. The next day everyone would know his name and picture.

It was an ironic twist that the body of Neil Hanlon was located less than a week later by gardaí. Mitchell was never charged with either murder. It was later revealed that he had kissed and made up his differences with the Westies. He was subsequently jailed for six years for armed robbery. When he came out of prison Mitchell was a broken man who was both an alcoholic and a heroin addict. He was never a gangland player again. In November 2022 he was found dead from a heroin overdose in a homeless hostel in Swords, County Dublin. In the room where his body was found there was €50,000 worth of heroin lying nearby. By the time Mitchell passed away his former partners and would-be killers had an almost eighteen-year head start on him.

By the beginning of 2003 the Westies were, as per the predictable cycle of gang life, running out of road and looked weak. In the treacherous, predatory world of narcotics there are always challengers waiting in the wings for the time to swoop and claim the crown. Sensing weakness, former associates brothers Mark and Andrew Glennon began to make moves to take over their patch.

In April 2002 they shot Bernard 'Verb' Sugg, Stephen's brother, who was hospitalized with a stomach wound but recovered. Around the same time Shane Coates was jailed for a number of road traffic offences. While the New Psycho was away the Glennons tried to kill Stephen Sugg when a hit man opened fire at him with a machine gun as he got into his car outside his home in the Corduff estate. He managed to escape unscathed but left the country and went into hiding in Alicante, Spain.

When Coates was released from prison he moved to live in County Meath to stay out of range of his enemies. He tooled up and prepared for war. The gangster had a narrow escape in May 2003 when gardaí raided a safe house he was using to hide out and store guns and drugs outside the town of Virginia, County Cavan. Coates was wanted in connection with the robbery of a firearms' dealer.

When the gang opened fire on gardaí a detective fired back hitting Coates twice in the leg. However, he managed to escape in the darkness across fields and was later understood to have been treated for his injuries by a rogue doctor. He then slipped out of the country to join Stephen Sugg in the gang's new Spanish base which they thought was a safe distance from their enemies. In their absence Verb Sugg took over the day-to-day running of the operation.

But then in August 2003 he was gunned down in the Brookwood Inn, the local pub where the Westies mob held court and intimidated the locals. Sugg became the sixteenth gangland murder victim in the year 2003. By the end of the year the figure had risen to nineteen.

The night he was murdered I was in the final stages of writing a chapter on the Westies in my new book *Crime Lords*. I hadn't intended on naming Westies in the book for legal reasons. Publishers were much more terrified of legal suits than we were in the *Sunday World*. After the shooting I consulted my lawyers Gerry Fanning and his partner Kieran Kelly, who also did the libel reads on my books. We reviewed everything I had written about the Westies. 'Fuck it Paul, go ahead and name them,' I still hear my late great pal Gerry telling me on the phone. I rewrote the chapter. As I was putting the book together that summer I had to rewrite two other chapters after other members of the cast died in similar fashion to Sugg.

I watched Stephen Sugg with a photographer from a distance when he turned up at his brother's funeral. With a baseball hat tightly pulled down on his head he cut a rather forlorn and isolated figure. The arrogance and brashness were no longer visible. I was looking at a dead man walking. The funeral was a small affair with only close family turning up to pay their respects. The underworld, the police and crime hacks like myself waited for the revenge attack which would surely come. Everyone knew that the Westies were planning to return to Dublin to settle the score, but they never got the chance.

Their reign of terror came to an abrupt end when they were lured to a warehouse five months later in Alicante in January 2004. The Westies' fatal mistake was that they thought they could throw their weight around in Spain like they had done in Blanchardstown. As already expressed gangland observes the rules of social Darwinism where only the fittest and most ruthless survive. Sugg and Coates were regarded as mad men who could not be controlled or trusted. Their criminal competitors and former business partners decided that they had to go.

As they walked into the warehouse, two other Irish criminals shot them dead and then buried their bodies under a concrete floor. The word quickly filtered back to Ireland that the Westies were no more. A source of mine in the Crime and Security section, who were generally the first to know what was happening, tipped me off that my favourite gangsters were dead. It was probably fitting that I got the chance to exclusively report the news of their demise. In the meantime life in gangland went on as the whip changed hands from the Westies to the Glennons. But they didn't last long either.

The brothers were shot dead in two separate assassinations in 2005. And in their place rose another gang, which was eventually replaced by another and so the story has continued. The remains of the once deadly Westies were eventually found in the summer of 2006 when police located the garage and dug up the secrets under its concrete floor. Twenty-six years after Shamie and Larry Dunne first brought smack to Dublin it was still claiming victims.

CHAPTER NINE

FINDING LARRY MURPHY

Gangland has produced its fair share of dangerous psychopaths who have little compunction about killing others. Some of these monsters enjoy dispensing pain and death to their rivals using the most gruesome of methods. But there is another rare breed of murderer that stands out from the rest of the pack at the apogee of the pecking order of evil. His very existence instils terror across all of society and even revolts the most violent and callous gangsters. He is a sadistic, misogynistic fiend – a serial killer.

Serial killings are largely defined as ritualistic, stranger-perpetrated, predatory murders carried out by men against randomly chosen women in pursuit of depraved sexual gratification and the thrill of dominating their victims. The typical modus operandi involves seeking out potential vulnerable prey and finding an opportunity to pounce like a predator stalking the Serengeti in search of food. In the study of criminology there is broad agreement that the serial killer is different from what are described as 'normal' single incident murders or the other types of multiple killings that occur in gangland. Another distinguishing characteristic is that murder in itself is the motive, and the perpetrator continues killing until caught.

The serial killer becomes the ultimate bogeyman because he hides in the shadows of society and is hard to catch. He tends to operate alone and has a 'killing field' – a geographical location where he feels comfortable, secure and in control – where he takes the victim to satisfy his primal urges before burying the evidence in an unmarked grave. In the absence of human remains there is no proof either of life or death and the victim is classed as 'missing'. Often the victim vanishes off the street leaving no clues for police to follow, and the monster remains free to find the next opportunity.

Detection is made even more difficult by the fact that the predator tends to hide in plain view behind the mask of an ordinary, law-abiding citizen in an apparently normal domestic situation – as a mere twig in the forest of life. In most cases the dark secrets are carefully hidden from spouses, families and friends. From Jack the Ripper to the Yorkshire Ripper, the serial killer has fascinated and scared society which is why their stories dominate the crime genre in popular culture, in books, documentaries, podcasts and dramas both fictional and based on actual happenings.

The term serial killer was first coined by agents attached to the FBI's Behavioural Science Unit (BSU), now made famous by, amongst others, the excellent Netflix series *Mindhunter* which dramatized the early work of the BSU. The unit was established in 1971 in response to the inadequacy of traditional techniques in the investigation of sexually motivated homicides in the USA. The unit studied the behaviour, experiences, and psychological make-up of criminals and suspects for patterns and insights that could help solve cases and prevent future crimes, especially serial murders. The BSU became the centre of excellence in criminal profiling and assists law enforcement agencies across the world. In 1998 the gardaí were seeking assistance from the FBI manhunters after six young women vanished without trace between 1993 and 1998, sparking fears that a serial killer was operating in Ireland.

That year Garda Commissioner Pat Byrne ordered the establishment of Operation Trace to explore possible links between what have become the most high-profile unsolved cases in Irish criminal history, referred to as Ireland's Missing Women: twenty-six-year-old Annie McCarrick (1993), twenty-one-year-old Josephine 'Jo Jo' Dollard (1995), twenty-five-year-old Fiona Pender (1996), seventeen-year-old Ciara Breen (1997), nineteen-year-old Fiona Sinnott (1998) and eighteen-year-old Deirdre Jacob (1998). In all the cases the victims are believed to have been kidnapped and murdered across the vast geographical area of Leinster, dubbed The Vanishing Triangle.

Commissioner Byrne, a dynamic leader and former counter-terrorism officer who is credited with dragging the garda organization into the modern age, had trained with the FBI, as did Assistant Commissioner Tony Hickey, the country's foremost criminal investigator who took charge of Operation Trace. Hickey assembled a small team of some of the most experienced murder detectives in the country. Their mission was to establish if there was a serial killer at large – and to catch them. But the ultimate goal was to locate the remains of the missing and in the process give their anguished families some degree of closure. Their lives were, and still remain, suspended in time as they seek answers. Parents have gone to early graves still haunted by the disappearance of a cherished daughter.

In three of the cases – Fiona Pender, Ciara Breen and Fiona Sinnott – suspects were established early on after their individual disappearances. In each of the three cases the prime suspect is a man who was known to the victim. Suspects have been arrested and several searches carried out over the years. But in the absence of physical evidence or credible witnesses, the police have been unable to charge any of them. One suspect has since died. In two of the cases I attempted to interview the suspects. In 2015 I spent two days with a colleague, Joyce Fegan, watching the home of the prime suspect in the disappearance of nineteen-year-old Fiona Sinnott. She vanished in 1998 from her home in Ballyhitt, Broadway in County Wexford. We wanted to get an interview with the man, but he had gone to ground.

In 2022 the case of Annie McCarrick was extensively reviewed by gardaí and a new investigation launched after it was established that the last reported sightings of the American woman had been incorrect. In highlighting the new development detectives confirmed that the sightings of Annie on a bus in the village of Enniskerry, County Wicklow, and three miles away in Johnny Foxes pub in the Dublin Mountains were not accurate. They believe that she may have been abducted and murdered by someone she knew closer to where she lived in Sandymount Village in south Dublin.

Gardaí believe that the disappearances of the final two young women on the list, Josephine 'Jo Jo' Dollard and Deirdre Jacob, are connected to the same man – a serial killer. As part of their enquiries Operation Trace sought advice from the FBI's BSU. One of the unit's most experienced serial killer hunters, Special Agent Bill Hagmaier, reviewed aspects of the cases. At the time the information pointed to the possibility that only two of the disappearances, Deirdre Jacob and Jo Jo Dollard, were connected. But there was nothing upon which to build a profile of a suspect. In December 1999 I had the pleasure of interviewing Hagmaier, who was then the head of the FBI's National Center for the Analysis of Violent Crimes. The *Sunday World* editor Colm MacGinty and I spent a few fascinating days in Quantico, Virginia after accepting a rare invitation to visit the FBI's Academy. (See Chapter 11.)

As part of his pioneering research work Bill Hagmaier had spent four years interviewing Ted Bundy, America's most notorious serial killer, to gain insights into his motivations and personality to aid in future investigations. Bundy was estimated to have kidnapped, raped and murdered more than forty young women in the 1970s – he eventually confessed to killing thirty. His modus operandi involved randomly picking his victims out on the street and then luring them to a car which would be parked in a secluded spot. He would knock his prey unconscious with a blow to the head and place handcuffs on them before driving to a remote area where he raped, killed them and then disposed of their bodies. A 2021 movie *No Man of God* was based on transcripts of Bill's conversations with Bundy, up to the time of his execution in Florida State Prison in 1989. He was played by Elijah Wood and Luke Kirby was Bundy.

Special Agent Hagmaier's secretive unit was based in an anonymous office suite a few miles from the FBI Academy to avoid unwanted attention. From there his profilers and analysts were assisting in scores of investigations of missing women and children across the US, which is considered to be the natural habitat of serial predators. He told me about his work and the experiences of getting into the head of Bundy. I still recall his answer when I asked him to describe a typical serial killer. 'Sir, they are godless, predatory creatures who murder because they like it and because they can,' he replied in a soft Southern drawl.

In February 2000, less than three months after our visit to Quantico, Ireland's first suspected serial killer was unmasked and immediately became a 'person of interest' to Operation Trace. He was caught following the abduction, multiple rape and failed attempted murder of a random woman he had spotted on the street. Up to that time he had been the quintessential Mr Nobody. The image he portrayed to the world was that of a taciturn, hard-working tradesman, married with two little boys and a third child on the way, living quietly in the village of Baltinglass, County Wicklow. His name is Larry Murphy.

The father-of-three holds the distinction of being the most notorious sexual predator in Irish history. His notoriety has endured over time and is reflected in the media-anointed moniker, the 'Beast of Baltinglass'. Twenty-five years after he was dragged from the shadows the mere mention of his name still evokes fear in Irish women. Ireland's premier bogeyman is etched in the national psyche, and he still haunts society. His notoriety was such that after his eventual release from prison in 2010 panic broke out in communities across the country when numerous false sightings of him were reported. Gardaí had to reassure the public in certain areas that he was not there, and that they knew where he was. I was to spend two years searching for the Beast to get his side of the story.

Murphy is unusual in that even though he was never convicted of murder he is a household name as a suspected serial killer. The police have publicly stated that he is the prime suspect for the abduction of Deirdre Jacob and sent a file to the Director of Public Prosecutions (DPP) recommending that Murphy be charged with her murder. In 2022 the DPP decided that there was insufficient evidence to support a charge. Murphy was also identified as a strong suspect in the disappearance of Jo Jo Dollard. The gardaí say that Murphy remains a 'person of interest' in the investigations which are still live in 2024.

Europol has issued several alerts to police forces all over Europe describing Murphy as a 'serial murder suspect and sexual deviant' whose activities should be monitored closely. Whenever he produces his passport at border controls it is immediately flagged with law enforcement in that country and alerts are issued about his presence there.

The Beast of Baltinglass ticks all the boxes in the profile of a serial killer. Some of the top criminal psychologists and analysts in the world who were consulted in various cold case reviews of the missing women over the years agree with the diagnosis. Profilers have described him as a 'self-obsessed, schizophrenic who portrays himself as the victim'. Despite the absence of hard evidence, he fits the frame for Bill Hagmaier's description of predatory creatures.

Murphy may have been a different league of monster compared to Ted Bundy but the modus operandi and traits of the crime he was caught for in February 2000 are chillingly similar to Bundy's. Everything about Murphy's sadistic crime marked him out as a practised predator. It was an act of evil in its purest form. Another interesting but perhaps unrelated fact is that no other women went missing after his arrest.

So how did Larry Murphy become the Beast of Baltinglass?

———

Shortly after 8 p.m. on the evening of Friday, 11 February 2000, a twenty-eight-year-old businesswoman finished work and walked to her car in a public car park in Carlow Town. As she entered the well-lit car park she spotted a man loitering twenty feet away. He appeared fidgety and impatient, and a bad feeling swept over her.

As the woman quickly opened the car door Larry Murphy suddenly pounced, snarling at her 'give me the money'. He had clearly been watching her because he knew she was carrying the day's takings from her business. When the woman tried to pull the door closed he punched her twice hard in the face, fracturing her nose. The victim screamed for help and tried to fight back. Murphy grabbed her around the throat and bundled her into the car and over to the passenger seat. He got behind the wheel, pulling the door closed.

As she tried to reach for the handle of the passenger door he grabbed her by the hair and slammed her head off the handbrake, fracturing her cheek. Murphy then drove his victim's car to a secluded corner of the car park where he had left his own car out of sight of any passersby, indicating that the attack was premeditated and planned. Murphy, who had marked his thirty-fifth birthday a few days earlier, had been renovating a house in the town. Gardaí believe that he randomly picked his victim on the street and began stalking her. The predator had been on the prowl for a potential victim and waited for his opportunity.

He forced the terrified woman to strip, tied her hands with her bra, gagged her and then bundled her into the boot of his car. Murphy drove ten miles north of Carlow Town where he pulled onto an isolated side road in an area called Beaconstown. At that location – which again was clearly part of his plan – Murphy raped his victim, as blood oozed from her broken nose. The callous monster ignored the woman's pleas to be let go and instead casually talked about himself as if nothing had happened. He said he was married with two sons, aged four and two, and that his wife was pregnant with their third child.

She later told the police that this is when she realized that by sharing so much information that could identify him later, Murphy had no intention of letting her go. He was going to kill his victim so that no one would ever know what had happened. He gagged her again and ordered the naked woman back into the boot. He then drove into the wild expanse of the Glen of Imaal, stopping on an isolated track in remote woodland. It was an area which he knew intimately from growing up in nearby Baltinglass. By then it was around 10 p.m.

Here Murphy raped his victim twice more. She was in so much pain and agony that she told gardaí that she said to Murphy: 'If you have a gun use it now because I can't take it anymore.'

Murphy began to feel sorry for himself again. 'I'll never see my wife and children again,' he moaned prophetically. He told her that his name was 'Michael' and that he was from Baltinglass. It confirmed her fears that he was going to kill her.

As he ordered the woman back into the boot she fought frantically for her life. One of her hands came loose from the binds and her fingers found a can of furniture polish. She tried to spray it in Murphy's face but it was empty. He was furious and slammed the boot lid down. He returned a few minutes later and placed a plastic bag over his victim's head to suffocate her to death. As she tried to get out of the car he slammed the door on her legs.

The Beast of Baltinglass had no reason to worry about the commotion: it was a cold winter's night in the middle of nowhere, far from the nearest main roads or houses. No one would hear her desperate pleas. But just then fate intervened. Ken Jones and Trevor Moody were out hunting foxes in the remote wilderness when they heard screams which they initially thought were those of an injured wild animal. They decided to investigate further.

Spotting the oncoming lights of the hunter's car, Murphy got into his car and drove off at speed leaving his terrified victim behind. In her desperation to get away from the killer the naked,

seriously injured woman became entangled in rusted barbed wire as
the two hunters came to her rescue. They reassured her that she was
safe and they were going to bring her to the local police station for
help. Fortunately the two heroes had instantly recognized Murphy
and his car. They knew him of old. The hunters drove the victim
to Baltinglass garda station from where she was taken to hospital.
In the meantime Murphy had arrived at his home drunk and later
had sex with his wife.

A major investigation was launched. At the time gardaí spoke of
how incredibly lucky the victim had been that night. One senior
officer involved in the investigation later told me:

> She was abducted from the last place you'd expect someone
> to be abducted – in a public, well-lit car park in the middle of a
> busy town – and no one saw it happening. Then she was taken to
> one of the most remote and isolated places in the country to be
> murdered, and two hunters just happen to be in the right place at
> the right time.

If the hunters had stayed at home that night the victim's name
would have been number seven on the list of Ireland's Missing
Women. And Larry Murphy would have remained free to kill.

His brother Thomas would later reflect on how well Larry had
concealed his monstrous side. The revelation had left Murphy's
family devastated. In an interview a decade later Thomas said:

> No one would ever think that Larry Murphy would do something
> like that. You'd think, to speak to Larry, that butter wouldn't
> melt in his mouth. He was very well liked. He had never been
> in trouble. Never, never, never. He liked his football. He liked
> socializing, never was in any sort of trouble.

The following morning gardaí arrested Murphy and brought him to Baltinglass station for questioning. He had been caught bang to rights. Gardaí had two solid eyewitnesses, the statement of his victim and a wealth of forensic evidence including conclusive DNA that would prove beyond any doubt that Larry Murphy had perpetrated the shocking crime.

That afternoon he gave the police his version of events. He attempted to manipulate the situation to his own ends which is another classic trait of the serial killer. Murphy tried to give the impression that the crime had been a spontaneous impulse that he could not explain. He said he wanted to rob his victim and dressed it up as a robbery gone drastically wrong.

Murphy was anxious to steer the investigators away from believing that he had planned it all. But the testimony from his victim and the circumstances of the attack demonstrated that the crime was predatory and premeditated. He admitted the first rape but bizarrely claimed that the other sex had been in some way consensual. In a statement to the gardaí he said:

> I was walking down the path and I saw this girl walking towards me. I had never met the girl in my life. I don't know what came over me. I just flipped. I said to her, 'Give me the money.' She said, 'Fuck off.' I hit her then. She had stopped to open the door of her car. I hit her with my hand on the side of the face. She stumbled back to the seat in the car. I pushed her over on to the other seat, the passenger seat. I asked her where her keys were. I found her keys on the seat. I moved her car over to where my car was. She was sitting in the car beside me with her head on my knee. At that stage, I tied her arms. I asked her to remove her bra. I used the bra to tie her arms. At that stage, I took her out of

the car. She walked out. I told her to get in the boot of my car and she sat in.

At this stage, I took off up the road. I don't know why I did. I don't know. I suppose I drove for about twenty minutes. I travelled out the Athy Road. I stopped in a lane. I raped her. First I took her out of the boot of the car. I put her in the seat of the car. I removed her trousers. I just raped her. When I stopped the car the second time I took her out and sat her in the car. She started talking to me. I told her I had two kids and she said she would like to have kids herself someday.

She asked me to take her home and said she would do anything I wanted if I took her home. I told her I would leave her home. So she told me she would make love to me. I had sex with her but that was her own choice. We made love in the car. I didn't try to kill her at all. I had sex in two places with her but the second time was her own choice.

At 8.05 p.m. that evening Larry Murphy was formally charged with rape and abduction. He was also charged with attempted murder. Murphy was remanded in custody and did not seek bail. His statement to the police was the only explanation he ever gave for the brutal attack. When his brother visited him in prison and demanded to know why he did it, Murphy's only reply was, 'I flipped.'

Murphy became the centre of attention for Operation Trace. Everything about him, his personality and modus operandi, indicated that he fit the profile of a serial killer. He had stalked his randomly selected victim before making his move when she was vulnerable. The most sinister aspect of the incident was that he brought his victim to the Glen of Imaal where the chances of being discovered were practically non-existent, suggesting it was his killing field where he felt most in control.

Faced with a mountain of evidence Murphy subsequently pleaded guilty to all the charges at the earliest opportunity which prevented any further public scrutiny of his behaviour and motivation. On 11 May 2001, the Beast of Baltinglass was jailed for a total of fifteen years on charges of false imprisonment, four counts of rape, assault, robbery and attempted murder. It hadn't taken long for word to filter out about Murphy's initial arrest and the horrific crime was widely reported. Journalists knew that he was a serial killer suspect but could not write about it while his trial was pending. Once he was convicted we could share that fact with the public.

Murphy served his sentence in Arbour Hill Prison which exclusively caters for child abusers, rapists and sex killers to keep them segregated from the rest of the prison population for their own safety. Prison officers said that he was a model prisoner and kept to himself. Murphy knew that keeping his head down safeguarded his automatic entitlement to have a quarter of his sentence shaved off for good behaviour, meaning he was only required to serve ten-and-a-half years. In any event sex offenders tend to be much more peaceful than the rest of the prison population and the likelihood of losing remission is remote. Significantly it would later transpire that throughout the years he never expressed any remorse for his actions. Nor did he participate in any rehabilitative programmes or counselling. He just wanted to do his time.

Since he was sentenced Murphy had become a household name in Ireland as a suspected serial killer. The media regularly featured his story which kept his name in lights. There were so many unanswered questions that the public had a right to know about.

The gardaí had continued their investigations in the hope of uncovering evidence to put him away for life. Murphy's wife and family disowned him. She got a divorce and he signed a legal agreement never to have contact with her again.

As the date of his release loomed into view – 12 August 2010 – there was huge speculation as to whether or not Murphy would have to register as a sex offender upon his release from prison. Under the Sex Offenders Act, which was signed into legislation a month after Murphy was sentenced for his crimes, the police have powers to maintain post-release supervision of dangerous sex offenders. The offender is bound by law to notify the police where they are living at all times and can be jailed for three months for not doing so.

Such was the level of angst about his release back into Irish society that gardaí had to reassure the public that Murphy would be supervized. However it emerged that the provisions of the Act were not retrospective even by a month – it didn't apply to Murphy. He was a free man. The authorities could not go near him, officially at least. Secretly the gardaí were preparing to keep him under surveillance from the moment of his release but they would not have the resources to do so indefinitely.

The one person who was more terrified at the prospect of Murphy's release than anyone else in the country was his victim. The brave woman had recovered as best as anyone can from such a horrific, life-changing experience. In the days leading up to Murphy's release gardaí deployed a full-time special patrol near her home and place of work to reassure her that she was safe. I was aware through my sources that senior officers decided that Murphy's movements would have to be monitored to ensure that he didn't try to make contact with the victim even though it was thought he was unlikely to do so.

A large media posse had been waiting patiently outside the prison for two days when Murphy finally emerged into a barrage of camera flashes. In the TV images he cut a solitary figure, looking gaunt and grey, when he walked through the prison gates wearing dark glasses and a baseball cap to prevent his picture being taken. He jumped into the back of a waiting taxi as a garda helicopter clattered overhead. His first hours of freedom were spent trying to escape from reporters and photographers who pursued him on motorbikes through the city. The predator had become the hunted. At the time I watched and read the coverage like any other punter. Joining in the chase would have been a pointless exercise because he wasn't going to talk and would just keep running. The spectacle of the hunter being pursued through the streets was a piece of macabre theatre.

The garda units watching him were more discreet. Everyone wanted to know where he was going and what he was going to do next. Murphy's first port of call was to Coolock garda station in north Dublin to complain that he was being harassed by the media. After that he slipped out of view and began moving between locations with the help of the probationary service which is obliged to assist all released prisoners.

Back in his home village of Baltinglass the community held an emergency meeting to discuss their concerns that Murphy might return home. Despite reassurances from his brother Thomas that the family wanted nothing to do with him, they received anonymous threats that their home would be burned down if Larry moved in. Murphy's infamous crime had also victimized his completely innocent family. In order to protect them from vigilantes Thomas Murphy was forced to give media interviews to convince the public that the family had no ties to Larry. In

an interview with the late Charlie Bird of RTÉ, Thomas left his
brother in no doubt about how the family felt.

> And he came out of Arbour Hill last Thursday morning with his
> head held high and I think if he had any decency he would have
> least stopped at the media and said sorry to this woman involved
> – the victim. There was never even a sorry, there was no remorse.
> And I don't know how anyone could carry out a crime like that
> and not at least say sorry to the victim.
>
> Larry never thought about what he was doing to that girl. That
> girl has a life sentence. She will never forget what happened to
> her – and his own family, his own kids, his wife, the sentence that
> they carry for the rest of their lives, it's something that's there
> on them two little boys and it'll never leave them. I would say it
> has destroyed our whole family. He didn't think of his sisters, his
> mother or father, or myself, either. My kids are suffering for the
> crime that Larry committed. It's a knock-on effect for everybody.
> He couldn't tell me the truth of what he did. He wouldn't have
> counselling when it was provided to him. The man refused help.
> A person who doesn't want to help themselves can't be helped.

Asked what he would say to his brother if he was listening to the
interview, Thomas said:

> I would say to Larry, number one, he was wrong to refuse help
> when he was in Arbour Hill. It was readily available for him.
> Number two, I think Larry Murphy should be very, very ashamed
> of himself. He has [duped] everybody who was any way involved
> with him down to the ground… I don't want him in my life and my
> sisters, I'd say, would be talking on the same lines themselves…
> he won't be accepted back into their homes.

The suspicions about Larry Murphy being Ireland's first serial killer had intensified while he was still in prison. Four years before his release Murphy had been elevated to the status of prime suspect for Deirdre Jacob's disappearance. In 2006, Detective Sergent Alan Bailey, a member of the original Operation Trace team, interviewed a prisoner who had asked to see him. The inmate claimed that Murphy had once confessed to Deirdre's murder while drunk on prison hooch. He had boasted about abducting a woman in Newbridge, County Kildare. The last confirmed sighting of Deirdre was of her walking alone in the direction of her rural home at Roseberry, about 1.5 km outside Newbridge, at 3 p.m. on the afternoon of Tuesday, 28 July 1998. Within the next thirty minutes or so she vanished without a trace – it was as if she had been swallowed up into thin air.

The prisoner claimed that Murphy said he had stopped alongside the student teacher and asked her directions on a map. When she reached in he grabbed his victim and dragged her into his van and hit her with a hammer. The prisoner said Murphy told him he buried the young woman's body in the Wicklow Mountains. Detective Sergent Bailey, who believed the prisoner, subsequently wrote about the allegations in a memoir of his distinguished career, *Missing, Presumed.*

Testimony from prisoners is generally viewed as at risk of being unreliable without corroboration. There wasn't enough in what the cellmate told them to charge the suspected serial killer with any crime. However, the detectives were able to establish that Murphy was working in the Newbridge area at the time and would have driven along the same road on his way to work. The information matched the modus operandi of the abduction of the woman in Carlow – and fitted the profile of a serial killer. The cops visited Murphy before his release but he refused to talk to them. There wasn't even enough evidence on which to arrest him for questioning.

In the meantime Murphy was feeling great sympathy for himself. He was totally alone in a hostile world and being hunted like a fugitive. Officers from the Garda Domestic Violence and Sexual Assault Unit (DVSAU) approached Murphy to find out what he was up to. He complained bitterly that he was being hounded by the media and had been rejected by his family:

> They have left me all alone and disowned me. I don't have a
> family now and will likely never speak to them again. Right now
> I have more important things to think about than therapy. The
> whole situation is a fucking nightmare. I served my time and
> I don't need any help. I am under no legal obligation to get
> treatment or keep in contact with the probation services.

A month after his release Murphy left Ireland for Europe, vowing never to return. Concerned that the Beast would strike again the DVSAU issued urgent alerts to Europol and national police forces across Europe to keep an eye on him.

But in Ireland the fact that Murphy was out of sight did not mean that he was out of the public's mind. Over the subsequent weeks and months false sightings of him reported by social media fuelled panics and near hysteria in parts of the country where he had apparently been spotted. Newsrooms including our own also received calls from concerned citizens claiming to have seen him. All of them proved to be bogus.

After each sighting the gardaí were forced to issue statements to reassure the public that he was not in the country and that they knew where he was. This was done to prevent a totally innocent individual being mistaken for Murphy and ending up either seriously injured or even killed by a lynch mob. The Beast of Baltinglass was big news – everyone wanted to know where he was and what he was doing. Over the next few years I did everything I could to do to find out just that.

———

By the time that Murphy was released from prison I had moved from the *Sunday World* to work as the crime editor of the Irish edition of the *News of the World*. Like every other news organization in town, we wanted to bag that elusive scoop. We put out feelers to contacts everywhere to find out where Murphy was. Every cop who met a reporter was asked the same question: where is Larry Murphy?

A few months later the *News of the World* exclusively revealed that he had been living in Amsterdam, the sex and drugs capital of Europe. He had been spotted by an Irish tourist in the Hoopman Café in the city centre where it turned out Murphy was a regular drinker. The tourist phoned the news desk with the story when they returned. We were able to confirm that the story was true and that the Dutch police had been secretly monitoring Murphy since he arrived in the Netherlands from Ireland a few months earlier. We didn't have an address for where he was living or working. He left Amsterdam after that and the trail went cold. At home the sightings of the bogeyman continued unabated.

Then in May 2011 the trail to Larry Murphy suddenly got hot again. I was at home writing *Bad Fellas*, a history of organized crime in Ireland, when a well-placed contact phoned me with exciting news – Larry Murphy was returning to Ireland the following day,

Wednesday, 25 May. The source said that Murphy had been living and working in Barcelona since leaving Amsterdam.

On the previous Saturday a pickpocket had stolen his passport from a backpack as he walked through the centre of Barcelona which is notorious for street crime. Murphy carried the passport with him everywhere just in case he had to flee again at a moment's notice. By all accounts he was frantic when he discovered the document was gone and went to the police to report it stolen. He could run nowhere without a passport. Following a routine computer check the Spanish cops realized who he was and contacted Europol and the gardaí. Murphy went to the Irish Consulate in Barcelona where he was supplied with a temporary travel document. He would have to return to Ireland within seven days to apply for a new passport.

This would be the first time that Murphy was in Ireland since leaving the previous September. The tip was pure gold. He was booked on the 10.10 p.m. Ryanair flight from Barcelona to Dublin on Wednesday night. I called the paper's Irish editor Jeff Frazier and a plan was hurriedly put in place to welcome the Beast home. If it worked out we would have the scoop of the year. But it would have to be kept a closely guarded secret within our own small team in the *News of the World* – *The Sun* newspaper was down the corridor and its editor, Mick McNiffe, could hear the grass grow, especially if it was a hot story.

Together with the news editor, the genial Ciaran McDaid, we nominated journalist Debbie McCann and photographer Niall Marshall to go to Barcelona to keep watch for Murphy. Even though the tip off was from an excellent source there is always a chance in such cases that the target decides at the last minute not to turn up. We needed to have eyes on the other side to make sure he got on the plane. They were booked on the first flight to Barcelona the following morning and were to shadow Murphy on the return that night. Once they spotted Murphy they would stay back and not spook him. Niall would photograph Murphy when he was sure it was safe to do so without blowing their cover.

Once it was confirmed that he was on the flight I and two more photographers, Padraig O'Reilly and Ciaran McGowan, would be waiting in the arrivals hall at Dublin airport. The plan was to keep a low profile because we didn't know if someone else would be waiting for Murphy. If everything went to plan I would confront him as he left the building to see if he would say anything. I was wired up with a recording device to capture his every word. All we had to do was sit and wait and hope that it all worked out.

Two hours before the Barcelona flight was due to depart Debbie McCann phoned me with the magic words: 'He's here… we have him.' Larry Murphy had just walked through the doors of Girona Airport. The nine months of freedom and his time in the Barcelona sunshine had done him good. Debbie said she had to take a second look to be sure because he had changed so much. He was fit and tanned compared to the gaunt appearance he had when he left prison.

Murphy was obviously confident that no would recognize him. He wasn't wearing his trademark baseball cap and dark sunglasses. He was dressed in a green t-shirt, black tracksuit bottoms and grey Asics runners. The fugitive had a black rucksack on his back and a large pull-along bag with all his worldly belongings. By arriving early Murphy avoided contact with the other Irish tourists by checking in and passing through security before them. He did not speak to anyone. Debbie and Niall went through security behind him.

As he waited for the flight to board Murphy read a newspaper, scribbled in a little address book and texted on his mobile phone. He went outside a few times to smoke. He also made and received several phone calls. In one conversation, which was overheard by our undercover reporter, he confirmed to someone that he was on his way. Murphy was obviously nervous about the homecoming which was why he had deliberately booked the late flight home. He said:

> I'm just about to board now. I had a sleep earlier so I'm feeling OK now. Everything is going fine, no problems here. I hope it'll be alright over there. I'll see you on the other side.

Debbie texted to warn us that someone was waiting for him in arrivals. As he queued to board the flight Murphy was careful to conceal the identity on his temporary passport from other passengers. But his new look didn't fool a group of middle-aged Irish women who recognized him. One of them could be heard asking: 'Is it him? I don't know?' Another said: 'It is him – look.'

Murphy sat alone on the plane next to the window, close to the front. He listened to music on his iPod earphones and ignored cabin staff when they came around selling drinks and scratch cards. When the plane landed just before midnight he was one of the first passengers to disembark. Debbie kept the phone open to give us live updates as he went through passport control and baggage reclaim, heading for the exit.

Gardaí took the unusual step of checking the passports of all the passengers on the flight as they entered the terminal building. The two uniformed immigration officers checked the rapist's temporary identification before letting him go on his way. In the arrivals hall we recognized a number of detectives from the DVSAU watching the passengers.

There were a lot of eyes on Larry Murphy when he emerged. He was greeted by a man who turned out to be a prison chaplain, doing his Christian duty. Murphy had asked the priest to meet him. He was also in contact with members of a state-funded group who helped former prisoners re-settle in the community and avoid trouble. They were the only friends he had in the world. As they walked out of the arrivals building I made my move – for once the plan had worked to perfection. Murphy showed no emotion and said nothing when I approached him and the cameras began flashing. He smirked and remained silent as he hurried to get away from us.

I walked alongside bombarding Murphy with questions as the huddle entered the car park:

Larry, why did you kidnap that woman in Carlow and then try to kill her? You have been accused of some of the most appalling crimes in history. Have you any comment to make? Are you an innocent man? Why is every woman so scared of you? What have you to say about the fact that the police believe you murdered Deirdre Jacob and Jo Jo Dollard? Do you not want to say something about this... surely you want to clear your name?

Murphy remained silent. He got in the car and drove off at speed. We didn't need to follow – we had our scoop.

We kept the story under wraps until Sunday morning when we shared it with the rest of the world. The front-page headline declared: 'THE BEAST IS BACK – We catch rapist Murphy as he tries to sneak into Ireland'. That weekend the *News of the World* sold out across the country. The story ignited a media storm as talk of his return filled the air waves and newspaper front pages. Finding where he was hiding out became the priority in every news organization. We later discovered that Murphy panicked after we confronted him and with the help of the chaplain checked into a hotel near the airport to lay low. He left two days later when someone recognized him and a reporter from another newspaper phoned his room.

Murphy complained to his minders that he was afraid the media attention would lead to him being attacked. Gardaí also met him to discuss his safety concerns. He was mystified as to how we had tracked him down and accused the police of leaking the information. Murphy said that he was going to 'escape' Ireland as soon as he had his new passport and vowed to never again set foot in the country.

The suspected serial killer was moved between hotels and safe houses over the following month as he waited for the new passport to be issued. He was helped by State-sponsored services who assist post-release prisoners. The gardaí were also keeping an eye on him to ensure that he wasn't attacked. The operation was a success because he eluded the media and the public.

On Wednesday, 22 June 2011, Murphy finally got the passport and his ticket to freedom. This time he was determined to leave Ireland more discreetly than when he had entered it. He decided that the safest way was to go by ferry. Murphy was booked on the 9.30 p.m. sailing from Rosslare to Cherbourg the following evening. He wasn't spending a minute longer than he had to in the country. On the same day as the passport arrived my contact phoned again with Murphy's new travel plans. We had another scoop in the making.

This time the plan was to send photographers O'Reilly and McGowan to shadow Murphy on the ferry and record the departure of the most feared man in Ireland. As a team they were as competent as any police surveillance unit only with much more limited resources and support. As there was little point in trying to confront him again I stayed in the office co-ordinating the operation with the lads on the ground. Our story was that Murphy had left the country again and the public – and several editors – could relax. It was a fitting bookend to a major exclusive.

Murphy was driven to the ferry port in a car with blacked out windows. Our team watched from a discreet vantage point as the driver spent several minutes checking out the car park and terminal building in case there were photographers lying in wait. Thinking that the coast was clear Murphy got out and quickly boarded. He was wearing dark glasses and had a baseball hat pulled down over his face. For good measure he also wore a hoody over the hat.

During the twenty-hour crossing the lads watched Murphy who was constantly on his guard, avoiding all human contact with other passengers. When he arrived in Cherbourg the next evening he booked into a cheap hotel. The following morning he took the train to Paris, with the photographers still in tow. By the time he arrived in the French capital he appeared more relaxed and had ditched the sunglasses, cap and hoody. He was photographed buying a ticket for the Metro underground. The guys later lost him in the bustling Metro but by then the job was done. The headline on the front page that Sunday simply said: 'Good Riddance'. Inside we published a sequence of pictures taken of him in Rosslare, on the ferry, in Cherbourg and in Paris. The spread carried the headline: 'Au revoir… & don't come back'.

———

A month after the Murphy exclusives – fifteen months after I joined the paper – the *News of the World* closed down after it was revealed that the paper had been illegally and criminally hacking the phones of crime victims, celebrities and politicians for several years in the UK. For the next year I was transferred to work with *The Sun* and a new Sunday version of the paper. I accepted a redundancy package in the summer of 2012 and began working freelance, setting up my own media company.

Larry Murphy was still a huge story. In the year since we'd published the stories false sightings of the Beast had continued. The gardaí had been repeatedly forced to reassure the public that the sightings were incorrect. Finding Larry again was going to be my first project, if for no other reason than to prove to the public that the bogeyman wasn't lurking in some quiet village in the west of Ireland. I didn't know where he was, but the one place I was sure he wasn't hiding out was Ireland. After rustling through my contacts I made the breakthrough in July 2012.

A contact told me that after leaving Paris Murphy worked for six months in Spain before moving back to Amsterdam in November 2011. He was living in a suburb in the north of the city where he had been working since January 2012 as a storeman with a local logistics firm who knew nothing of his sordid history. Most importantly I was given his new address. This time I wanted to have him photographed and filmed while confronting him so that we could use the footage in press and TV reports.

My company hired Padraig O'Reilly to do the initial reconnaissance and paid for flights, accommodation and a hire car. I also hired film and sound recording equipment. It was an expensive operation. Being freelance for the first time in my career meant I no longer had the luxury of someone else footing the expense bill. O'Reilly first went to Amsterdam in July and staked out the address. Within hours he had spotted the Beast of Baltinglass. The game was on.

I then brought Ciaran McGowan in, to team up with O'Reilly. They made two further trips spending a number of days each time monitoring Murphy and compiling a picture of his daily routines and haunts. Over the weeks we built up a treasure trove of photographs and footage. But we were not going to rush the job.

Murphy spent all his free time in the company of another man, a lanky, bald individual who looked Irish. They always looked very rough and unkempt as if they were heavy drinkers. The mystery man collected Murphy for work every morning at 4 a.m. on his scooter. Whenever the suspected serial killer went he travelled with his friend on the bike. The two men were also filmed going fishing together and, on another occasion, taking a train from Amsterdam's Central Station to an unknown destination.

At the weekends the mystery man, who lived in another apartment ten minutes away, would regularly stay with Murphy in his apartment in a quiet suburb where the residents were mostly immigrants and people kept to themselves. It was a perfect hiding place for a man with a dark past.

We really had to find out who this man was, especially as he was someone who spent his time in the company of a suspected serial killer. In Dublin I hawked around his picture to garda sources to see if anyone could identify him. I eventually made a chilling discovery.

The man in the pictures was forty-four-year-old Rory O'Connor, a violent sex offender and double rapist from Dublin who befriended Murphy while they were doing time in Arbour Hill Prison. In 2001 O'Connor raped two women at knife point and held them hostage in an apartment in Rathmines in south

Dublin. In what was described as an 'absolutely horrific' attack Murphy's friend assaulted the women with the knife before taking turns raping them. O'Connor was arrested a short time afterwards by police and a year later was sentenced to ten years after pleading guilty to four counts of rape and false imprisonment.

Just like Murphy had done, O'Connor pleaded guilty at the earliest opportunity and offered no explanation for his savage act. Prior to that he had never come to the attention of the police. He had been another twig in the forest. In prison Murphy and O'Connor were described as very close pals. When O'Connor was released in 2008 he was placed on the Sex Offenders Register but had kept in touch with his fellow predator which is in breach of the sex offenders' legislation. We discovered that O'Connor helped Murphy get the job in the logistics centre where he was also working.

When I dug deeper I discovered that the gardaí were aware that the two highly dangerous sexual predators were together in Amsterdam. The Dutch police had been keeping tabs on them and officers had visited the pair on at least one occasion to check their documentation. However there was nothing the cops could do about it unless they attacked someone. Suddenly the picture of Larry Murphy's new life looked a lot more sinister.

In October I went with McGowan and O'Reilly to Amsterdam – it was time to let Murphy know that he was going to be famous again. We knew that we would have to confront Murphy on the street and that he was unlikely to talk. But the 'doorstepping' would round off our efforts. His daily routine involved going for groceries to a local shop and next door for a takeaway – he ate a lot of takeaways.

On Saturday, 6 October we were watching Murphy's building when he and O'Connor returned from a trip on the bike. We were parked in two cars at different ends of his road. There was no point attempting to approach him there because he just had to walk inside the door and, with the element of surprise lost, he wouldn't be coming out anytime soon. The two notorious rapists disappeared inside and from what we knew of their routines they were unlikely to emerge again until the following day.

In many ways in our hunt we were observing some of the methods of a serial predator although we only wanted answers. We had one brief chance with Murphy so we needed to get him alone on the street some distance away from the apartment. It meant that once I approached him I could physically stay close to him as he tried to get away. The only opportunity would be when he went for his takeaway and shopping.

The following morning, Sunday, we took up position at first light and then we waited – and waited. Around 6 p.m. O'Connor emerged and took off on his scooter, presumably going home to his apartment. A few minutes later Larry appeared and headed for the shops. By the time he got there the two photographers were in position in the car with cameras ready. I was wearing a baseball cap and rambled into the shop beside him and then waited on the street when he went next door to get his food. It was all about timing.

When Larry Murphy walked out I sidled in beside him and introduced myself. Unlike in Dublin Airport this time he seemed to be momentarily startled. His only words were, 'oh yeah?' as I began to ask about the accusations against him. Then literally in the flicker of an eyelid he pivoted on his left foot and sprinted off in the opposite direction like he was running for his life. He disappeared.

We took up position again at his apartment and filmed his eventual return. I rapped on the door several times and left a note.

No answer, but we'd got everything we came for. It had been a worthwhile effort.

The Murphy investigation appeared in the *Irish Independent, The Herald* and *The Star* newspapers and was the subject of a special report for Virgin Media's (then TV3) *Midweek* programme. The story caused a sensation, especially the disturbing revelation about Murphy's association with O'Connor. But it did succeed in quelling public fears at a time when false sightings of him were rife.

On the weekend that I confronted him in Amsterdam I got a call from a friend in Leitrim telling me that Murphy had 'definitely' been spotted in Carrick-on-Shannon. I could assure the caller that the story wasn't true but couldn't say why I knew. Around the same time it emerged that companies in a Kilkenny industrial estate had hired extra security staff after rumours spread that he was living and working in the area. In another town a man was forced to seek refuge in a garda station because a mob thought he looked like Murphy.

The scoop also caused a stir in Amsterdam. All the main news channels covered the story and carried our footage of Murphy. Local people and politicians told how they didn't want the Beast of Baltinglass living amongst them. As a result of the furore that ensued Murphy and O'Connor left the Netherlands and went in different directions. The Beast of Baltinglass moved to live in London soon afterwards. In 2014 it was reported that he was living under an assumed name and in a relationship with a businesswoman. But he could never outrun his notoriety and was spotted on occasions by Irish ex-pats on the street. Murphy is believed to be still living in London and avoids contact with Irish people.

The gardaí have never forgotten Murphy or his crimes. In 2021 an investigation team based at Naas station, backed up by the garda's cold case review team, submitted a file to the DPP recommending that Murphy be charged with the abduction and murder of Deirdre Jacob. Part of the case revolved around the evidence of a second prisoner who claimed Murphy once admitted to 'killing' and discussed hiding places in the Wicklow Mountains. He reportedly said that the police were clueless and would never find his DNA 'because he didn't leave any'.

Around the same time there was another twist in our story about Murphy's rapist friend Rory O'Connor. In August 2021 O'Connor murdered his Scottish partner Diane Nichol in a savage sustained attack at their home in Hawick in southern Scotland. He repeatedly kicked, stamped and struck his victim's head against a floor. Evidence showed that she suffered multiple injuries consistent with a car crash. In April 2022 O'Connor pleaded guilty and was jailed for a minimum period of fifteen years before he could be considered for parole.

Diane Nichol's sister, Gail Atkinson, later revealed her shock when she saw a YouTube video of our footage of O'Connor and Murphy together in Amsterdam. Even though the rapist was pixelated in the report she recognized him straight away. She said she had confronted him about his past and his connections to Murphy. But her sister would not accept the warnings that she was living with a monster.

Detectives investigating the murder of Deirdre Jacob interviewed O'Connor about his relationship with Murphy. The rapist and killer had expressed a desire to work with the gardaí but then refused to divulge any of his pal's dark secrets.

Four months after O'Connor was sentenced the DPP decided that there was not enough evidence to prosecute Larry Murphy. After twenty-four years there was no body, no proof of death, no forensics and no irrefutable witness testimony. Prosecuting Murphy would be the evidential equivalent of climbing Mount Everest. There was the additional difficulty that he could not get a fair trial in Ireland where everyone feels they know the truth about him – that he is a cold-blooded, predatory killer.

Murphy's guilt or innocence may never be established beyond all reasonable doubt. Only time will tell. In the meantime he maintains his right to silence. But one thing is for sure, the final chapters in the story of the Beast of Baltinglass have yet to be written.

CHAPTER TEN

THE FBI: A HERO, 9/11 & THE HUNT FOR WHITEY BULGER

The world froze in stunned disbelief as it watched two commercial airliners smash into the twin towers of the World Trade Center in New York on 11 September 2001. The most powerful nation on earth was shaken to its very foundations as the iconic buildings collapsed in an apocalyptic cloud of dust and smoke on live TV. The aftershock that washed over America hadn't been felt so profoundly since the Japanese attacked Pearl Harbor in 1941. To paraphrase Franklin D. Roosevelt's speech on that occasion, 9/11 is a date that will live forever in infamy.

Most people remember where they were when the single worst terrorist attack in human history took place. The tremors reverberated through the democracies of the Western world. It was a message that the nihilists of Islamist fundamentalism would target them next. Just over 3,000 people perished on 11 September 2001 when groups of al-Qaeda terrorists, working on the orders of Osama bin Laden, simultaneously hijacked four commuter flights after they took off from airports on the east coast, turning them into weapons of mass destruction.

The third aircraft slammed into the Pentagon, the HQ of the US Department of Defense claiming 125 souls. The final aircraft, Flight 93, was headed towards Washington DC when passengers overpowered the terrorists and forced it to crash in a field in Pennsylvania with the loss of another forty lives. The heroic act prevented a fourth incident of mass murder that day.

The vast majority of the casualties died in the attacks on the twin towers. The death toll included citizens from over 100 countries including Ireland, reflecting the global melting pot that is the USA. Knowing someone who died in such a monstrous atrocity humanized it. He was a counter-terrorism legend of the FBI, who had been a contact and a friend for a number of years. His name was John Patrick O'Neill.

John's death at the hands of Osama bin Laden was one of the most tragic ironies of 9/11. He had taken up the post of chief of security at the World Trade Center only a week earlier after he was effectively forced to retire from the Feds. John had been overlooked for promotion a number of times after falling out of favour with his superiors who saw him as a maverick. Up to the time of his retirement in August 2001 he was the FBI's foremost expert on bin Laden and al-Qaeda, the terror group the fundamentalist founded.

O'Neill had spent the previous six years on the trail of the world's most infamous terrorist. He had led the investigations into a series of suicide bombings carried out by al-Qaeda at a US military barracks in Saudi Arabia, the US embassies in Tanzania and Kenya and against the Navy destroyer, the USS Cole, in Yemen. John has been deservedly memorialized in books, film and documentaries as 'the man who knew' because he was obsessed with Osama bin Laden long before most people had ever heard of him. I remember him talking about bin Laden and the threat he posed over dinner three years before 9/11. Eighteen years after his death actor Jeff Daniels played the part of John in the series *The Looming Tower*, which was adapted from the Pulitzer Prize-winning book by journalist Lawrence Wright who meticulously charted the build up to 9/11. For those who had the honour of knowing him, Daniels' portrayal of his dynamic personality was uncanny.

John had repeatedly sounded the alarm of the rising threat posed by bin Laden, warning that he had terror cells operating in America and was planning a major attack on US soil. His last days in law enforcement were spent fighting a losing battle to convince FBI HQ of al-Qaeda's lethal potential. He wanted the agency to begin a hunt for the hidden cells. But fed up with John's brash, no bullshit style the powers had stopped listening to him.

It was later discovered that the CIA had withheld vital intelligence that supported O'Neill's hypothesis. They knew that al-Qaeda suspects had been training at a flight school in the US but did nothing about it. If they had heeded O'Neill the subsequent attacks might have been averted.

The night before the outrage John famously confided to a friend that he feared al-Qaeda were about to launch a major attack. He said: 'We're due, and we're due for something big.'

John O'Neill was forty-nine when he perished in the twin towers. He had been an FBI agent for three decades. A law enforcement man to his toes – a cop's cop – he joined the Feds within days of his high school graduation in Atlantic City, New Jersey. One colleague I spoke to after 9/11 recalled how he 'could move heaven and earth if it was in his way' to catch the bad guys. He first emerged as a rising star as the head of a special strike force set up to take on the mafia and organized crime in Chicago during the 1980s. In 1995 he was promoted to chief of the FBI's counter-terrorism section and assisted in the arrest of Ramzi Jousef, the bin Laden associate who had masterminded a 1993 car bomb attack on the World Trade Center. John immersed himself in the world of Islamic extremism and earned a reputation amongst admiring colleagues as 'America's pit bull on terrorism'.

In January 1997 his expertise was acknowledged with a promotion to the Assistant Special Agent in charge of the FBI's powerful National Security Division based at Federal Plaza in New York which put him in charge of 350 agents. It was from there that he spearheaded the investigations into bin Laden and first put his name on the international terrorist radar. John's work enabled a grand jury to indict the Saudi terror leader with murdering US citizens in the embassy attacks in Africa and 'conspiracy to attack defense utilities of the United States'. Thanks to his efforts, Osama bin Laden was placed on the FBI's ten most wanted list. It was as a result of his work in the area of Irish terrorism that I first met John O'Neill.

For decades the FBI was heavily involved in monitoring the activities of Sinn Féin and the IRA in the US where the Provos had a strong support base to raise funds, source weapons and hide fugitives from the police. John O'Neill had worked closely for over a decade with the Garda Commissioner of the day, Pat Byrne, and they had become close friends. O'Neill and Byrne were key backroom players in a major undercover sting operation which saw an FBI agent, David Rupert, planted at the highest level of the dissident terror gang, the Real IRA. It ultimately led to the arrest and subsequent conviction of the group's leader, Michael McKevitt, who had been responsible for ordering the Omagh bombing in 1998 which claimed the lives of twenty-nine people.

Byrne had spent most of his career as a member of the anti-terrorist Special Detective Unit (SDU) and studied at the FBI Academy. Prior to his appointment as Garda Commissioner in 1996 he was the Assistant Commissioner in charge of counter-terrorism and national security in Ireland. In 1998 Pat Byrne introduced me to John O'Neill suggesting that he was 'the only guy to know if you want to find out about international terrorism'. We first met in person in a Manhattan bar when I was in the Big Apple with my wife for the launch of the movie *The General*. Tall, impeccably dressed, with hair slicked back, he was an exceptionally warm, charming, fascinating character and great fun to be with. He liked to remind people that he was Irish himself and said it explained why he was so stubborn and loved to party.

Over dinner he gave us a crash course on the dynamics of international terrorism and the emergence of a new type of Islamist threat. That was the first time I ever heard of Osama bin Laden. John said that he also believed that within the new world order of terror, Irish subversives were part of the same milieu as the twilight world occupied by Jihadist groups. We remained in touch on a regular basis after that.

Then towards the end of 1999 John organized the trip of a lifetime for a crime reporter, inviting me to visit the FBI Academy in Quantico, Virginia, with my *Sunday World* editor Colm MacGinty. We were picked up by Federal agents when we arrived at JFK Airport in early December, along with John Farrelly, the head of the garda press office at the time. That night John O'Neill brought us for dinner to the famous Elaine's restaurant in midtown Manhattan, a popular haunt for celebrities.

As the FBI's flamboyant head of counter-terrorism John clearly enjoyed a degree of fame himself. As we talked away a small man who was walking by said, 'Hi John, it's good to see you' in a voice that was instantly recognizable. 'Hi Woody,' O'Neill replied with a beaming smile as Woody Allen stepped over to shake his hand. The eccentric moviemaker said nothing else and then left.

The next day John brought us to his office in Federal Plaza where he gave us a rare – very discreet – tour of the counter-terrorism operations room and the command centre set up to coordinate security for the upcoming millennium celebrations in Times Square. In one large room we saw lines of booths where people of all nationalities sat with earphones and typed into computer terminals. He explained that each person, most of them civilians vetted and hired by the FBI, were listening to bugged conversations between hundreds of Middle Eastern individuals suspected of being part of the al-Qaeda network. The secret listeners were experts in colloquial Middle Eastern and Asian dialects and could pick up nuances and information from the recorded conversations that an ordinary linguist would not understand.

At the time, although we didn't know it, O'Neill was leading a massive investigation in a race against time to prevent a number of bomb attacks then being planned by bin Laden's acolytes. A few weeks later the operation thwarted a plot to bomb Los Angeles International Airport. O'Neill's efforts also foiled a second bomb attack planned for Times Square on New Year's Eve 1999 where over two million people were due to gather. It was described as 'the most comprehensive investigation ever carried out before September 11'.

Garda teams in Dublin were part of that international operation. On 21 December 1999 they arrested Hamid Aich, one of the suspected conspirators with links to bin Laden. However, much to the annoyance of the Americans, there wasn't enough evidence to charge Aich and he subsequently left Ireland before the 9/11 attacks. Documents and computers seized in Aich's home were shared with the FBI and other intelligence agencies worldwide.

Despite the tense investigation he was running John still found time to bring us to the FBI and Secret Service Christmas party. He introduced us to members of the NYPD Joint Terrorist Task Force who worked as part of John's team. We then left New York and O'Neill to spend a few fascinating days at the FBI Academy near Washington DC, a criminal investigation centre of excellence.

One of the first things that struck me was the large numbers of police officers from all over the US and the rest of the world who were there on various training courses. The FBI lays great emphasis on building relationships with law enforcement around the world and sharing the latest methodologies in crime investigation. When they discovered we were Irish the special agents we met in the different departments would ask after senior gardaí they had regular dealings with in Dublin.

The friendships had built up over decades as a result of the war against the Provos and then the dissident republican gangs. At the time the gardaí were assisting the FBI in a nationwide investigation of organized fraud and theft rackets being controlled by gangs of Irish Travellers who were categorized as an organized crime group. As the Irish State's national security agency, the garda also shared intelligence on the movements of international criminal and terrorist gangs through Ireland. It made me realize how the Irish security services were very much a part of the global law enforcement community.

We had a tour of the vast firearms ranges where students were trained in the use of every type of weapon and tactics. At a huge 'kill house' we watched helicopter-borne members of the FBI's

Hostage Rescue Team swoop from the skies to mount assaults using live ammunition in training for the real thing. There was also an extensive racetrack where extreme driving conditions were simulated to teach agents how to handle a range of vehicles.

One of the most interesting experiences for me was a visit to the FBI's National Center for the Analysis of Violent Crimes which specialized in investigating serial sex offences and murders. I interviewed the head of the unit, Special Agent Bill Hagmaier who was one of the most experienced criminal profilers in the world. At the time Ireland had just set up a special investigation to discover if we also had a serial killer and had sought advice from the unit concerning the cases of Ireland's Missing Women. (See Chapter 9.)

Following the memorable trip I kept in touch with John O'Neill and met him on a few more occasions in New York. He had promised himself an overdue trip to Ireland. In the meantime he had been very busy. One of the last times we spoke he talked about the emerging global fundamentalist terror networks that were a new iteration of evil in the world. The new groups were part of a sophisticated, inter-connected network that operated between several countries. He said they had sleeper cells operating in every western country including Ireland. This was valuable information for a crime hack. It became particularly useful in covering the aftermath of the 9/11 attacks.

In October 2000 John O'Neill was sent to Yemen by his new FBI boss, Barry Mawn, to head up the investigation of the al-Qaeda suicide bomb attack on the *USS Cole* which killed seventeen sailors and almost sunk the warship. By then, however, John had more enemies than friends in the hierarchy of the FBI and the CIA whose toes he regularly stepped on while trying to get the job done. He had also crossed swords with Barbara Bodine, the

US ambassador in Yemen, who bad-mouthed him back home in Washington.

Around the same time he was placed under investigation after temporarily losing a briefcase containing classified reports which had been quickly retrieved intact. A story that the high profile FBI man was subject to an internal inquiry was deliberately leaked to a New York newspaper to further discredit him. The story had served to undermine his reputation and led John to re-consider his future. In August 2001 he retired to take a much better paid, prestigious job as chief of security at the World Trade Center.

The last time I spoke with John O'Neill was to wish him well after his departure from the Feds. No matter how busy he was he would always take time for a call and a bit of banter. He was upbeat about the new job and invited my wife and I to come see him next time we were in New York. He said he'd give us the grand tour of the World Trade Center and we would have lunch later in the famous restaurant, Windows on the World on the 106th floor of the north tower. All he wanted was a few days' notice.

On the morning of Tuesday, 11 September, John was two weeks into the new job. He was in his 34th floor office in the South Tower when the first hijacked aircraft hit the North Tower at 8.46 a.m. Seventeen minutes later the second plane crashed into the South Tower. Within minutes John O'Neill was outside the burning building helping to co-ordinate the first, and tragically last, serious incident in the job. He phoned a friend and his son JP, who I had met with him, to say he was ok just before re-entering the South Tower to help evacuate people and to do his job. Minutes later the South Tower collapsed and John O'Neill was never seen alive again. The North Tower came down thirty minutes later. John had been killed by his nemesis in the attack he had warned was coming.

Back in Dublin the normally noisy newsroom of the *Sunday World* was unusually silent apart from gasps of shock as people gathered round TVs to watch what was unfolding live in New York. From the time of initial impact to collapse the terrifying events took just 143 minutes, the same length as the average horror movie. As the dystopian drama unfolded over the following hours I tried John O'Neill's phone but it wasn't connecting as most of lower Manhattan was cut off from the world. I called some other Irish friends to check how they were. Millions of similar calls were being made from around the world at the same time. Due to the damage to the communications network and the huge amount of phone traffic, getting through to anyone was hit and miss.

I then called Kenny Hieb, a New York cop who was a member of the Joint Terrorist Task Force. John had introduced me to Kenny two years earlier. Kenny was one of the surveillance specialists on John's team and had been with him in Yemen. He was on a day off but as we spoke he was driving towards Manhattan which was smothered under a cloak of dust and smoke. Like every other cop and firefighter in the city, he was going in to do his bit. Kenny said it was feared that John may be amongst the dead.

'John called and said that he was okay but was going back into the South Tower to ensure that all his people had gotten out,' Kenny said, recalling the last conversation he had with his friend and former boss immediately after the first strikes. 'He said he would see us later and have a beer. He didn't sound scared or anything, he was just doing his job. A few minutes later the building collapsed and we haven't heard from him since.'

I was horrified to realize that I had actually watched as John O'Neill was being killed. It was heartbreaking news. The hard-bitten, experienced city cop was clearly shocked and emotional. Kenny lost a lot of friends and colleagues that day.

In the following days the world's media descended on New York including a large contingent from Ireland. Given my contacts in the FBI I was dispatched to cover the story, along with my colleague Roy Curtis who, apart from being the doyen of sports writers, is also a master of rich, colourful prose. Charlie Bird was there, as were Joe Duffy and Gerry Ryan who both broadcast their shows from New York that week. We were covering the biggest story in the world.

———

The epicentre of the collapse of the World Trade Center became better known as Ground Zero. Over fourteen acres of lower Manhattan was turned into an apocalyptic wasteland. It was a smouldering volcanic mountain of twisted steel and rubble, belching clouds of highly toxic dust and smoke hundreds of feet into the air, blocking out the sun. The exposure to carcinogenic fumes would later claim many more lives than the actual 9/11 attacks with over 10,000 cops, fire fighters and paramedics later diagnosed with cancer. Some estimates claim that in the decades since 2001 the attack has had a knock-on effect on the health of four million people. Bin Laden had achieved carnage beyond his most depraved dreams.

The dust clouds had dissipated and settled by the time we arrived a week later on Tuesday, 18 September on the first flight we could get after the resumption of air travel to the US. The following morning I went to Ground Zero like everyone else. My guide was an old school friend from Leitrim, Mick O'Rourke, who had joined the NYPD after leaving home in the late 1980s. We had also served in the army reserve together.

As we walked through the side streets from the direction of Wall Street, every surface in lower Manhattan was caked in the dust that had engulfed the entire downtown area south of Canal Street. As I got closer the ground was cloaked in a carpet of dust and bits of paper from the offices in the towers. Walls full of pictures of human faces were everywhere I looked, as desperate families sought information on missing loved ones. New York was a city engulfed by grief, shock and anger.

As we drew closer Mick warned me to brace myself. When we turned the corner I realized why. No matter how gruesome the non-stop coverage of the Ground Zero images were, nothing could prepare me for the sight of the grey mountain standing there like a mausoleum of death. Frozen to the spot I was looking into the pits of hell. It left its mark on me and on everyone who witnessed it.

Turning the corner a blast of intense heat washed over us, as if someone had opened a giant oven door. Smoke seeped up everywhere through crevices in the pile as rescue workers resembled ghosts in the acrid mist. A shower of rain began to gently fall on the ruins turning into pillars of steam. Burning ash singed my nostrils and the clammy air carried a sickly-sweet scent that clung to my clothes, skin and hair. You could damn well taste it. I asked Mick what it was. He said it was the smell of human flesh cooking in the intense heat of the burning cauldron buried beneath the rubble. The grotesque reality was that the sources of the smell were to be found in the faces of the missing a block away.

The skeletal remains of the buildings assailed all the senses at once. It was the sight, smell, feel and taste of death against the sounds of machinery and voices of hundreds of volunteers and first responders still clawing their way through the rubble in the hope of finding people still alive. Over twenty-three years later the sights, sounds and particularly the smell of Ground Zero remains burned in my memory. Two days later the body of John O'Neill was recovered from a stairwell in the ruins of the South Tower.

Despite the intense horror of it all we had a job to do. And even though it was the biggest story in the world a newspaper still requires a new angle. I had arranged to meet Kenny Hieb and some of John's other colleagues to write a piece about him. I was also hoping to talk to some Irish cops and first responders to record their experiences.

The last thing I expected was a major exclusive. Then the phone rang. It was Commissioner Pat Byrne in Dublin. He had been deeply shocked by the loss of his friend and the way in which he died. I'd told him we were going to New York and asked if he knew someone involved in the investigation. It was a very long shot given the gravity of the situation where the major players would be too busy to talk to reporters, especially one from a little newspaper in Ireland.

But it turned out that Barry Mawn, the officer in overall command of the mammoth investigation, was a good friend of Pat's. They'd met many years earlier when they attended a specialist counter-terrorism course in Quantico and had worked together on joint investigations between the FBI and garda, including the Real IRA sting. Pat had spoken to Special Agent Mawn and he had agreed to give me a brief interview if I wanted it. The fact that I had been a friend of John O'Neill had been the deciding factor. I couldn't believe it. Pat gave me a mobile number and said goodbye.

Mawn had been appointed Assistant Special Agent in charge of the FBI's New York bureau a year earlier. John O'Neill had desperately wanted the job but his enemies in Washington were determined he wouldn't get it. However it wasn't personal between the two men and they got on well together. Against the wishes of the hierarchy Mawn had sent O'Neill to Yemen after the *USS Cole* attack in October 2000.

I was astonished when a voice picked up and gruffly announced: 'Barry Mawn.' I told him who I was. 'Oh you're the guy who is a friend of Pat Byrne and I believe you were a friend of our John O'Neill,' he said straight away. 'I'm not doing interviews but if you come down I can give you ten minutes.'

I couldn't believe my luck. Mawn told me to take a cab to West 26th Street and someone would give me directions from there. He had only one proviso, that we wouldn't reveal the location in the paper. John Shiels, the then managing editor of the *Sunday World*, came with me.

An hour later the taxi driver dropped us on the corner of a quiet New York backstreet, leading to the Hudson River shoreline. We reckoned at first that he had made a mistake. He told us he'd never heard of an FBI building around here. We thought we were lost. It didn't look like the kind of place to find the nerve centre of the biggest criminal investigation in the world.

Confused, we walked to the end of the deserted street. A large dumper truck painted in pink and loaded with huge chunks of concrete was parked across the road. Then suddenly a member of a SWAT team, with a pistol strapped to his leg, jumped from a jeep with blacked-out windows. Behind him were similar pink coloured dump trucks parked defensively. We learned later it was to prevent attackers ramming their way through with a vehicle loaded with explosives. The cop asked who we were, as the area was cut off from the public.

'Oh you're the Irish guys, you are expected,' he said.

He directed us to the bottom of the street facing out onto the Hudson and told us to wait beside a steep ramp which led up to what looked like a large warehouse. As we got closer there were heavily armed troops and police on machine gun posts in a protective ring around the area. Police boats patrolled the river and a military helicopter circled overhead. Further down the riverbank was the *USS Intrepid* aircraft carrier museum which we later learned had also been pressed into service as a secret command centre.

Even though we were in the middle of New York there was very little traffic in the area and the place seemed deserted.

Just then a smartly dressed FBI agent came down to meet us and introduced himself as the press liaison officer. He shook his head as he led us back up the ramp to the darkened entrance of the garage:

> You guys are the only media who have been invited here. None
> of the US media has been allowed through to Barry... we've
> turned down the *Washington Post*, the *New York Times* and
> CNN... I don't know who you guys know.

We were just as surprised as he was.

It was called the 26th Street Garage, the New York FBI's automotive garage used to park and repair federal vehicles. It had been hurriedly pressed into service as the investigation centre. Within minutes of the attacks, Mawn and his senior staff realized that their HQ at Federal Plaza, just around the corner from the World Trade Center, had been rendered inoperable in the catastrophe.

At the top of the ramp we were greeted by an astonishing sight. Over 500 cars had been moved to make way for up to 1,000 personnel. They worked at lines of trestle tables bedecked with computer terminals, linked to miles of cables draped from the

roof. Their jackets identified them as members of several law
enforcement agencies – FBI, ATF, NYPD, DEA and NSA. A
forklift was moving pallets of food and water to sustain the huge
force of investigators.

We had never seen anything like it before but we weren't
allowed to take pictures for understandable security reasons. While
researching this book I discovered that amongst the hundreds
of TV documentaries made about 9/11, only one highlighted
the significant role played by the garage headquarters in the
investigation, *The 26th Street Garage: The untold story of the FBI on
9/11*. We had witnessed another piece of history in the making.

Every lead, even the tiniest piece of information, that came in
from around the globe was funnelled through the 26th garage.
When a name came up every bit of information pertaining to that
individual's life was downloaded, from vehicle registration, health
insurance, to financial, phone and police records. Teams of agents
across the country would then be sent to interview the person.
It was the kind of tedious, meticulous work involved in every
criminal investigation only on a vast scale. The initial objective was
to identify and profile all the hijackers and the sequence of events
on 9/11. Then the huge team trawled through the background
of each terrorist to trace those working with them. It was vital to
prevent any further attacks and bring those involved to justice.

Top of the suspect list was Osama bin Laden and al-Qaeda.
'Nearly 98 per cent of the leads come to nothing,' our guide
explained, as we walked through the bustling garage which smelt
of oil and grease. 'But you have to keep looking for that two per
cent which will crack the whole thing open.'

Barry Mawn, a tall bluff man with fair hair and glasses, was
sitting in a makeshift conference room overlooking the Hudson

River. He gave us a warm welcome and said he considered himself Irish before introducing his top officers. There were a number of TV screens and cameras standing on tripods where the G man and his senior people were preparing for an online conference with senior Government officials including President George W. Bush, the Secretary of State and the heads of the FBI and CIA. In 2001 this was as sophisticated as communications could get.

'We are at the highest state of alert right now and that is why we are not advertizing where our command centre is,' said Mawn, whose CV included the hunt for the notorious domestic terrorist the Unabomber.

But before talking about the investigation he had his own story to tell about 9/11. Mawn had almost perished in the immediate aftermath of the collapse of the towers. He had been close by at the same time that John O'Neill died when the South Tower came down. The FBI boss recalled his experience:

> It was surreal. I was working at my desk at Federal Plaza when I heard an aircraft roar past overhead and seconds later there was a tremendous boom. At first I thought it was a military jet which had broken the sound barrier as it flew down the Hudson River. Then my secretary started screaming that the World Trade Center had been hit by an aircraft. I decided that I was going to go down and see for myself what was going on. I met with the New York police commissioner and his deputy. The fire and emergency services were arriving. The fire department and the police had started evacuating the first tower which had been hit.
>
> We were standing there looking up at the fire for a short time and then we saw the other aircraft coming from the south and it was obvious that it was heading right for the other tower. As it

smashed into the building a huge fireball came from the north side of the building. We all turned and started running because there were chunks of concrete and steel girders raining down on top of us. We sought cover under an ambulance and stayed there until the debris stopped falling.

The Assistant Special Agent began finding bodies and torn limbs scattered through the debris.

As I left the cover one of my officers drew my attention to something that could be a piece of material evidence in the street. It was a leg which had been severed at the knee cap. Then there was another tremendous roar and the first tower block started falling right above our heads. I was with my Head of Intelligence and two firefighters. We had seconds and as they ran to get out of the way of the falling building, I followed them.

We got shelter behind a huge girder and the firefighters told us to grab hold of one another. Then suddenly we found ourselves in total darkness - the bright morning became so black that you could not see anything. It was black night. The dust and smoke were so intense that I thought we were all going to choke to death. Someone in a building near us opened a door and yelled at us to come towards him. A person began flashing a camera so that we could follow the light through the darkness.

You couldn't see your hand in front of your face. We got into the building which was the World Trade Center Seven block and made it into the basement. We got out through a loading dock of the building. It was around this time that the second tower came crashing down. I got separated from my own people in all the commotion and sheer chaos and thought they were dead. They also thought that I was dead. I suppose I cheated death a few

times that morning like so many others. I eventually got out of the
area and began organizing our response.

With Federal Plaza disabled Barry Mawn's first objective was to
find a base for the investigation which automatically fell to him
and his FBI team.

> We effectively evacuated all our staff from the building. We really
> didn't have a place to go and that is when we picked this large
> garage. It was a really major logistical operation to set up. From
> there we were co-ordinating with every FBI field office in the US
> and throughout the world, and every law enforcement agency
> in the world including the garda in Ireland. The garda played a
> significant role in this hunt.
>
> The thrust of our investigation was to identify all the hijackers
> and retrace everything they did. We investigated their support
> systems and what they did since they came to this country. This
> attack was a whole new level of terrorism which went beyond law
> enforcement alone, but every one of us was determined to solve
> this crime. We needed to do this for the sake of the whole world.
> Terrorism of this kind cannot be allowed to flourish.

Sitting across a table from Barry Mawn, his relaxed confident
demeanour belied the enormity of the responsibilities he carried.
Stoicism is a quality that unites cops all over the world.

He said, 'John's death is very upsetting to all of us in the FBI and
the manner of his passing is a bitter irony almost beyond belief.'

When Roy and I returned to file our copy on the Saturday
morning we reckoned the significance of the story might be lost
on the readers. It was the kind of mega scoop that you would have
expected to read in the *New York Times*. Colm MacGinty ran it as the

splash across the front page under the headline: 'We go inside secret FBI terror centre'. Inside we also ran a two-page tribute to the life and extraordinary career of John O'Neill. Under the heading, 'My journey of pain through dark streets of New York' Roy Curtis produced a deeply moving and emotionally raw account of Ground Zero.

The next time I came into contact with the FBI was a very different experience but it was about another terrorist on their most wanted list.

In 2003 I wrote an exclusive story which revealed that the gardaí had joined the international manhunt for James 'Whitey' Bulger, the head of the Irish mafia in the US and second on the FBI's ten most wanted list – next to Osama bin Laden. From second generation Irish stock Bulger was the head of the powerful Winter Hill Gang which controlled the criminal underworld in South Boston or Southie. During his reign Bulger, who was also a secret FBI informant, murdered at least twenty-one people. The FBI task force set up to track down Bulger flew me to Boston to see if I could help with the case. At the time they believed that America's most wanted man was being hidden in Ireland by members of Sinn Féin and the IRA.

Bulger went into hiding in 1994 when John Connolly, a corrupt FBI agent who grew up next door to Bulger, tipped him off that he was about to be charged with serious criminal offences including extortion, racketeering, drug trafficking and murder. Connolly had been protecting Bulger for years and in return he was paid handsomely. Bulger also gave information to Connolly which the FBI used to smash his opposition.

In one incident, in September 1984, Whitey had organized the shipment of seven tonnes of explosives, firearms and ammunition to the IRA. The Provos had no moral qualms when it came to dealing with organized crime on either side of the Atlantic. In South Boston Whitey's support for the Provos underlined his patriotic credentials. The arsenal was shipped on a trawler, the *Valhalla*, which transferred its cargo to another fishing vessel, the *Marita Ann*, off the south Kerry coast.

It was later widely believed that Bulger had tipped off Connolly about the shipment to give the FBI agent kudos with his bosses. The Irish Navy intercepted the *Marita Ann* arresting a leading Provo and latter day TD, Martin Ferris, who was jailed for ten years for his crime.

Connolly was later convicted of taking bribes, obstructing justice and second degree murder. It was a dark episode in the history of the FBI and a source of great embarrassment to the agency. Bringing Bulger to justice was a top priority. They offered one million dollars for information leading to his arrest.

In December 2002 two FBI agents arrived in Dublin to liaise with Garda HQ in the hunt for the now seventy-three-year-old mob boss. As part of the probe they had located a safety deposit box in a Dublin bank vault. I reported that the discovery came after a similar seizure by Scotland Yard in a London bank. Amongst documents and £50,000 in various currencies, the UK detectives found a legitimate passport containing Bulger's picture and a false name. They also found a key which led to the search at the Dublin bank.

Bulger's brother William, a former president of the Massachusetts State Senate, was listed as the contact person for the safety deposit box in London. He refused to tell a congressional committee if he knew of the whereabouts of his mobster brother.

The gardaí had established that Bulger had spent time in Ireland in 1993 and 1994 holidaying in posh hotels. Intelligence suggested that despite suspicions he may have been an informant, Bulger had maintained good relations with senior players in the IRA and Sinn Féin.

At the time I interviewed one of the FBI agents who confirmed that there was a high possibility that Bulger was in Ireland. He told me:

> Ireland is one of three countries, including the UK and
> Switzerland, where we believe he has been lying low. Bulger was
> spotted in London in September (2002) and we have a strong
> suspicion that he is somewhere in the Irish Republic. We took the
> decision to go public because someone may recognize him or
> know his whereabouts.

The FBI also issued an appeal for information on RTÉ's *Crimeline* programme in January 2003. However, nothing came of it and the Whitey Bulger story fell silent again.

Over a year later I received a call from Mike Kradolfer who identified himself as a member of the Bulger Fugitive Task Force, a joint effort comprising the FBI, the Massachusetts State Police and the Deputy US Marshal Service. Kradolfer said he was reaching out to see if I could help in their investigation and that they were particularly interested in my knowledge of the republican movement. He wanted to know if I would be interested in travelling to meet the team in Boston. They would pay for the flights, accommodation and expenses. Although I doubted that I would be of much help, a trip to Boston was an offer I could not refuse. I arrived in the windy city on 30 January 2005.

The next day the officers brought me to their investigation HQ which consisted of an open-plan office behind a steel door in the coastguard building overlooking the waterfront. The location had been picked because it was secure and discreet. The only indication that there was something sensitive going on was a big CCTV camera perched over the door. The nerve centre of one of the America's biggest manhunts was surprisingly messy and unkempt. The reason, I was told, was that they could not allow cleaners in. It made sense.

The investigators revealed that it was their strong suspicion that Bulger was being protected in Ireland by republicans. They had mapped out the connections between the mob boss and republican supporters in South Boston and named Sinn Féin and IRA members in Ireland. I was getting more information than I had to offer. It was a fascinating insight.

Mike Kradolfer and his colleagues took me on a tour of Southie, pointing out the locations where Whitey once presided and where his associates still lived.

Of more interest was an Irish bar whose owner had direct links to Bulger and Sinn Féin, particularly Martin McGuinness. The team's belief was that Whitey's disappearance was connected to the bar and McGuinness. Their intelligence showed that whenever McGuiness visited the US he would slip away for clandestine meetings in the Southie bar. The Feds were even able to describe the windowless room at the back where the meetings took place. I suspected that they had probably planted bugs in the room but they weren't sharing that information.

The FBI secretly watched McGuinness and Gerry Adams, who were still classified as terrorists, whenever they visited the States in the early 2000s. The US authorities were also concerned by revelations that the IRA had given bomb-making training to

Colombia's FARC terror group, a sworn enemy of the US at the time. FARC also controlled a large portion of the cocaine trade in South America. A US investigation had found that the republican movement was paid over twenty million dollars for their expertise. The whole operation had been planned through communist Cuba. It was easy to see why the FBI considered the republicans to be a threat.

I spent a day with a group of investigators including an analyst from Quantico, answering questions and laying out what I knew about the Provos. Many of the questions were more illuminating than the answers I gave. The information I had was the same as theirs – it came from the same sources. The hypothesis that the mobster could be hidden in Ireland was certainly feasible.

Following the public appeal for information in 2003 there had been a rush of callers claiming to have spotted Bulger in different parts of Ireland. Each sighting was thoroughly checked and found to be inaccurate. The Feds were particularly interested in two places: Kerry, where Martin Ferris lived, and South Armagh. The Provos loomed over Bandit Country like local criminal mafia bosses and no one dared break the code of *omertà* they'd set. Whitey could walk up and down the main street of Crossmaglen, Co. Armagh, and no one would admit to seeing him.

When I returned to Ireland I asked sources about Whitey Bulger. Senior gardaí I later spoke to were adamant that he was not being hidden by the IRA – if he was they would have known. The story went dead for another six and a half years at which point the Irish cops were ultimately proved to be correct – and my very enjoyable trip to Boston had been a waste of Federal resources.

On 22 June 2011 the Bulger Fugitive Task Force finally caught up with their man. Whitey Bulger's remarkable sixteen years spent evading capture ended when he was arrested in Santa Monica, west of LA. It turned out that he and his girlfriend, Caterine Greig, had lived there in an unremarkable apartment block since shortly after he went on the run. Santa Monica was a much warmer place to hide out than rain-sodden South Armagh. While the FBI was scouring the world their target had being hiding openly behind an unassuming lifestyle. He paid for everything in cash, didn't drive a car and limited his social interaction with others to small talk. The breakthrough came after the FBI launched a media campaign for information in 2010 and a former neighbour tipped them off.

In 2013 Bulger was convicted of racketeering, firearms possession and eleven murders. The man who tried to arm – and then disarm – the Provos was sentenced to two life sentences. In 2018 he was beaten and stabbed to death by a group of other inmates in the US penitentiary in Hazelton, Virgina. At the age of eighty-nine the once powerful godfather was attacked in his wheelchair and was so badly disfigured that he was left unrecognizable.

For once everyone had been wrong about the IRA.

CHAPTER ELEVEN

THE ERA OF THE NARCOS

The first years of the new century marked the beginning of an unprecedented boom time for organized crime. The underworld cashed in to feed the Celtic Tiger generation's insatiable appetite for illicit drugs, particularly cocaine. As Irish society shook off the shackles of decades of economic decay it became one of the most prosperous countries in the developed world. But it had a dark underbelly as people fell in love with recreational drugs. If heroin was synonymous with the gloom in the eighties, cocaine was the poison of choice in Ireland for the good times of the noughties. Gangland had discovered a new Klondike gold rush.

From 2000 up to the present day, more Irish people per capita are snorting the Colombian marching powder than anywhere else in Europe. Within a few short years the unprecedented demand for narcotics had created an alternative Irish economy worth an estimated €1 billion which has grown exponentially ever since. Cocaine became available in every parish, village, town and city in the country causing an epidemic of addiction and other health problems. The bad habits of law-abiding citizens ushered in a new era in the history of organized crime in Ireland that has continued to thrive and prosper over the last quarter of a century. We are living in the era of the Irish narco.

The likes of Martin Cahill or the Dunnes would not have recognized the gangland that emerged in the millennium. The Westies were the pathfinders of the new drug subculture and personified the changing psyche of the average criminal. From 1999 onwards gangs sprouted up like mushrooms as a new generation of greedy, reckless and volatile criminals emerged. The proliferation of drug dealing mobs was accompanied by an unprecedented upsurge in violence and murder.

I chronicled how the rise of the narcos created the new phenomenon of the gang war which became the deadly by-product of the drug trade. Violence and murder became the tools of choice for dealing with problems in the new order and the level of feuding became a barometer to gauge the amount of criminal activity on the streets.

There was no shortage of reckless killers or guns available and the new breed showed they were prepared to intimidate or murder anyone, whether a rival, an innocent civilian or even a cop, who got in the way of their avaricious ambitions. Would-be killers honed their skills practicing on ranges in the US and Eastern Europe. The Glock automatic replaced the less sophisticated sawn-off shotgun. The new gangs demonstrated that there were no longer any boundaries beyond which they were not prepared to cross.

As criminals became more emboldened and arrogant, feuds sprung up like bush fires. They would claim the lives of over 150 people, including innocent civilians, in the first decade alone. As a journalist watching from the sidelines it was astonishing to observe the dramatic trajectory taking place. I estimate that I covered at least 200 individual gangland hits over the years. Chronicling the explosion in organized crime and murder became a constant race just to keep pace with what was happening. Crime reporters were amongst the busiest staff members in the daily and Sunday newspapers.

From the mid-1990s the *Sunday World* had become the newspaper that the public read to find out what was happening in the underworld. Apart from sport and showbiz, crime was our speciality and biggest seller. I remember at a luncheon hosted by Tony O'Reilly he asked Colm MacGinty about the elements that made the paper a success. The Independent News and Media (INM) board were there including the former Canadian Prime Minister, Brian Mulroney. I'll never forget the puzzled look on his face when Colm explained as he counted on his fingers: 'It all boils down to three elements – Gee, Gaa and Gore.' To those outside our tabloid bubble that meant sex, sport and murder. We were the law and order newspaper. We adopted an aggressive campaigning style which exposed criminals as parasites who were not untouchable or invincible.

We continued to get some criticism from academics and others that we were glamorizing the mobsters. If we were, why then had they murdered one journalist and were making serious threats of violence against others? I saw my role as raising awareness of a social crisis that was spiralling out of control and infecting the lives of countless numbers of victims. There was plenty of reasons why it became so personal.

In 2001, four years after the murder of Veronica Guerin, a loyalist drug gang gunned down Martin O'Hagan who worked as an investigative reporter in the *Sunday World's* northern office. On the night of 28 September he was shot dead in his home town of Lurgan, County Armagh, while walking home from the pub with his wife Marie. He was fifty-one years old and the father of three daughters.

Working under his fearless editor Jim Campbell, and later Jim McDowell, Marty had been a thorn in the side of the loyalist and republican paramilitaries since the 1980s. He specialized in exposing the criminal rackets controlled by the mafia-style terror gangs on both sides of the sectarian divide. They reciprocated by regularly threatening his life. The Provos, the terrorists supported by the so-called democratic party Sinn Féin, once kidnapped Marty and held him for two days to interrogate him about his sources.

In 1992, long before I began pissing off the gangland thugs, the company moved Marty to work in the South for his own safety. It followed a bomb attack on the Belfast office by terrorists loyal to the UVF leader, a psychopath and sectarian serial killer called Billy Wright. Marty had also been physically attacked by the terrorists. The bomb attack was the second at the *Sunday World* office in Belfast. In the first attack in 1984 the then Northern editor Jim Campbell had been shot and seriously injured by terrorists who disagreed with the paper's campaigning style. The UVF delivered a message from Wright to Marty O'Hagan warning that he would be killed if he didn't stop writing about them.

Marty stayed with me and my family in Dublin before he got fixed up with more permanent accommodation. He was then moved to Cork where he worked for two years before returning north again because the threat had died down. Gently spoken, charming and great fun, Marty loved nothing more than to sit in the pub with his colleagues and chat about writing 'wee stories' over copious pints. His murder came as a numbing, heartbreaking blow to all of us in the *Sunday World*.

I remember receiving the awful news that night when I got a call from my colleague and friend, Paul Reynolds, RTÉ's crime correspondent. I couldn't believe that this was happening all over again. After Veronica, I genuinely thought that we would never see another journalist being killed in the line of duty. Marty's murder at the hands of terrorists was profoundly shocking especially coming as it did less than three weeks after the 9/11 attacks in the US. His assassination was condemned by political leaders of all hues as the loyalist paramilitaries were supposedly involved in a ceasefire and the peace process.

Marty's colleagues across the media in Britain and Ireland united in grief and over 2,000 mourners attended his funeral on 1 October 2001, including the entire staff of the *Sunday World* in Dublin. With colleagues from across the media world, we took turns to carry Marty's coffin on the long walk from his home to the local graveyard. One of the things that rankles all these years later is that Marty's murder did not generate the same level of public or political outrage, anger or resolve as that which followed Veronica Guerin's assassination.

The people of Northern Ireland were more accustomed to terrorist outrages than their contemporaries in the Republic. The view from the South was that Northern Ireland was a complicated, terrorist-ridden, sectarian enclave that was a completely different world from the prosperous, more civilized Irish Republic. Such atrocities were seen as normal 'up there'. The shooting dead of journalist Lyra McKee, while she was observing a riot in Derry in April 2019, was another shocking precedent for the whole island of Ireland. When I heard the awful news I instantly thought of Marty.

The fact that the two murdered journalists worked for the same newspaper group, Independent News and Media, stiffened the resolve of everyone in the *Sunday World* to continue shining a light into gangland's darkest corners. Brophy and MacGinty provided the leadership and all-important resources to wage our campaign exposing organized crime. Since Veronica's murder we'd begun tracking down criminals who had moved their operations to places like Holland and Spain, secretly photographing them and revealing their whereabouts.

Our brilliant lawyers, Gerry Fanning and Kieran Kelly, were key members of our small team. They navigated a path through the Irish defamation laws so that we could tell the stories that no one else would. When criminals did attempt to mount legal actions our intrepid 'consiglieri' would make it clear that we would not be legally intimidated. Sadly, in 2004 Gerry who was a dear friend died suddenly at the age of fifty. Kieran Kelly has steered the ship ever since and is highly regarded as the country's top libel lawyer for several branches of the media. He has kept me out of more trouble than either of us care to remember.

By 2001 I had developed an investigative template when compiling stories about organized crime. I had a large cross section of reliable, well-informed sources in the gardaí, the criminal community and wider society. The public, including people close to particular criminals, came forward with tip offs because of our coverage of crime. Running an exposé on an individual or a story on a major crime would also prompt people to pick up the phone and share information they had.

The information coming to us was kept within a small number of people including the editor, news editor and the photographers who worked with me to ensure confidentiality, particularly around the protection of our sources. Protecting informants was paramount as the intelligence they often gave us would result in certain death for them if they were discovered. Sometimes we had to drop big stories for fear that they might compromise the sources and put their well being in jeopardy. None of my contacts were ever rumbled.

I built an extensive database of information on the major players in the gangs as they emerged, which was constantly updated and included their pictures, activities and associates. As the years went by I gradually filled four filing cabinets with the information. It gave us an edge in exposing what was going on in gangland. Despite the inherent risks the work was all-consuming and rewarding. It was also exciting and good fun.

At times during the early 2000s the pace was frenetic as I was often covering the activities of up to ten gangs and several feuds at the same time. The background to gangland murders became a regular staple of our front page crime coverage. The new players on the block were literally blasting their way into the headlines and the public's awareness. In weeks when we hadn't a strong front page story someone would say: 'The week's early there's bound to be someone killed before Saturday.' As the bodies piled up the sadistic godfathers were too blinded by hubris and greed to realize that it was bad for business. The murders drew unwanted attention from the police and the media as the killers were elevated in the gardaí's most wanted list.

Photographic surveillance on the funerals of those killed in the spiralling madness were still a fruitful source of information as they were the only events where large numbers of criminals congregated together. We had got good at keeping well out of sight while watching the burials. The pictures often helped identify gang members and to piece together their roles and connections. Over the years the funerals of major gangland players were turned into mafia-style spectacles, with no expense spared on the trappings including caskets and limos. The associates of the dead would be decked out in matching designer suits which they wore like a uniform.

The optics of the garish, vulgar displays of wealth were intended as a show of strength and defiance to their rivals – and a contemptuous two-fingered gesture to the rest of society. The theatrics around the gangland funeral came to exemplify what criminologists describe as the 'carnival of crime' – a ritualized celebration of the mob's oppositional value system.

Gang funerals often gave us an opportunity to strip the big players of their cherished anonymity by publishing their names and pictures. The more egotistical narcissists revelled in the notoriety but I knew that most of them hated it. Media attention brought even more police heat down on them. As the gangs grew more powerful and corrosive in society, it became a personal goal to make their lives as difficult as possible. Some critics have said it was a personal crusade. At times it was. Interviewing the desperate families of innocent victims and those trapped within the grip of the gangs made it so. The new mobs effectively imprisoned whole working-class communities where they sold dope, waged war and bullied everyone.

As the era of the narcos progressed the number of victims being intimidated, injured or murdered jumped dramatically. Innocent parents and children in crime-ravaged estates were left traumatized by the violence they witnessed. Parents were often involved in a desperate battle to keep their kids out of the clutches of the local godfathers. The crime boom created another new phenomenon where children were groomed by drug dealers to do their dirty work in much the same way paedophiles groom their victims.

The motivation for gardaí passing on information to the media about the criminals was that they were also sickened by what was going on and wanted to see them exposed to the public. They wanted people to know what they were up against. It had worked in the past. Cops who were frustrated by the lack of powers to investigate John Gilligan's ill-gotten wealth tipped off Veronica Guerin because publicity was the only weapon to force the authorities to take action. It took her needless death to finally force the Government to introduce legislation that gave birth to the Criminal Assets Bureau.

The murders of Veronica and Marty gave us the impetus to go after the bastards in any way we could. Many perpetrators were free because people were too scared to testify against them. Highlighting the victims' stories and exposing the narcos' more shocking crimes sometimes prompted people to contact the police with important information. In many cases members of the public had recognized the criminals after seeing their picture in the papers. The spotlight provided a small bit of justice in a cruel world.

The evolution of the CAB made it possible to jettison the blacked-out faces and reveal the drug dealers' real names. Since 1996 the CAB had been targeting the wealth of gangsters even though they may not have been convicted of serious crimes. The criteria for an individual to become a target of the Bureau is that they possess identifiable assets which could be linked to criminality. Seizing the proceeds of crime is done under civil law where the burden of proof required operates at the lower level, on the balance of probabilities, as opposed to the proof that applies in a criminal case which is beyond all reasonable doubt. The defamation laws also come under the civil law.

Using the backdrop of a CAB case meant that we could finally expose criminals whose identities had been previously withheld for legal reasons. Defamation laws, which are seen as draconian in Ireland, have always been used by people from all walks of life to prevent the truth coming out by shutting down legitimate journalism through the threat of legal action.

One of those many targets I wrote about was Gerry Hutch, the Monk, the last of the genuinely ordinary decent criminals. He was clever enough to see the transformation taking place and made a conscious decision to retire. Nevertheless, his notoriety as the country's most successful armed robber made him a prime target for the CAB when it was set up. In 2000 he was forced to pay €2.1 million in 'satisfaction of all taxes due by him'. Our headline on that story was 'The Monk Comes Out to Pay'.

The tax demand was based on the record-breaking multi-million-euro robberies he masterminded in the 1980s and 1990s for which he has never been prosecuted. But Hutch was much cleverer than his contemporaries. He was happy to pay up because the settlement made him a legitimate – and very wealthy – businessman who would go on to enjoy the fruits of his investments in property.

In the CAB's first decade in operation Hutch and his network of associates paid over €40 million in tax settlements. In the same period they took over €100 million from the Irish underworld. A CAB investigation also offered an opening to expose the likes of George Mitchell who had become one of the biggest drug traffickers in Europe. In 2006 I wrote the bestselling book *The Untouchables* which told the inside story of how the Bureau was established and chronicled its first decade in operation. CAB's success was due in no small part to its three founders: Detective Chief Superintendent Fachtna Murphy (later Garda Commissioner),

Detective Superintendent Felix McKenna (later chief of CAB) and Barry Galvin, the indefatigable former state solicitor for Cork who was the bureau's legal officer. The courageous lawyer was the subject of an assassination plot by associates of the Kinahan cartel and became the only civilian ever allowed to carry a police firearm for his own protection.

Since the early 1990s when I got more involved in digging deeper into the underworld I had been regarded as a hate figure for the mobsters and thugs. In the new narco gangland that hatred seemed to go into overdrive. I was making deadly new enemies who joined the ranks of the old ones. Crime journalism in the era of the narcos became an even more hazardous profession. The arrogant gangsters had forgotten the unprecedented backlash in the wake of Veronica's murder when the gardaí turned the underworld upside down.

In those years between the crackdown and the early 2000s the criminals had realized that targeting journalists wasn't good for business and there were relatively few threats. The most serious incident that I experienced in that period took place in May 1997 when the team investigating Veronica's murder picked up intelligence that forty-seven-year-old veteran drug trafficker Tommy Savage had returned to Ireland intent on having me killed. Nine months earlier I had written the first major exposé about Savage which revealed him as one of the pioneers of the modern drug trade. I told how he had earned the nickname the Zombie from other criminals because of his reputation as a dangerous psychopath and gangland serial killer.

Savage had been a founding member of the INLA and later an even more dangerous breakaway criminal grouping, the Irish People's Liberation Army. At the same time the convicted armed robber was one of the first to move into the hash business in the 1970s. Together with his long-time partner in crime Mickey Weldon, a former Irish soldier, INLA comrade and killer, they had become the most successful terrorists-turned-drug dealers in the business. Savage and Weldon were among the first Irish villains to establish links and supply routes with cannabis suppliers in Holland, Morocco and the Middle East.

The Zombie carried out the first ever drug-related Irish murder in 1982 and was credited with killing at least three other villains. He and Weldon were also linked to the executions of several old comrades in the INLA during a number of internecine feuds in the late 1980s. The republican crime gang has the distinction of murdering more of each other than they did British soldiers. Fearing that he was going to be whacked Savage and Weldon moved their operation to Holland in 1992. As a major influential figure in gangland for decades in 1996 I'd thought it was time to introduce the Zombie to the public. It appeared that he had a long memory.

Our local superintendent John McLoughlin called to our home one Monday night in early May. He seemed to be in a bit of a flap. John told me that he had been instructed to place two armed officers with me from the following morning. Tony Hickey's team at Lucan garda station had picked up intelligence that Savage was returning to Ireland to have me shot. It was considered a serious threat. Knowing Savage's capacity for violence I was genuinely worried that something might happen. For the next week armed detectives from Sundrive Road and Crumlin stations accompanied me wherever I went. The protection was taken off when Savage left the country again. It appeared that he had changed his mind.

As the narcos ascended in the early 2000s the sheer volume of stories inevitably caused a lot of annoyance for more bad people. As 2003 approached I didn't realize what a difficult and dangerous year it would turn out to be. But before the year began an unlikely old adversary decided to have my house attacked to let me know that he had not forgotten me or gone away. He also wanted to demonstrate that he hadn't learned any lessons from his previous ill-fated exploits – threatening and killing people.

And it was all down to Santa Claus and John Gilligan.

———

The trouble erupted on 22 December 2002 when John Gilligan read an article of mine in the *Sunday World* while sitting in his cell in Portlaoise maximum-security prison. In March 2001 he had been acquitted of the murder of Veronica Guerin but was handed an unprecedented twenty-eight-year sentence for drug trafficking which was later reduced to twenty years.

In the same year I wrote *Evil Empire*, which chronicled Gilligan's rise to power and how he and his gang plotted the journalist's murder. An updated edition of the book had been serialized in the *Sunday World* a week earlier but the article that caught Gilligan's eye had nothing to do with crime. On the same day the paper published a two-page spread about my visit to Santa's winter wonderland in Lapland with my eight-year-old daughter, Irena. Christmas has always been my favourite time of year, and the most magical ones were when the kids were young. The tongue-in-cheek, light-hearted headline parodied the crime brief by declaring that I had travelled to the North Pole to come 'Face to Face with Santa'.

The story was accompanied by a picture of Irena and me posing beside the great man himself. Over the years, on garda advice, I kept my wife and kids out of any limelight connected with my job so that they could not be identified. Gilligan's reaction to the picture proved the article to be a lapse in judgement on my part. It reminded him that I actually had a happy family life away from work. I later found out that the image irritated Gilligan so he decided to try and destroy Christmas for his hated enemy.

Gilligan, like so many other players who were locked up, had continued to run his drug business from prison with the aid of a mobile phone. He thought it was a closely guarded secret and had no way of knowing that the Crime and Security Branch at Garda HQ were listening to his every word. The authorities had deliberately turned a blind eye to prisoners having mobile phones because it produced a rich vein of invaluable intelligence.

The strategy seemed to work as the conversations from prison cells had already helped prevent serious crimes and led to huge seizures of drugs and guns. While serving a four-year sentence for receiving stolen cheques Christy Kinahan's secret phone calls from Portlaoise prison also revealed valuable information about his drug dealing empire. In particular, calls he made between 1999 and 2000 provided vital intelligence for a joint Irish/Dutch police investigation, Operation Plover, between the Garda National Drug Unit and the Amsterdam Serious Crime Squad which began in September 1999. It was targeting the Dutch-based drug trafficking operation controlled by his partner in crime, John Cunningham, the Colonel. Over a fourteen-month period alone, it was estimated that the Cunningham/Kinahan syndicate had shipped drugs worth more than €150 million from Holland to Ireland, and a large number of firearms. Cunningham was later convicted of drug trafficking and supplying weapons.

When Gilligan read the Christmas article he had a rush of blood to the head. He rang an associate in Dublin that night with orders that my house was to be shot at. He specifically wanted someone to fire a shotgun blast through the front downstairs window of my home before Christmas Eve. He wanted it done late at night to prevent injuries. Gilligan told the accomplice that he just wanted to put the family in fear and ruin our Christmas. That would be his festive gift to me.

The reason I learned this was because the next morning the officers in charge of the detective branch in our local division called at my home. As I was living on their patch Detective Superintendent Denis Donegan and Detective Inspector Tom Mulligan had the unenviable job of keeping an eye on me. The uniformed and plainclothes gardaí in the G District were still regularly patrolling our street, day and night.

Donegan and Mulligan were highly respected, seasoned officers who had spent practically all of their careers investigating organized and serious crime. They had also become good friends of the family and were determined that we would not be intimidated.

That morning Crime and Security had alerted them to Gilligan's phone call and an investigation was launched to prevent the threat being carried out. The officers knew the identity of the individual he had been in touch with and was keeping them under surveillance. When I heard the story I wasn't particularly worried and reckoned that it was just Gilligan letting off steam – the majority of threats made by criminals are done so in moments of rage and never materialize. Gangsters are capricious creatures.

Donegan thought Gilligan was serious but their intelligence was that no one was prepared to carry out the attack. They knew the heat that it would bring down on them and they didn't want the unnecessary hassle, especially at Christmas. In fact the spooks had heard Gilligan's pal describing it as a ridiculous idea in a call to another associate. They were aware that there was a regular police presence in the area. It wasn't worth the risk of getting caught and spending ten years in prison on Gilligan's malicious whim.

Donegan and Mulligan intended to send people to inform the man on the phone that he had taken the smart choice although he would never know how they found out. Gilligan's pal later reported back that there were too many cops in the area to fulfil the drug dealer's festive wishes. Nevertheless, the officers weren't taking any chances. Over Christmas Eve and the following few days two armed detectives escorted us if we left the house and nightly patrols were increased. Thankfully nothing happened and we had a marvellous Christmas.

Gilligan's secret phone conversations were to cause him a lot of bother over the following year. As he used the phone to organize drug shipments between Spain and Ireland the police in both countries were able to bust several of his new gangland associates.

It also resulted in the seizure of cocaine with street values running into millions of euros which ultimately rendered the former godfather irrelevant and powerless. I published stories linking Gilligan to the drug seizures and the huge financial losses. After the string of seizures his hopes of maintaining a position of influence in gangland from his prison cell evaporated. He was incarcerated for another ten years.

The Gilligan threat was quickly forgotten, however, as 2003 got off to a violent, bloody and hectic start.

CHAPTER TWELVE

LIVING DANGEROUSLY

The gangland murder statistics provide the starkest indication of the transformation in organized crime. In 1993 there were three gangland killings in Ireland each of which I had covered with shock headlines about the rise of the hit men. A decade later, in 2003, the death toll reached an all-time high of twenty as society began to become inured to the violence. It was one of the most violent years in the history of organized crime and saw the emergence of new alliances and seminal events which further changed the face of gangland. That same year was to prove to be a pivotal one in my career which I hadn't seen coming. It was a year of living dangerously as the gangs plotted to bestow on me the distinction of becoming their twenty-first victim.

One of the first gangland murders to take place that year confirmed the growing power of the Kinahan gang. On 28 January former drug dealer and addict Raymond Salinger, who once sold heroin for Christy Kinahan Senior, was having a pint in his local pub, Farrell's, in the south inner city. Salinger had fled to London after the Dapper Don was busted in 1986 with the largest shipment of heroin yet seized by the Garda Drug Squad.

Kinahan always suspected that Salinger had tipped off the cops about his operation. But in early 2003, as Kinahan was well on the way to becoming one of Europe's biggest narcos, Salinger returned from London believing that he had been forgotten. But the Dapper Don bore a deep grudge against his erstwhile dealer. As Salinger enjoyed his pint a lone gunman, armed with an automatic pistol, walked in and shot him four times in the chest at close range.

Investigations of gangland murders tend to draw unwanted police scrutiny on gangs that have not yet popped up on their radar. The Salinger investigation uncovered evidence that the murder had been carried out by a new gang of young violent cut-throats under the leadership of Kinahan's son, Daniel. The inquiry also revealed that Daniel was now running the Irish end of his father's massive drug trafficking empire.

Released from prison in 2000 Kinahan Senior had become a major target of the police in Ireland, the UK and the Netherlands, a fact that featured many times in my stories as I tracked his progress. A year earlier in August 2002 I'd exposed him as the international drug trafficker behind a haul of cocaine, cannabis and firearms which had been seized in a major operation by the Garda National Drug Unit. The drugs were worth €24 million in today's value. But while it may have been a blow it did little to stop Kinahan's ascension to the top of the global league of scumbags.

The inquiry into the Salinger murder provided a picture of the awesome extent of the Kinahan operation which was estimated to be supplying hundreds of millions of euros of ecstasy, cannabis, cocaine and heroin to a large network of gangs across the country. The inquiry confirmed that the Kinahans were at the epicentre of Ireland's burgeoning drug trade. The Salinger murder was a reminder to their competitors that they weren't to be trifled with.

The core of the Kinahan cartel was made up of a large complex network of dangerous young hoods from both sides of the city – all of whom were destined to become household names for the wrong reasons. It included Crumlin brothers Liam and David Byrne, their notorious cousin 'Fat Freddie' Thompson and brother-in-law Thomas 'Bomber' Kavanagh. At the time the Thompson/Byrne alliance was immersed in a ferocious feud with their former partners and friends, led by Brian Rattigan. It became known as the Crumlin/Drimnagh feud which I had been covering from the start.

The bloody conflict was a paradigm for the new gangland. It ignited in 2001 when a once close group of young drug dealers fell out following a garda drug bust. The spark that ignited the inferno occurred when Brian Rattigan stabbed his former friend Declan Gavin to death. It was followed by scores of tit-for-tat shooting incidents, serious assaults, arson attacks, as well as grenade and bomb attacks. Sixteen lives were ultimately lost in the mindless savagery. Many more criminals and innocent people were injured and traumatized in the ensuing madness.

The Kinahan gang also included two of the Monk's nephews, Christy 'Bouncer' Hutch and his brother Gary, who controlled the group's drug rackets on the north side of the city. The Salinger investigation uncovered connections between Gerry Hutch and the Kinahans. In total gardaí identified over thirty hard core members of the Kinahan organization including a number of prolific killers for hire. Years later, the mismatched Kinahan/Hutch feud which claimed another eighteen lives exploded after Gary Hutch eventually fell out with Daniel Kinahan.

The day after the Salinger assassination another major gangland story broke which I was to become immersed in for another decade. This time a feud that had been simmering for over two years exploded engulfing the city of Limerick. It started on the night of 29 January 2003, when Kieran Keane, one of the leaders of the Keane/Collopy drug gang, was abducted, tortured and murdered in a spectacular double cross.

It led to one of the deadliest blood feuds in Irish gangland history. Over the space of a decade over twenty people were murdered and hundreds more, including civilians and children, were injured, maimed and traumatized. The gruesome savagery that followed was unprecedented, especially the fact that a quarter of the murder victims were completely innocent people who were deliberately targeted. The names of Baiba Saulite, Sean Poland, Brian Fitzgerald, Shane Geoghegan and Roy Collins were added to the death toll by the most dangerous gang Ireland has ever seen.

They were the McCarthy/Dundons, a family of settled Travellers led by psychotic brothers Wayne, John and Dessie Dundon who were the principle architects of the savagery that ensued. They were best described as brutal creatures devoid of any semblance of remorse, empathy or humanity: what FBI profiler Special Agent Bill Hagmaier called: 'Godless, predatory creatures who murder because they like it and because they can.'

The Dundons were a gangland serial killing machine who instilled terror in the city that they tried holding to ransom. They were purely evil on a scale that I never witnessed in all my time investigating criminals. I dubbed them Murder Inc., and later wrote a book of the same name. *Murder Inc.* chronicled fourteen years of savagery in the Treaty City, whose motto is 'A city well versed in the art of war', before the gang were finally smashed by the police. I spent a lot of time in Limerick covering the brutal gangland war.

We had been expecting a dramatic development after Eddie Ryan Junior and Kieran Ryan disappeared on 23 January 2003 and were believed to have been kidnapped. They were the sons of Eddie Ryan, a brutal thug who had once been a key member and enforcer for the Keane gang, the biggest drug supplier in the mid west. In keeping with the human dynamics of the underworld Ryan fell out with his former pals after setting up a rival narcotics operation. The row escalated in November 2000 when he tried to murder his former boss and friend, Christy Keane.

Two days later Christy's brother Kieran and Philip Collopy blasted Ryan to death as he sat in the Moose Bar in the heart of Keane territory, close to Limerick's Island Field. It sparked a tit-for-tat war which included forty shooting incidents, attempted murders, bomb attacks and stabbings over the next two years. Miraculously there were no fatalities. But it suddenly escalated when Ryan's sons vanished.

The city held its breath as everyone expected them to turn up dead in a ditch somewhere. I had very good sources in Limerick. Shortly after the Ryans vanished I learned that Kieran Keane had offered the McCarthy/Dundons €60,000 to abduct the brothers and have them killed. The gardaí were closely watching Keane and his associates in a bid to rescue the brothers. No one expected what happened next.

Keane had acted to prevent the brothers getting to him first. The Ryan boys were cut from the same cloth as their father and were determined to get revenge. It was the oldest rule in the gangland survival manual – kill or be killed. Keane's arrangement with the Dundons was that once they had the Ryans held captive he wanted to personally execute them both to ensure his difficulties were over.

The notoriously perfidious killer clan, however, had been waiting to make their stab for power and was involved in a complex double cross. Up to then the McCarthy/Dundons had been customers of the Keane mob and had remained ostensibly neutral. The Ryan brothers went into hiding and the Dundons informed Keane that they were holding them in a house on the edge of the city. Keane and Owen Treacy, his nephew, fell for the trap. After handing over the bounty the pair was suddenly overpowered at gunpoint by six members of Murder Inc. They were then tied up and tortured for over an hour.

The gang tried to force the uncle and nephew to lure other key members of the gang, brothers Brian and Philip Collopy, into the same trap but they refused to comply. Treacy would later tell gardaí that they knew their friends would be murdered if they made the call. The plan was to wipe out the leadership of the Keane/Collopy gang in one fell swoop. A similar plan was at the heart of the Hutch gang's infamous attack at the Regency Hotel thirteen years later. It was a gangland concept inspired by the infamous Valentine's Day Massacre in Chicago.

The captives were taken to Drombanna six kilometres from Limerick where they were stabbed several times. Kieran Keane was dispatched with a bullet to the back of the head, while Owen Treacy was left for dead. Although critically injured, Treacy survived and lived to testify against five members of the McCarthy/Dundon gang, including Dessie Dundon, who were subsequently convicted of murder and jailed for life.

A few hours after the murder the Ryan brothers presented themselves to gardaí in Portlaoise, Co. Laois. They claimed that they had been taken hostage and managed to escape. It quickly became obvious that it was a set up. The murder of Kieran Keane and the 'release' of the Ryan brothers was major news. But it was also a very bad development for the decent people of Limerick and the gardaí on the front line.

When I arrived in the city the following morning there was a palpable sense of fear around the place. Gardaí were on high alert for the conflagration that would surely follow. There was a real sense of crisis in the air which I had never experienced before having spent a lot of work time in Limerick over the years. The whole city felt like a powder keg. As I drove through the deserted streets that night I was again witnessing another chapter of gangland history in the making.

For the first time ever on the streets of an Irish city heavily armed members of the ERU in paramilitary gear were deployed alongside uniformed gardaí at checkpoints. A police helicopter could be heard hovering somewhere in the dark. Intermittently a blinding shaft of light glowed from the belly of the invisible aircraft, illuminating the streets below. Never before had the authorities felt compelled to display such high-profile firepower and force against organized crime.

The unprecedented scenes were a stark illustration that the underworld posed a much more sinister threat to society than ever before. Limerick in those days felt like a war zone.

Over twenty years later serious crime has become so endemic that the sight of heavily armed cops on the streets of our cities and towns has become the norm. In the following weeks, months and years I wrote countless stories about the unfolding mayhem in Limerick. Before 2003 was over another three men were shot dead as part of the feud but it was only warming up.

Other old enemies who had targeted me in the past reminded me
that they had not gone away. On 14 June 2003, twenty-five-year-
old doorman Ronnie Draper was shot dead as he worked at a pub
on Eden Quay in Dublin city centre. He became the eleventh
gangland victim of the year so far. Draper was gunned down by
the INLA who also murdered his friend Pat Neville in 2000.
The killings were in revenge for a ferocious showdown between
the INLA and a south Dublin criminal gang that took place on
Wednesday, 6 October 1999.

The extraordinary confrontation was sparked when an INLA
gang led by Declan 'Wacker' Duffy ambushed a group of six
criminals in a factory unit in the Ballymount Industrial Estate in
west Dublin. The young hoods had been sent by their boss, Brian
O'Keefe, to collect payment for damage done to a truck in a feud
with a brother of the factory owner. Duffy, from South Armagh,
had previously murdered a British army recruiting sergeant in the
UK. I hadn't forgotten how he and his thugs had threatened me
in 1996 outside the cinema in Tallaght, after I revealed that his
INLA mob had been working as enforcers for the Gilligan gang. It
was the kind of publicity that they didn't need. In the days before
Twitter/X they regularly demonized me in their propaganda leaflets
and issued statements denouncing as lies everything I wrote about
them. I took it as a compliment.

Duffy and his associates, who were armed, stripped the six
young hoods and then subjected them to sadistic torture. The
men were beaten with a variety of weapons, sliced up by Stanley
blades and had boiling water poured over their gaping wounds.

It was one of the most horrific and unusual gangland stories I
covered. The incident quickly spiralled into an all-out bloodbath
when friends of the criminals arrived to rescue them. The

confrontation involved twenty-four men who milled into each other with swords, knives, baseball bats and guns.

During the ensuing fracas INLA member Pat Campbell suffered severe injuries after a sword sliced him so badly that his legs were hanging off. He later died from his injuries. Seven men were left seriously injured including one who suffered an eye injury when one of the INLA men opened fire. When gardaí learned of the astonishing incident a major investigation was launched to unravel what had happened.

The gardaí assigned to the case knew of my history with Duffy and the INLA. I was tipped off about the incident as officers were investigating multiple crimes including murder, false imprisonment, possession of firearms, grievous bodily harm and attempted murder. On the following Sunday we exclusively revealed everything we knew about the showdown and dubbed it the Ballymount Bloodbath. It was a major story that captivated the public.

Over the following weeks I travelled to London to meet members of the criminal gang who had fled to escape the wrath of the INLA. With their backs to the wall they reckoned that the only way of getting their message out was through gangland's favourite newspaper. The guys I met were genuinely terrified that they and their families would be murdered in revenge for Campbell's death and the organization's humiliating defeat at the hands of a group of nondescript petty criminals. They wanted it known that they only went to the warehouse to save their pals and never dreamt of coming up against the INLA. 'We thought they were Travellers,' one of them said.

Writing about the Ballymount Bloodbath gave me an opportunity to expunge any remaining notion that the paramilitaries were in some way a patriotic republican movement. I revealed how they were immersed in organized crime, particularly drugs and extortion rackets. As a direct consequence of the bloodbath ten members of the INLA, including Duffy, were subsequently jailed. Duffy had handed himself up on a plate to the police – and provided me with a wonderful splash.

When Duffy was arrested detectives found a comprehensive handwritten report on the incident which he had prepared for his bosses in Belfast. He had to explain how a so-called volunteer had been killed. In it he confessed to organizing the incident and described in graphic detail the horrific torture they had inflicted on the victims. He laid out the roles played by each of his comrades. He said that he brought firearms so that he could shoot someone. The discovery of the document astonished the gardaí. It gave the investigators the full unvarnished, blow-by-blow account of the Ballymount Bloodbath. Never before had a hardened terrorist actually written his own confession without police involvement or encouragement. He had even signed the document.

When Duffy was confronted with the document by detectives he could only laugh and admit that he had done the cop's job for them. Having been tipped off about the document and its contents I took a modicum of pleasure sharing Duffy's humiliation with the readers of the *Sunday World*. We ran the story on the front page under the fitting headline 'Ireland's Dumbest Terrorist'. Following the publication of the stories gardaí again advised me to be careful and increased patrols around my home when they learned that the INLA wanted to even up the score. But I knew they were being swamped by the gardaí and left powerless as most of the leadership were rounded up.

In 2001 Duffy was sentenced to nine years for his role in the Ballymount Bloodbath. Even though his victims were too scared to testify, the weight of evidence, including the statement, left him with no option but to plead guilty. I thought that we had heard the last of Duffy after he was jailed.

Then in May 2003 I got a tip off that the Department of Justice had secretly granted Duffy temporary release on six occasions over the previous seventeen months. It was an astonishing revelation given that he was only a year into his sentence for a brutal crime when he was first let out. The source revealed that Duffy had been released on three occasions in January, June and November 2002 for a total of nine days. In 2003 he had been freed for a total of four days, from 11–14 February. On the 8 and 25 April he was allowed out on his own for another two days. I confirmed the information with a number of other sources.

On 18 May 2003 I broke the story and revealed that the terrorist had somehow conned the Government into believing that he was helping to organize the INLA's move into the peace process. The Government and the Department of Justice wanted their shabby dealings with a criminal gang kept secret and had ignored the advice of the gardaí who knew better. The story was hugely embarrassing for the Department and its voluble minister, Michael McDowell. But if the publicity didn't stop Duffy's free days then the murder of Ronnie Draper certainly did.

In a follow-up story on 22 June I revealed that gardaí suspected Duffy of organizing the hit while out on one of his peace process jollies. It also revealed how two of Duffy's 'comrades', Dublin brothers Troy and Arthur Jordan, were partners in crime of the Keane/Collopy gang in Limerick. Originally from Tallaght in west Dublin they had been members of the INLA, while at the same cutting their teeth as drug dealers working for John Gilligan. After Gilligan was busted the Jordan brothers moved to fill the void and became major narcos in their own right while still maintaining their close links to the INLA.

Following the murder of Kieran Keane, the Jordans helped procure guns and a number of car bombs from their INLA associates for use in the Limerick feud. Luckily detectives intercepted the arms before they could be used. Arthur Jordan's efforts to create murder and mayhem came to an abrupt end in early May 2003 when the motorbike he was driving crashed into a tree in dense fog in County Kildare. Jordan died instantly. At the time he was awaiting trial for possession of firearms.

Troy Jordan took serious umbrage when he read the article. Still gutted by the loss of his brother, in a surge of anger he decided to come to our home with the intention of attacking my wife. The recurring theme in the personalities of the gangsters who create so much misery is that they are terribly thin-skinned and sensitive when they are called out. He was in a rage when he phoned a friend to say he was on his way to my home. Luckily, the garda Crime and Security Branch were listening in on his phones and a major security operation was put in place involving the ERU and local armed detectives who raced to our home while we remained blissfully unaware.

The secret listeners gave their colleagues a minute-by-minute update as they tracked Jordan's progress from his home in Kildare to Walkinstown where I lived. A friend called him several times and urged him to calm down. The pal presciently warned Jordan that he was likely to run into the cops and end up behind bars. As the gardaí braced for action, Jordan stopped off at his friend's home in Clondalkin and cooled off. He later told his mates that he would not interfere with my family but was determined to come after me.

I knew nothing about the incident until the following day when senior gardaí Tom Mulligan and Denis Donegan again called to see me. They had been informed by Garda HQ that there was now a credible threat from Jordan and the INLA. But in the days that followed the situation got a lot more complicated.

———

CHAPTER THIRTEEN

DANGER LOOMS

Around the same time that Troy Jordan was flexing his muscles I also came into the sights of another old foe, Martin 'the Viper' Foley, who happened to be closely connected to the Jordans and the INLA. For over fifteen years the Viper had harboured a grievance against me over the ongoing publicity I gave him in the *Sunday World*. Foley was a cowardly thug who liked to bully people and was also very thin skinned. Foley and his friend Seamus 'Shavo' Hogan had been behind plots to attack me in the past to intimidate me into silence.

It was difficult to avoid Foley when writing about Irish crime. He had a lot more enemies than the *Sunday World*. One of the reasons that I had given him so much coverage was that Foley had a knack of crossing swords with some very dangerous people. The Viper had an extraordinary capacity for irritating people and having lucky escapes, like in 1984 when he was rescued by gardaí after an IRA unit kidnapped him. Foley also fell out with Martin Cahill who suspected him of being a police informant and dangerously disloyal.

Apart from being malicious liars and masters of dissemblance, criminals are notorious gossips and scandalmongers. In the Dublin underworld Foley is considered to be one of the worst. 'An auld woman with a moustache – and an ugly auld woman at that,' was how one villain described him to me.

Incredibly by 2003 the Viper had survived no less than three assassination attempts at the hands of well-armed, professional hit men – in 1995, 1996 and 2000. In 2008 he survived a fourth attack in which he was again shot and seriously injured. No other Irish criminal had ever been shot so many times. Foley's name was engraved on every one of the forty bullets fired in his direction. The fit and physically strong veteran villain was wounded at least fourteen times. He lost the top of one of his fingers, a bullet was lodged in his chest and he lost his spleen.

The first attack was orchestrated by Brian O'Keefe of the Ballymount Bloodbath fame in a row over a lover. The second, in 1996, was carried out by Gilligan's henchmen, Brian Meehan and Paul Ward. Foley and Shavo Hogan were customers of the gang. But they had been putting pressure on John Traynor, the Coach, for money they claimed they were owed from the time of the General's gang. Foley crossed the line when he escalated the row with the Gilligan gang by spreading false rumours that they were selling heroin wholesale which drew unwanted attention from the IRA. The third incident in September 2000 was ordered by Christy Kinahan whose associates were also suspected of being behind the 2008 attack.

Foley, Hogan and another associate, Clive Bolger, had moved into wholesale drug trafficking after gardaí smashed John Gilligan's operation. Their main supplier was Chris Casserly who was a senior partner of John Cunningham and Kinahan. From Dublin's northside Casserly, who had no criminal convictions, was one of the new breed of major dealers who had emerged since the late 1990s. Their associations came to light during Operation Plover. (See Chapter 11.)

Before the police moved to nab Cunningham the investigation resulted in a string of large drug seizures in Ireland, Belgium and Holland. When Foley and Hogan lost a shipment and a consignment of cash they fell out with Casserly and threatened to have him shot.

The Salinger murder had shown that Kinahan had plenty of young gun men at his disposal to try to sort out the Viper. In the summer of 2001 they had more success when Shavo Hogan was shot dead at a club in Crumlin. The murder took place on a Saturday evening while I was on holiday with the family in Spain. I got a call from Dublin about the shooting ten minutes after it happened and filed the story for the following day's front page from our apartment. I couldn't ignore it given my knowledge of Hogan and his associates. Crime stories regularly interrupted our holidays over the years.

A month before Shavo was whacked Foley had been arrested by the ERU and a firearm was recovered. At the time he was in the midst of a bitter feud with Clive Bolger. The intense bromance that once characterized their relationship had turned to pure hate where they were trying to kill each other. It later emerged that the gun had been planted in Foley's car by an associate of Bolger's. The CAB was also on the Viper's case and had sent him an initial €200,000 tax demand. One Saturday morning in the newsroom I took a notion, and my life in my hands, by approaching him for an interview. When I phoned him the veteran villain went berserk and ranted:

> Are you fuckin' trying to get it up for me lookin' for a fuckin'
>
> interview after ten years writing about me? Meet me on your own
>
> in Bushy Park and I'll give you an interview that you'll never forget.

The 'interview' he referred to was the kind that probably would
have necessitated me being fed through a straw in a hospital bed
for the next six months. His angry tirade continued:

> I don't give two fucks what you print. If you say I am the
>
> Rathmines rapist or a child molester I don't give a fuck. You seem
>
> to enjoy upsetting me family. I'll call up to your house and then
>
> I'll give you a fuckin' interview. I know where you live. How'd you
>
> like that? Are you afraid of me? It'll be a long time before I lie
>
> down for the likes of you or any other fucker. I will keep getting
>
> back up.

I told Foley that I wasn't afraid of him and I was aware that he
knew where I lived. I told him he had been seen there skulking
around in the dark plenty of times. I put it to him that he had
plotted several times to attack me or my home. Of course he
denied this. I was more interested in getting an interview. I waited
patiently and gave as good as I got as it took the gangster about
half an hour to calm down. Foley didn't think that I would stand
up to him the way I did. I said I wanted to hear his side of the
story and we agreed to a truce of sorts. I got a laugh when I
suggested that we bury the hatchet metaphorically so to speak,
and not in each other! He invited me to his home in Crumlin
for a sit down and I agreed. I assured the Viper that I would be
alone. My news editor John Donlon thought I was mad.

When I arrived at his door Foley was cordial and the red mist
had cleared. Over cups of tea he seemed anxious to get across his

version of reality. He wouldn't talk about who had been responsible for the attempts on his life and wanted to make it clear he had no problems with the IRA. 'I have never accused them of anything. I have no problem with them,' he said.

Foley also went to pains to claim that he didn't owe the CAB any money, asking: 'Where are my criminal assets? Up me fuckin' arse is where. Just look around my house this is not the home of a wealthy drug baron.'

But when pressed Martin Foley will not confirm or deny that he is a drug dealer. He said in reference to a story I had printed about him:

> It was written that I was involved in an eight million pound drug seizure in France some years ago; well that's just not true. In the early 1980s everyone was naive about drug dealing and no one knew just how much devastation it would bring. I won't start denying being involved in drugs because the more you deny it the more people believe that you are involved. Fuck them – they can think what they like. I've told my side of things.

Foley was particularly annoyed with his nickname, the Viper, which he blamed me and Gilligan's sidekick and former Cahill gang member, John Traynor, for inventing. But I explained that the nickname had come from Martin Cahill himself in an interview several years earlier because he believed Foley was an informant. Foley had been a key member of the Cahill gang for several years and gave me his version of the story:

> I walked away from Martin Cahill in 1991 because Martin went off the rails. It had nothing to do with money or informing. But the reason me and Martin Cahill parted friendship I will carry

that secret to the grave. I don't want to dig up old sores. I walked

away from Martin Cahill because I wasn't happy with something

that he done and somebody else went and got involved. Despite

what has been claimed Martin never accused me of being a tout,

an informant, a rat, a grass or whatever you want to call it.

We parted on good terms and I had just bagged an illuminating scoop. We ran the story on the front page under the headline: 'Viper Talks – Gangster Martin Foley speaks out for the first time to Paul Williams'. The truce, however, didn't last long.

Foley was involved in so many criminal incidents and rows that it was hard not to write about him. He stopped taking my calls. One of the reasons why he got agitated about me in 2003 was that I was in the process of writing my fifth book, *Crime Lords*. It was a contemporaneous exposé of organized crime as it then stood. The book told the inside stories of the INLA, the Limerick feud, the Cunningham and Kinahan syndicate and the Westies. I was also researching a long chapter about the life and crimes of the Viper which he got to hear about. It was to include details of Foley's drug activities and the real reasons why he had been shot so many times, which was something he was always coy about. He also held a grievance over the fact that the *Sunday World* had run a report and pictures of his wife Pauline's funeral which took place in January 2003.

Around the same time as the threat from Troy Jordan I had been tipped off about an attempt by Foley and his associates to nobble a jury to get a long-time friend off a major criminal charge. Sean Fitzgerald, a fifty-seven-year-old veteran con man known as the Fixer, had been on trial for burning out a stolen car. The case was an embarrassing climb down for the duplicitous fraudster who saw himself as a gangland sophisticate and cleverer than the rest of the rabble he looked down on. A long-time associate of the Viper, Fitzgerald was also the best friend of Foley's enemy John 'the Coach' Traynor. The pattern of relationships between criminals is complex and fluid to say the least.

Fitzgerald was involved in the stolen car racket with another criminal called Jason Black. Detectives from Crumlin had set up a camera to secretly record the comings and goings at a lock up the villains were using. The pair had been videotaped moving the car before it was set alight. They had been caught bang to rights.

The jury bribery attempt was hatched in the Submarine pub in Crumlin on the evening of 4 June 2003 between Martin Foley, Fitzgerald and another criminal associate, forty-five-year-old former soldier Jimmy Walsh from Rathfarnham, south Dublin. The two-week trial in the Circuit Criminal Court had just ended that evening and the jury were sent to spend the night in a hotel. At the time juries were sequestered under guard in hotels while deliberating on cases to prevent anyone influencing their decisions. Fitzgerald was terrified of being sent to prison. Nobbling the jury was a last-ditch bid to scupper the trial.

Senior gardaí were so concerned that the Fixer and his mob would try to intimidate the jury that they arranged extra security around the courtroom to protect them. On the first day of the trial they informed the presiding judge that Jimmy Walsh had been spotted writing down details of the jurors as they were being selected. On a separate occasion a bench warrant was issued for another associate, Stephen Costello, who was twice observed purposely standing beside the door of the bus used to ferry jurors to and from their lunch. Costello claimed he was only taking a call and Walsh said he was merely noting the breakdown between male and female jurors. In the latter stages of the trial, gardaí observed the Viper watching the court building while hiding in the back seat of a car.

From studying the jury list and watching them in court Walsh recognized the chairman of the jury and realized that he had been in the army with his brother, Thomas McGrew. The villains decided that they had nothing to lose by contacting McGrew.

Walsh phoned his old army buddy and came straight to the point, asking: 'How much would it cost to return a not guilty verdict?' McGrew, who left the army to become a prison officer was outraged and bluntly told Walsh to 'fuck off'.

Thomas McGrew didn't know that his brother was on jury duty and didn't make contact with him. He immediately reported the phone call to Detective Sergeant Joe O'Hara, one of the lead detectives involved in the case, along with another garda legend, Kevin 'Bridie' Dolan who first cut his teeth as a member of the Tango Squad. Walsh had seriously underestimated Thomas McGrew who was prepared to give the gardaí a full statement and wasn't afraid to testify in court. The mob had made a fatal mistake.

The following morning the jury who were unaware of the contacts made by Walsh, returned guilty verdicts against Fitzgerald and Black for which they later received sentences of five years.

A source later showed me CCTV footage from the pub which was recorded around the same time as the bribery call was made. It showed Foley, Fitzgerald and Walsh deep in conversation. The footage showed Walsh making the call to McGrew, while standing next to the Viper. Walsh was subsequently charged with the bribery attempt. He was convicted by another jury after a trial in 2005 where his former army comrade testified. Before sentencing Walsh to five years Judge Donagh McDonagh described it as an 'attack on one of the fundamental pillars of the Irish criminal justice system'. Attempting to bribe a jury is a very serious offence which undermines the rule of law. It is one of the reasons why major gangland trials are now heard before three judges in the non-jury Special Criminal Court.

That same week I published the images of the villains plotting together on the front page. It was a major story, particularly given the cast of dubious organized crime veterans involved. The fact that the plot failed was just icing on the cake. When I began looking into the background to the case I spoke to Thomas McGrew who showed no fear of the thugs involved. I decided to contact Jimmy Walsh to get his side of the story before going to print.

On Tuesday, 17 June 2003 I called to his home and spoke with his son. I left my name and phone number. On Friday 20 June I got a call from a man purporting to be Walsh. He wanted to know what I was after. I explained that it had to do with the Fitzgerald case and the fact that the gardaí brought the incident to the attention of the trial judge. The voice on the other end claimed it was just a big mistake and that the cops had gotten it wrong. I said I would like to interview him and he said he would come back to me.

A week later, on Tuesday 24 June, the day after gardaí alerted me to the threats from Jordan and the INLA, I got a call on my mobile from a withheld number. It was from the same man. This time he was threatening and abusive, although there was nothing new or particularly shocking about that. I often got threatening calls which I ignored. The male voice asked: 'What happened ya prick ya, why was there no information in the *Sunday World* about me, ya gobshite?' Then he hung up.

The following day I got another call. It was the eve of the seventh anniversary of Veronica Guerin's death which was obviously on the villain's mind. The voice snarled:

> If you write anything about me in the *Sunday World* you will be
> joining Veronica Guerin, I mean that. I said if you write anything
> about me in that paper, you will be meeting Veronica Guerin
> head to head, and I mean that you fuck.

This time I took the threats more seriously than before because I knew the people involved and their connections. The fact that it was coming so quickly on the back of the other threats was a bit overwhelming. I reported it to Detective Sergeant O'Hara who happened to be one of the local officers looking after us and was also investigating the attempt to nobble the jury.

That afternoon O'Hara invited Jimmy Walsh to Crumlin garda station to quiz him about the phone calls and the jury episode, all of which he denied. Walsh then left, as he was not under arrest.

Minutes after Walsh left the station I got another call. This time the voice said: 'I have just been pulled in by your fuckin' mate Joe O'Hara and I am tellin' ya you won't be walking very much longer you cunt... you won't be walking for long, ya fuckin' cunt.' The phone went dead before I had time to respond.

Some days later Walsh rang me and denied that he had been threatening me on the phone. His voice appeared to have changed somewhat. How did someone else know I called to his home and left my number with a message to call me, I asked him? I suspected that he had been disguising his voice in the previous calls. He later complained to gardaí that I had threatened him.

Walsh was subsequently charged with making the threats to kill but was eventually acquitted following three jury trials before the Circuit Criminal Court. It later emerged that the suspected mystery caller was an associate of Walsh. A senior garda gave evidence that he was talking to Walsh at the same time as one of the calls was being made. Phone evidence backed him up. The officer, who was above reproach, had received the call from Walsh who he knew. However the same phone evidence showed that Walsh's official phone was in close proximity to the phone used to make the threatening calls. It also showed that the phone had attempted several times to gain access to my message minder.

The main concern for me at the time was that there were three distinct groups on my case – the INLA, Jordan and Foley's mob. It was all getting a bit uncomfortable. At a meeting with Colm MacGinty and senior editorial staff we decided that the only course of action open to us at that stage was to publicize the threats on the front page in a bid to scare off the thugs and let them know that they had been rumbled. Through the years we rarely if ever highlighted threats unless it was absolutely necessary. The gardaí told us that they were very concerned about the threats being made. They agreed that a story highlighting the threats and emphasizing that my family were now under armed guard might calm the situation down and scare off the thugs.

On 29 June 2003 the front page headline bluntly declared: 'Gang Plot To Shoot Williams'. Written by the then deputy editor Neil Leslie the story revealed that gardaí had uncovered the plot and identified Declan Duffy, Foley and mentioned a 'major cocaine dealer', which was a reference to Jordan. The story was also picked up by other newspapers which got the message home.

The following week a garda phone tap overheard Foley talking to a reporter from a newspaper outside the INM group in which Foley was being encouraged to stage a protest outside my home which would then be publicized. While it may have made for a story such an act of overt intimidation was a very worrying development, especially because my home was where my family lived and they had nothing to do with my work.

The fact that another journalist was involved in choreographing the event was sickening. However, the gardaí were determined that Foley's publicity stunt was not going to happen. Detective Inspector Tom Mulligan, who was closely monitoring the situation, gave orders that Foley was to be arrested as soon as he turned up. If the reporter turned up with him he was to be arrested as well. I wasn't told about the development until some days later. The following week in a newspaper interview Foley denied knowledge of any threats to me, stating that he was planning to place a picket at my home to protest against the 'constant barrage of stories'. But the Viper backed off from the idea – he was smarter than that.

The escalation of tensions could not have come at a worse time for the mob. Two days later the world premiere of Joel Schumacher's movie *Veronica Guerin,* staring Cate Blanchett, Ciarán Hinds, Brenda Fricker and Colin Farrell, took place in Dublin. I remember it as a glittering occasion and my wife and I had a wonderful night meeting all the stars. The publicity around the movie refocused attention on gangland.

At a press conference before the premiere Cate Blanchett referred to the recent threats on my life and said that it was worrying to think that despite the backlash in the wake of the Guerin murder, Irish criminals still felt that they could intimidate journalists. It further convinced the mobs that their campaign was bad for business.

While I was researching *Crime Lords* a source had come out of the woodwork with information about Chris Casserly, Foley's now sworn enemy. Casserly had fled the country in March 2000 after the arrest and imprisonment of John Cunningham in Amsterdam. At the same time in Dublin Casserly's entire operation was shut down with the arrest and subsequent convictions of several of his associates. In the process millions of euros worth of drugs and a large number of weapons were seized. Gardaí wanted to question him in relation to the bust.

The informant revealed that the gangster was back bigger than ever and working with Christy Kinahan. Independent reliable sources confirmed that the information was correct. Casserly had been involved with Kinahan in the €24 million shipment of cocaine and hash that had been seized by gardaí in August 2002. An associate of his told us that Casserly was operating from a luxury home in the south of Spain but we didn't know where. Three years later the source finally found out where Casserly was living. I had him secretly photographed in Sitges, just outside Barcelona, and ran it on the front page.

On 20 August 2003 I ran a two-page investigation which named Casserly for the first time. It also revealed his involvement in the drug trade and his elevated position in the narco hierarchy alongside Kinahan. I also revealed the background to his row with the Viper and why Kinahan had Foley shot. The story led to a very bizarre visit from the gardaí.

The National Bureau of Criminal Investigation (NBCI) is the garda equivalent of the FBI and is responsible for the investigation of major and serious crime on a national level. Two senior officers requested to meet me in the company of Detective Superintendent Donegan as the head of the detectives in the Southern Division.

They had a very strange story to relate. They said that their intelligence sources had revealed that another criminal grouping was hatching a rather exotic plot.

Apparently this unnamed group, which I later discovered included elements of the Kinahan cartel and Martin 'Marlo' Hyland's mob, was considering setting up a bogus organization which was going to invite me to attend a crime conference of some sort in Eastern Europe. They planned to print a glossy brochure about the event and offer me a large fee to attend as a speaker. When I got there I was to disappear.

The officers suggested that the plotters had contacted Christy Kinahan for advice and that he was the one who had come up with the elaborate ruse. In fairness over two decades later I still believe that because the Dapper Don was the only gangster with the sophistication to come up with such an imaginative idea. The NBCI officers emphasized that while this idea was only being discussed by the mob it underlined that I was pissing off a lot more people than anyone had thought.

The detectives claimed that they didn't as yet know the identities of the group which I found hard to believe. Gardaí are not obliged to inform a person about the identity of a threat although I was usually informally told by friendly sources. They left after instructing that as soon as anyone approached me with an invite to another country I was to call them immediately. I was never invited to any conference. Either it had just been gangsters venting hot air, the gardaí had intervened – which they often did without my knowledge – or the gang had decided I wasn't worth the hassle.

Sometime later the same NBCI officers contacted me again. This time the information they came to impart was more sinister.

They told me that the same plotters had another idea. This time I was to receive a call from an unidentified source offering me 'rock solid' inside information on a gangland story. Over time the same source would gain my trust by supplying strong tips that stood up. Then, when my guard was down, they would arrange to meet face to face at a location where I would be shot.

The senior detectives didn't offer any further information only to say that they were taking the information seriously and would keep me abreast of any developments. They suggested that I exercise extreme caution when dealing with sources which I already did as a matter of course. Whenever I met with dodgy sources it was always in a public location of my choosing. At the time I remember wondering how I was expected to work in such circumstances. It was a surreal situation.

I listened to the security advice from the police. Over the years I became something of an expert in the area of personal protection. To such an extent that I have often been asked for advice by people in similar predicaments. It requires maintaining a healthy degree of paranoia and always being coiled to expect the unexpected. As the old saying goes – just because you are paranoid doesn't mean they are not out to get you! Looking back now it was a state of permanent stress. To think that someone out there wants to harm you or your family is rather daunting and sobering. There were times when I was scared but I couldn't show it. I particularly didn't want my wife and kids to know how I felt.

Our home was well protected by CCTV cameras, bullet-proof glass and panic alarms installed by the company following the events of 1996. The alarms were monitored by a security company which was directly connected to the Garda Command and Control centre in Dublin where we were officially classified as being a 'very high risk priority'. I sometimes wore a bullet-proof vest and friends with a particular skillset gave me a short course in the art of evasive driving and self defense. Basically, they trained me how to get away from an ambush in my car or to fight my way out of a hostile situation.

At the time, watching for suspicious followers, especially motorbikes, was second nature. At traffic lights I automatically left a car length between me and the car in front in case I had to make a sudden getaway. As I waited for the lights to change my eyes remained fixed in the mirrors. I also learned a number of counter-surveillance techniques in case I was being followed that have stood me well on occasions.

Wherever I went out for dinner with the family or met friends for drinks, I instinctively and discreetly scanned the place for potential problems. I always had an eye on who was coming through the door. The first rule of self defense is to be fully aware of the environment you are in. The staff in the *Sunday World*'s local pub, Brady's in Terenure, even became part of our security blanket. The barmen would keep an eye out for suspicious strangers or known villains coming into the pub. On occasions over the years when they had concerns they would immediately call me or the local gardaí.

The taxi company I used, Orchard Cabs in Rathfarnham, added another layer to the security precautions. The company was owned by a friend and former detective, John Maunsel, who employed very trustworthy drivers, most of whom were also ex-cops. When I booked a cab the standing procedure was that the dispatcher assigned the job to a trusted driver. It was done over the phone rather than the radio to prevent others hearing the message. Writing about it at this far remove in time really makes it sound like a rather crazy way to live.

The public tend to be unaware of the fact that unlike any other area of civilian employment, risks to personal safety are an occupational hazard for crime journalists everywhere. And as global organized crime has become more powerful the risks have grown exponentially. In the recent past scores of crime journalists have been murdered around the world for doing their jobs, particularly in Central and South America. Journalists have also been murdered in Europe. At least four other crime journalists in Irish newspapers have received serious threats from gangsters over the years. As part of their obligations to staff it is now standard practice for media companies to pay for the installation of security systems in the homes of crime reporters.

———

Back in 2003 the queue of enemies and threats coming from all directions was bad enough but then the situation was suddenly exacerbated by, of all people in the land, the Minister for Justice of the day, Michael McDowell. A founding member of the Progressive Democrats (PDs), McDowell was an accomplished senior counsel and former attorney general. Following the 2002 general election the PDs entered coalition to form a government with Fianna Fáil and McDowell was appointed to the ministry that he had always wanted. In the run up to that election the party had asked me to run as a candidate for them in Dublin. I respectfully declined the offer on the grounds that politics terrified me and I wasn't suited to it. I turned down a similar offer from Fine Gael five years later.

The controversial politician, whose combative outbursts tended to get him in hot water, characteristically barged in with a sledgehammer to reform the gardaí. He was soon in conflict with the crime reporters. The row began when he decided to include a section in the 2005 Garda Síochána Act making it a criminal offence for a garda to share information of any kind with anyone outside the force, including journalists.

The draconian move was attributed to an incident when a family member was assaulted near McDowell's home in Ranelagh, south Dublin, in 2003. The story was broken by *The Star's* crime editor, Mick O'Toole, a distinguished journalist and author, and the article was sympathetic, showing that not even the justice minister's family was immune from crime. Mick had also penned a previous exclusive about the erection of a security wall around McDowell's home which the minister had complained about to Gavin O'Reilly, the then CEO of INM as *The Star* was half-owned by the company, with a view to having the story spiked.

O'Reilly dutifully contacted the editor of the paper, Ger Colleran, to enquire about the story and relate McDowell's discomfiture. Colleran was a hard-bitten, no bullshit Kerry man who believed in the principle of print and be damned – as long as it was legally safe to do so. He assured O'Reilly that the story was watertight so they published it. When the paper then contacted McDowell about the assault he again phoned O'Reilly to complain. Colleran and O'Toole stood over their story and the right to print it. O'Reilly didn't try to prevent the publication of that story either.

But the minister hadn't finished. He kicked up such a stink that an internal garda inquiry was initiated to identify the source of O'Toole's story. In June 2003 senior gardaí interviewed Mick and sought to access his phone records which amounted to an appalling assault on the freedom of the press. They probably secretly accessed records anyway without the journalist's knowledge which, by 2024, is done routinely by a number of Government agencies but particularly by Garda HQ and the Garda Síochána Ombudsman Commission (GSOC). In 2024 it emerged that GSOC had secretly accessed Mick O'Toole's phone records and those of other journalists even though none of the journalists had been implicated in any crimes. McDowell can take a fair share of the blame for that. But for some strange reason the mainstream media seems to have capitulated and done little to highlight this egregious breach of the principle of a free press in a democracy.

Around the same time that *The Star* was under pressure a source gave me a copy of an internal garda report which revealed how McDowell, in a fit of anger after the assault story appeared, told an officer on duty outside his house to 'hop it' from his premises. It was a great story.

As *The Star* guys had put their necks on the block I reckoned that it would be only fair if they broke the story. I handed the document to Colleran over a pint. He passed it on to Mick O'Toole without telling him where it came from and the paper had another great scoop. Unsurprisingly it irked the combative minister even more. But this time there was no way that anyone would ever find the source of that particular leak. McDowell later denied being rude to the garda but in a front page editorial *The Star* asked its readers whether they believed the cop or the minister.

In May I had been a guest on RTÉ's *Questions and Answers* programme with McDowell. During the debate I criticized the Government for failing to implement an election promise to recruit 2,000 more cops. There had also been cutbacks in garda resources at a time when gangland murders were increasing at a dramatic rate. Although these were facts McDowell dismissed me as a 'tabloid journalist' suggesting that what I was saying was untrue or exaggerated. After that the *Sunday World* editor decided that we would not hold back in our criticisms of the minister. Ger Colleran in *The Star* made the same decision. The tabloids were fighting back against the elite.

At the same time as his spat with *The Star* I ran a story about the spike in crime rates in McDowell's south Dublin constituency. The figures were compiled by a local neighbourhood watch group and showed a big rise in muggings, assaults and robberies, including the one where his son had been attacked. The crime wave was newsworthy in light of the fact that there were extra police patrols in the area since McDowell had become justice minister.

On Saturday evening, 14 June, the first editions of the paper hit the streets with the story splashed across two pages. That evening I was one of the guests at a barbeque in Gavin O'Reilly's home in Killiney, south County Dublin, along with other senior editorial INM staff. It was a yearly event to mark the end of the group's AGM. Gavin approached Colm MacGinty and me to say that he had just taken a call from a very irate justice minister.

He told us that McDowell was concerned the *Sunday World* and *The Star* had a vendetta against him. O'Reilly merely wanted us to know about the call and, while he didn't suggest that we lay off, the subtext was that perhaps we might go a little easier on McDowell in future. To my utter surprise the minister publicly apologized for his comments to me on 18 July when he addressed the 700 guests attending the retirement function for the outgoing Garda Commissioner Pat Byrne. It was a magnanimous gesture. But then the minister went on the attack again.

In August Diarmuid Doyle, a columnist with the now defunct *Sunday Tribune*, wrote an extraordinarily venomous opinion piece in which he baldly declared: 'I can name five journalists who pay gardaí for stories.'

The allegation was completely baseless and without a shred of evidence which was clearly intended to demonize a small cohort of journalists, including myself. It was one of a number of comment pieces by Doyle in which he made no secret of how much he detested crime reporters. I remember being taken aback at the level of hostility from a fellow hack who I had never met or spoken to. It caused more upset than any amount of underworld intimidation.

In the midst of an already very tense situation Doyle, for reasons known only to himself and his editor at the time, was opening a new war front in our own backyard. The truth was that if a garda ever asked for money, which never happened in my career, I would run a mile because such an individual could simply not be trusted. A crooked cop is lower than the worst criminal. I would have more time for the Viper than for an officer of the law offering himself to the highest bidder.

The fact that the loss-making *Sunday Tribune* was part of INM and depended on the profits from the likes of the *Sunday World* and *Sunday Independent* for its survival simply beggared belief. Doyle had seriously libelled a clearly identifiable group of about seven crime journalists, in print and broadcast, whom he effectively derided as being criminals themselves.

Michael McDowell immediately seized on Doyle's unfounded claims to justify putting manners on the cops and the reporters. As an eminent senior counsel McDowell was all too aware of the importance of actual evidence when making an accusation. He repeated the slur as a fact in a number of subsequent media interviews. The claims caused intense anger amongst INM editors who saw it as a flagrant attack on the integrity and reputation of their newspapers. If crime journalists were bribing cops or indeed anyone else, the money would have to be sanctioned by their bosses.

But despite legal advice that we each had a *prima facie* case to sue Doyle and the *Sunday Tribune* no one wanted to take legal action against one of our own newspapers. However, *Sunday World* lawyer Gerry Fanning insisted on writing a letter to the paper outlining how they had seriously libelled me. Anything further would have been hugely costly for a foundering newspaper which was already haemorrhaging money. There was also a fear that the INM board might use the controversy as an excuse to finally put the *Sunday Tribune* out of its misery and shut it down. No one wanted that on their conscience.

In a subsequent column Doyle was forced to row back on his comments using legalistic prose which suggested it had actually been written by lawyers. Doyle wrote:

> For the record, I did not claim two weeks ago, nor do I now,
> that security correspondents on any Irish paper or in any Irish
> broadcasting organization pay or have paid for stories… I repeat,
> I never claimed, suggested, implied or believed that any of our
> security correspondents are involved in cash-for-stories scandals.

But by then the damage had already been done. The commentary from Doyle and the Justice Minister had not been lost on my enemies. The gangsters saw it as an opportunity to undermine my reputation in the eyes of the public.

Criminals always want to drag their adversaries down to their own level, particularly those who can do the most harm to them – cops and the media. Dealing with criminals is a dirty business. I always had a strict unwritten rule when chronicling the activities of organized crime – never, ever sink to their level. If you do then you become fair game. There always needs to be a high moral wall between the sides.

Michael McDowell and Doyle's words weren't lost on Foley either. He was reported to have told a detective: 'Williams is a criminal just like the rest of us.' The gardaí then received more confidential information that he and his associates were planning to 'teach Paul Williams a lesson' as a result of the unwarranted police attention brought on them by the articles.

CHAPTER FOURTEEN

THE BOMB SCARE

An uneasy calm resumed when the storm of controversy and recriminations had passed. But ultimately it proved to be the calm before an even bigger storm. In the meantime I finished writing *Crime Lords*. It was a hard-hitting exposé of the major players in gangland and it was about to upset quite a few of them, all at the same time. I didn't have long to wait to find out who was most offended.

On 26 October 2003 the *Sunday World* published exclusive extracts from *Crime Lords* in a special twelve-page supplement. Four pages of the supplement were dedicated to the Viper. He decided to take affirmative action and sent his young gang of cut-throats out to do his dirty work. Three days later in the early hours of 29 October one of Foley's thugs poured acid over my car. The CCTV footage showed that it had taken less than three seconds before the attacker ran off into the night.

It was discovered by a milkman around 3 a.m. He heard the acid sizzling as it melted the paint across the car roof and the boot. The damage had been extensive. The milkman alerted a passing garda patrol who then woke me up to tell me about the incident.

The car was sealed off as a crime scene. Everyone knew straight away who had been involved. It was a startling escalation. The following day the car was taken for forensic analysis and then on to the garage to be repaired. At least the incident showed that Foley was not intent on causing me any physical harm but had opted instead to cause as much harassment as possible. For the next few nights local armed cops were on duty outside our home to prevent a recurrence.

Two days later, shortly after midnight on the morning of 31 October, one of Foley's associates placed a hoax call to Dublin Fire Brigade. The Viper always used other idiots to do his dirty work for him so that he was a safe distance away from a charge sheet. The caller said that there was a fire at my home and smoke was billowing out of the attic – although they said the address was number 34 which did not exist. At the time we were at number 35.

The intention was to cause me more annoyance. Two fire tenders were dispatched on the bogus call in the busiest period of the year for the fire service. Martin Foley didn't care if someone lost their life because the fire brigade could not respond in time to a genuine emergency. The fire tenders were met by the gardaí on duty outside the house and it was quickly assessed as a hoax. We heard about it the following morning.

Two days later the protection was downgraded to half-hourly passing attention. I trusted that the police knew what they were doing.

The day following the acid attack, senior gardaí invited *Sunday World* managing director Michael Brophy to a meeting in Crumlin station to discuss what was happening. Chief Superintendent Eddie Rock told Brophy that the gardaí had serious concerns for my safety. They explained that the concerns were based on intelligence reports which had been coming to them for months from diverse sources. They said that I was writing about 'very dangerous people' and that the coverage was 'driving them mad'. They gave Brophy the clear impression that the Viper was not the only gangster on the case. The officer wondered if I could be convinced to pull back. He said he would have armed officers watching the house at night but could not say for how long. The problem was that garda resources had been cut by the Department of Justice.

Michael Brophy approved a major upgrade of the security system at the house after an audit by a garda crime prevention officer. The CCTV footage of the incident was too grainy to help identify the perpetrator. Brophy was also considering hiring private security guards to maintain a twenty-four-hour presence. He offered me the alternative of moving out of our home to rented accommodation at the company's expense as well but after consulting my wife I turned down the proposal. I didn't want to inflict that inconvenience on my family and anyway, as strange as it sounds, we were probably safer at home.

I also talked the situation over with Michael and Colm. We agreed that there was no point in me suddenly pulling back and starting to write about politics. If you did that then you were giving in to the bully boys and showing that intimidation worked. I wasn't prepared to do that. What about the memory of our two colleagues who were murdered? Capitulation by the biggest selling newspaper in the country, with a reputation for hard-hitting journalism, would embolden the thugs to think they could go after any reporter who upset them. I have always believed that the media has a responsibility to highlight those who try to undermine civil society. Like the police, we were an occupational nuisance to the criminals. The likes of the Monk reckoned so and that was why he never made threats. In fact I would find out much later that his associates had actually tipped off the gardaí about other threats. Also I knew that if I did pull back as the gardaí advised there was no guarantee it would stop the harassment. Gangsters have long memories and an acute sense for detecting weakness in an enemy.

People have often asked how I could be so irresponsible with my family's safety and what did my wife Anne think about it. The answer was that she wholeheartedly supported me because she already knew what it was like when powerful forces tried to silence the messenger. Anne was a multi-award-winning journalist in her own right before she opted to be a homemaker. She was one of the first women in Ireland to win a journalism award in a time when the business was dominated by men. Decades earlier, as a young trainee reporter with the *Longford Leader* newspaper, she incurred the wrath of the Catholic Church when she wrote in her column that women had a right to choose if they wanted an abortion.

In the late 1970s it was considered to be heretical, inflammatory commentary for a national newspaper to publish but coming from a provincial newspaper in conservative, rural Catholic Ireland it was considered unconscionable. The editor and owner of the *Leader* was Lucius Farrell, a ground-breaking maverick who was before his time. He believed that provocative commentary created constructive social debate. It's what newspapers do. He also believed in challenging the hegemony of the church. The hierarchy complained bitterly to Farrell but were rebuffed.

Then the local bishop sent one of his boot boys to visit Anne's mother in Leitrim, a sweet, gentle woman who wouldn't harm a fly. Katie Sweeney was, like the rest of her generation, deferential and respectful to the men of the cloth. But the visit from a holy priest complaining about her jezebel daughter left her deeply upset. It was an act of blatant, bloody-minded intimidation designed to force Anne's silence. Katie loved her Church but she never told any of her children what to think. She stood by her daughter.

The Church then doubled down in their efforts to humiliate and isolate Anne when a diocesan newspaper ran a front page editorial excoriating the young journalist under the headline, 'No, No Anne Sweeney'. But she never backed down from her feminist principles and continued to be a voice in the dark for the women of Ireland. She was happy for me to face down the bullies for the same reasons.

Three nights after the acid attack the garda protection was again pulled. The local garda chiefs didn't have the resources to maintain a full-time presence. In the past security alerts tended to last a few days and then receded but this time things felt different. Garda HQ only place individuals under armed full-time protection as a final option because it gobbles up resources and is costly. My position was that they were the experts and I had to trust their judgment. The car incident was well known through the media, police and criminal grapevines but we ensured that there was no publicity. I was later told that this annoyed Foley. Publicity was key to his plan.

On Tuesday 4 November Chief Superintendent Rock and Detective Inspector Colm Fetherstone called to the *Sunday World* offices and asked to see Michael Brophy and Colm MacGinty. The senior garda told them that they still had serious concerns that various criminal elements and the INLA posed a threat to my safety. He suggested that the company should go ahead and bring in a private security company. Michael called me after the meeting. He was furious to hear that the garda protection had been taken off at the weekend despite the fact that the police had just told him the situation was becoming extremely grave.

The following evening the trouble was forgotten when *Crime Lords* was officially launched at a party attended by over 400 guests. The crowd included colleagues, senior gardaí, a few judges and friends. The book had gone straight to the top of the bestsellers list and the distributors said it was the year's fastest selling book. They reported that in Limerick, where the gang war was raging, it reportedly sold out within an hour and a half of going on the shelves. The Irish public were hugely interested in true crime.

The recently retired Garda Commissioner, Pat Byrne, launched the book and the MC for the evening was Joe Duffy. During his speech Pat deliberately distanced himself from Michael McDowell's claims that reporters were bribing cops. He said that he had never found that journalists had jeopardized an ongoing investigation into serious crime. Joe Duffy, who has been a friend for over thirty years, also took aim at the minister. 'Most of you here tonight [gardaí], he [McDowell] is your boss, and for the rest of you [the media] he wants to be your boss and he's getting there very quickly. He knows what nobody knows,' he said to rapturous applause. It turned out to be a great night.

The next day Michael Brophy met with representatives of a specialist security company which employed former members of the Army Ranger Wing to do close protection. The company bluntly told Brophy that if I was to be attacked by criminals or terrorists they would do so with guns. Their operatives were experts in firearms and tactics but the law forbade them from carrying firearms in the Irish Republic. In other words, they would not be of any real use in the circumstances and they could not place their employees in such a potentially dangerous situation. Michael Brophy was doing everything humanly possible to help his reporter, which I have always greatly appreciated.

On Friday 7 November he decided to write a personal letter to Michael McDowell:

Security considerations concerning Mr Paul Williams Crime Editor of the *Sunday World*

On Friday last, 31st October, I was invited to Crumlin garda station to meet Chief Superintendent Eddie Rock and Superintendent Manley regarding our crime editor Paul Williams.

Chief Superintendent Rock informed me that the gardaí had serious concerns for the safety of Mr Williams. They based their concerns, they said, on intelligence reports which had been coming to them for some time from diverse sources.

They said that Paul's work was being read by very dangerous elements and was 'driving them mad'. I was asked if there was any possibility that I could, in his own interests, get him to pull back.

Chief Superintendent Rock said that the previous week Paul's car had been the subject of an acid attack and that a fire brigade had been called to the house in the middle of the night. He added that they would have men protecting his house during the hours of darkness but did not specify for what period this protection would be maintained.

We discussed the general security surrounding Mr Williams and I informed the gardaí that I had authorized a €30k upgrade on his home security system which was being implemented immediately following garda recommendations.

I asked would any purpose be served in putting one of two security men on his home both day and night and we discussed moving him from his home to rented accommodation, which would be provided by the company.

I was informed that in general these would be matters for myself. It was stressed, however, that the gardaí were taking the threats very seriously and it was important that I discuss the matter with Paul. I said that I would discuss the matter with Paul at the earliest opportunity following a round of radio and TV appearances he was making to publicize his latest book.

The meeting ended on that note.

On Tuesday 4th November Chief Superintendent Rock and Detective Inspector Featherstone visited the offices of the *Sunday World* at lunchtime at their own invitation and met myself and the Editor Mr Colm MacGinty. The tone of statement from the gardaí was similar to that of the previous Friday. Chief Superintendent Rock said that he was very concerned for the safety of Paul Williams. That there were criminal elements and INLA elements who posed a threat to his safety.

There followed a general discussion on security matters surrounding Mr Williams and the meeting concluded with Chief Rock reminding me that I had suggested private security for Mr Williams at the previous meeting at Crumlin Garda station. He said that it might be a good idea if that was implemented.

Some hours after this meeting I met with Paul Williams to inform him of events surrounding him which had taken place. He informed me then that the garda security, which had existed at his home over the weekend, had been withdrawn and was not in place the previous night. This, despite the fact that I had been informed, just hours earlier of garda concerns about Paul Williams safety.

In a follow-up discussion with gardaí regarding private security, I met with a firm of security consultants on the afternoon of Thursday 6th November. They produced a proposal for personal protection for Mr Williams but pointed out that if Mr Williams was to be the target of any attack by subversive or underworld elements, it was a certainty that these elements would be armed and it was impossible for them to respond with armed protection due to national laws.

The situation therefore is that there are ongoing garda concerns for Mr Williams' safety and as of today there are no adequate security structures in place.

Michael Brophy,
Terenure,
7 November 2003

On the following Sunday evening we returned from a family meal to discover an armed detective waiting at our front door. It appeared that the letter had trickled down to Garda HQ from the minister's office and there had been a panic. However the protection was lifted again the next day. In the meantime regular armed and uniformed units continued to patrol around the house at half-hour intervals. In a statement by the Garda Commissioner Noel Conroy to a Dáil committee a month earlier he'd told them that he did not have enough resources to combat organized crime. It was the kind of honesty that the Department of Justice did not like.

The local officers who knew what was happening on the ground expressed their frustration that the situation was spiralling out of control and would require a decision to mount a permanent presence before it was resolved. Garda friends who carried firearms in the job offered to take turns staying at the house. I didn't think it was right for them to put themselves out and trusted that Garda HQ knew what it was doing.

There were times I was scared of what might happen. Giovanni Falcone, the Italian prosecutor blown up by the Corleonesi mafia, once said that 'only the stupid aren't scared'. Some nights I sat up watching the security cameras with a baton close by. I also had a Gurkha knife which had been presented to me by the Nepalese contingent on a visit to the Irish UN troops in Lebanon. If anything was going to happen the danger hours would be between midnight and 4 a.m. I thought that it would probably involve another attack on the car. The regular garda patrols meant that the thugs would only have minutes to do anything or risk getting caught.

A week later, in the early hours of Friday 14 November, Foley decided to have another go.

———

It was shortly after 3 a.m. when I heard the door ring. When I answered on the intercom it was one of the local detectives from Crumlin asking, 'Paul, can you come down to the door now?' I instantly recognized his voice. It was calm but urgent and I got dressed quickly.

When I opened the door he stepped into the hallway and spoke almost in a whisper. He and two colleagues had been patrolling the area. They had actually decided to remain on duty for another hour or so even though their shift had ended. He said:

We've just found something under the car outside. It looks like
a bomb. We want you, Anne and the kids out of the house now
while we sort this. We have to call in the Bomb Squad.

At 1.12 a.m. the CCTV footage captured a lone male attaching the
device underneath the rear of a replacement car I was using since the
acid attack. It had been deliberately made to look like a real bomb,
something Foley's associates had plenty of knowledge of. While it
came as a shock it was not unexpected. I quickly woke Anne and the
kids and told them to get dressed, that we had to leave the house. It
was like we had rehearsed this moment because everyone got up and
dressed without saying hardly a word. The only family member that
didn't want to leave was our dog Sally who resisted as our thirteen-
year-old son Jake scooped her up in his arms.

Inside the front door the detective was waiting for us to gather
ourselves. He was a friend of the family and the kids loved him.
'Turn off the mobile phones just in case it activates the thing.
Right, let's go.' Outside other detectives were standing in silence
waiting for us.

As I passed the car I could see the large device sticking out from
the back. The officers shepherded us down the road where they
placed us in two squad cars that were sitting in darkness. The cops
were cool, professional and totally in control. It was like something
from a movie but this was sickeningly real.

The gardaí had decided to maintain radio silence because they
suspected that Foley and his pals might be listening on a scanner.
As garda outriders escorted the Bomb Squad from Cathal Brugha
Barracks in Rathmines, south Dublin, they had been ordered not
to use sirens only blue lights. The whole operation was to be done
as quietly as possible.

I sat in the back of a squad car and cuddled my daughter. As tears welled up in my eyes I wondered what to fuck was I putting my family through this for? This was my fault. As the squad cars ferried us to the safety of Crumlin garda station I was very fucking angry. A friendly female garda led us to the recreation room where she produced mugs of piping hot tea.

As she left us alone I was experiencing one of the lowest points in my life. The other times that I had felt like this was after hearing the news about Veronica Guerin and Marty O'Hagan. The job had taken over our lives and despite all my experience I had never really expected that the family would be so directly affected. Although they weren't showing it I knew they were scared. I looked at my family and said 'sorry'.

I remember Anne declaring: 'You can't stop now. These bastards are not going to put us out of our home.' The kids said almost in unison: 'Dad, we don't mind… the bad people won't get us.' I was so proud and ashamed at the same time. They were strong and brave.

The moment was broken when the inspector in charge came in to give us an update at around 4 a.m. The Bomb Squad had arrived at the scene and X-rayed the device which they believed to be a viable bomb.

I later discovered that the 'bomb' was contained in a tin box containing circuit boards, batteries and other components found in a viable device. It had been attached to the car with a large magnet. Dough was used to resemble a real explosive substance. It had all the hallmarks of a terrorist device.

The Inspector told me that the army explosives ordnance disposal (EOD) officer had ordered the evacuation of all of the 150 neighbours who lived in our cul de sac. We had lived there for fifteen happy years and many of them were great friends. When I heard that I suddenly wished that the ground would swallow me up. It was one thing to intimidate my family but a whole different matter when the mob also caused innocent men, women and children to be forced out of their beds in the middle of a cold winter's night. This too was my fault.

I phoned a detective who was helping with the evacuation to find out what was happening. In the background I could hear one of my neighbours telling the guards that her little daughter was not well. I can still hear the fear and upset in her voice twenty years later. Another neighbour had just come out of hospital after treatment for testicular cancer. Even though he didn't look ill the poor man had to explain to the garda rushing him out of the house with his family that he was too weak to carry his little child. Remembering that night still brings on a knotted spasm in my gut. After the incident I spent a lot of time going around the neighbours to apologize.

That night the neighbours were taken to the nearby school hall at Greenhills College where the kind nuns, who had also been roused from their sleep by the police, made them as comfortable as possible.

At 4.30 a.m. a controlled explosion was carried out on the device to make it safe and everyone returned to their homes. Martin Foley had achieved his goal.

The whole purpose of the exercise was to harass, intimidate and instil fear in as many people as possible at the same time. It was never intended to cause any physical harm. He wanted to turn me into a pariah in my own neighbourhood. No one would want to live next door to someone who could bring danger into their lives. The subsequent garda investigation established that the plot involved Foley and three of his younger gang members.

After the device had been attached to the car he waited in a gang member's apartment a short distance away listening to a radio scanner to hear if the cops had found it yet. The whole purpose of the elaborate exercise was for the device to be found. If the 'bomb' wasn't spotted by me it could simply fall off the car the next morning on the journey to work and he would have to do it all over again.

Getting impatient, at 2.45 a.m. he instructed one of his minions who was involved in the plot, a twenty-four-year-old small-time criminal called Michael Keating, to phone a garda he knew in Rathfarnham. Keating had been one of the detective's informants in the past. He tipped the garda off that he had 'just found out something' that 'something has been put under Paul Williams' car. When the garda pressed him to know what exactly had been placed on the car Keating replied, 'some device or something'.

He said he was only ringing so that nobody would get hurt in the morning. Eight minutes later the hood sent a text message to the garda informing him: 'You did not hear that from me. I can't say where it came from but it's 100 per cent. Text me back let me know you got this.'

The detective decided to check out the story for himself and drove to my estate. When he got there the device had just been found.

Foley's associate then phoned the 'friendly' journalist who had tried to choreograph a protest outside our home four months earlier. He is what they used to call in the Cold War era a 'useful idiot'. The journalist didn't pick up on the call. Keating later told detectives that the Viper was anxiously listening to the garda radio networks for news that the device had been found. He was 'agitated and hyper' the tout said. Foley assumed that the radio silence meant that the device had not been found. Shortly before 4 a.m. a taxi picked him up to bring him home to Crumlin.

As the cab drove onto Whitehall Road it met the army Bomb Squad team with its garda escort under blue lights. Gardaí were told by a confidential source that Foley got excited and ordered the cab driver to go down a side road. The cowardly godfather slumped down in the back of the car as the convoy of police and military vehicles sped past.

The following morning Foley got what he wanted. The bomb hoax caused a media storm on the front pages and was the lead item on TV news channels. It was an attack on society in general and on all journalists and a free press in particular. In the public mind it conjured up memories of the Guerin murder. When it was later publicized that Foley was the prime suspect it confirmed his place as one of Ireland's most reviled criminal figures.

In 2024 at the age of seventy-two he still is causing trouble and fear for people as he uses his notoriety to run a debt collection business, Viper Debt Recovery. Through the years I took pleasure in exposing the so-called law-abiding citizens who paid for the thug's services. It is incredible that there are no laws to ban a convicted criminal from the role. His very presence has terrified people. On one occasion, in 2009 during the economic crash, a former developer took his own life after a visit from the Viper. Foley has also come to the attention of the police for threatening behaviour. In February 2024 Foley pleaded guilty to threatening and abusive behaviour when he went to a man's home in Wexford Town. The judge gave him a suspended three-month sentence on the stipulation that he did not enter the town for twelve months.

Shortly after the bomb scare I was contacted by an army friend who had served with the Ranger Wing. Over previous years I had spent a lot of time with the special forces guys including an exhausting week on an exercise in the Wicklow Mountains and a trip to the jungle of East Timor. He wanted to meet for a chat. When we met he offered to 'deal with' Foley and his pals. My friend and some of his comrades, who were all highly trained, would bump into the Viper in a pub and start a fight. Given their skillsets these guys made the hardest gangster look like a choir boy. He assured me that no one would be killed but said Foley and his friends were very likely to end up in hospital. He wasn't joking. All I had to do was say the word. It was a very thoughtful and genuine offer but if I had agreed to that then I would have been no better than the gangsters themselves. It would be stooping to their level. I politely declined. Foley had no idea how much grief I had just saved him.

In the meantime the gardaí turned up the heat on Foley and his associates and the CAB landed him with a new bill for close to €1 million. In 2024 the CAB sought an order seeking possession of Foley's home to satisfy his tax debt. His stunt ultimately backfired.

The incident also proved to be rather embarrassing for Michael McDowell as the bulk of the coverage focused on the fact that full-time protection had been pulled due to a lack of resources even though there was intelligence of an imminent serious threat. In newspaper editorials the rhetorical question was asked, was it going to take the murder of another journalist to wake the Government up to the existential threat being posed by organized crime? After all, 2003 had been the bloodiest in the history of organized crime with twenty murders already. In official statements the gardaí said the incident was a worrying escalation, describing it as a 'serious and sinister development'. A spokesperson for Michael McDowell was quoted in the *Evening Herald* as saying that my security was not his responsibility, yet the spokesperson confirmed the minister had been kept 'fully briefed' on my security.

Over the hours that elapsed after we had been first awoken my shock had turned to white hot anger – likely fuelled by a few glasses of brandy. In an interview with Joe Duffy on *Liveline* I declared that the 'bastards are not going to put us out of our home or stop me doing my job' and if they wanted to know where I would be that night, I would be in the same place as I was when they came with the bomb.

The bomb squad officer in charge of the operation was Commandant Ray Lane. He was one of the army's leading experts in EOD who had been disarming terrorist bombs along the border since the outbreak of the Troubles. Ray was recognized internationally as one of the top EOD specialists in the world and he had trained US troops in IED counter measures in Afghanistan. The morning after the incident he phoned a mutual friend, Jim Cusack, the security correspondent with the *Sunday Independent*. Ray wanted to convey the message that the bomb was a 'very serious warning… the next time it could easily be the real thing, that man is on borrowed time,' he said. Ray subsequently told me the same thing in person but thankfully he was wrong about the borrowed time bit. His opinion was that whoever made the device knew exactly what they were doing. In 2024 Ray published a stunning memoir of his life as one of the world's top bomb experts, *Only a Soldier Knows: Life on the Front Lines with the Irish Defence Forces*.

Needless to say the *Sunday World* gave the incident huge coverage with the front page and four pages inside. I wrote a piece describing how I would not be scared off and that it was time that the scumbags were shown that they were not omnipotent. In a two-page spread the headline ran: 'How We Warned Minister McDowell Of Threat Just Days Before Attack On Williams'. Michael Brophy's letter to the minister was reproduced in full to avoid any confusion.

There was also a huge reaction from the public. Over the following weeks I received bundles of cards and messages of support from ordinary decent people. There were prayers, and medals and rosary beads sent. It reminded us that the most positive aspect to humanity is that the good people will always outnumber the bad ones.

On the day after the hoax I decided to take the family away from the drama and we escaped for the next four days or so to an apartment in the K Club with the support of the company. We picked the resort in Sallins, County Kildare, because Shea Dempsey, a dear family friend, was Michael Smurfit's then head of security and ensured that we were safe. No one apart from friends and the police would know we were there. It was a good distraction for Anne and the kids while I tried to sort out the next move. The whole incident had left me very nervous and unsure.

On the Friday evening and Saturday morning I had a number of meetings with Chief Superintendent Rock and Detective Superintendent Donegan. They expressed anger and frustration that due to the budgetary situation they could not provide personnel to prevent a further attack. They had sent several reports to Garda HQ informing them of the situation. There was already a wealth of intelligence from the Crime and Security Branch and NBCI to substantiate their concerns. A source later told me that when the senior spooks listened back to recordings of conversations between a number of different criminals they realized the threats were much more serious than they had previously thought.

The following Monday Michael Brophy and Colm MacGinty met with Michael McDowell to discuss the issues. I heard that a fairly frank exchange of views had taken place. Michael Brophy could be very scary when he was angry. McDowell emphasized that the security of a journalist was not his responsibility, that it was a matter for Garda Commissioner Noel Conroy. The meeting ended with McDowell saying that he was due to meet the commissioner to discuss the issue.

It appeared that Foley may have done me a favour in the end. According to my source in Garda HQ who had access to the most sensitive intelligence, the attack had convinced one gang to drop a convoluted plan to have me shot in November. This was the same unnamed group officers from NBCI had warned me about during the summer when I was told they wanted to gain my trust by passing on high quality information with the intention of luring me into a trap. The spook source was able to tell me that the most recent information I had received from the group concerned a major drug trafficker called Sean Dunne. The voice on the phone had given me some solid information about Dunne's operation including that he was to be targeted. Dunne was embroiled in a money laundering scam involving other criminals and members of the IRA. A short time later, on 4 November, Dunne was shot and critically injured outside his home in Ratoath, County Meath. The information could not have been more solid.

Just before the acid attack on my car the next stage in the plan involved meeting me in the Central Hotel on Exchequer Street in Dublin city centre. Scouts were to keep watch to see if I had an escort or was being followed. The plan was that the hit man was going to keep me under surveillance and, after the meeting, follow and shoot me. With the publicity around the other threats, suspicion would automatically fall at the door of the INLA and the Viper. The gang abandoned the idea when they heard of the acid attack on the grapevine because they reckoned I would be surrounded by armed protection after that.

Around the same time I was approached by a completely separate source, a senior garda who is now retired and confided the same information. It turned out that he had been the original source of the intelligence. The officer, a highly regarded detective throughout his career, was known to have excellent sources in the Hutch gang. In light of a recent scandal involving another former garda with improper links to the Hutches, it is important to clarify that it was not the same officer. Although I have no evidence to corroborate it, my belief is that the information came from either the Monk or some of his family. If it did I owe them one.

While trying to put the bomb hoax behind us in the K Club Detective Chief Superintendent John O'Brien from Garda HQ came to visit. O'Brien was in charge of the International Liaison and Protection Office which was responsible for all personal protection assignments in the police. The sensitive portfolio included the personal protection of senior Government figures, the President and the witness protection programme. Placing an individual under full-time protection is always a last resort for the police. It is expensive and a drain on resources.

He informed me that following a comprehensive risk assessment of the existing threat levels it had been decided to place my family and I under full-time police protection for the foreseeable future. I suspected that the decision had also been influenced by Michael Brophy's meeting with the minister. The security regime would involve me being accompanied everywhere I went by two armed members of the anti-terrorist, Special Detective Unit (SDU). My home was to have a permanent garda presence provided by the local district, with a uniformed officer on duty between 8 a.m. and 8 p.m. An armed detective would take over for the other twelve-hour shift during the hours of darkness, when attacks were most likely.

He warned me that it would be a dreadful intrusion on our lives but said that it was the only alternative in the current climate. When the two-member SDU team met me for the first time the next day they were wearing bullet-proof vests. They later confided that they had been warned that there was still a strong possibility at that stage that the INLA or the other criminal gang were going to shoot me, regardless of the protection. The officers were warned that the threat level was 'very high'.

It took some time to acclimatize to the fact that everywhere you went, even in the pub or restaurant, two armed officers would be nearby. It was an enormous, life-changing inconvenience and a constant physical reminder that the job I loved had literally taken over our lives. As part of the security regime, the police had to know what I was doing and where I was going from day to day and week to week. If we went home to Leitrim for a weekend the chief of the local division would have to be informed a number of days in advance. Two armed local officers would then be assigned to take up duty when the SDU men clocked off. Some people used to think it was glamorous having armed police around you all the time but in reality I was like a prisoner. It was the equivalent of being in a witness protection program. One of the few fringe benefits, however, was that I never had to worry about a lift home from the pub. The gardaí organized to have a hut and outside mobile toilet positioned on the property for the officers on the permanent post. The Tardis-like ugly structure stuck out like a sore thumb in our estate and became an object of public curiosity as people drove by just for a look.

We gave them a TV and hooked them into the cable to make their lives a little easier. SDU were to stay with me for over two years before the close protection was pulled. The permanent presence at our home continued for over a decade.

Apart from a few incidents over the years we were left in peace. In August 2004 a now defunct magazine, *Irish Crime*, reported that gardaí had foiled an elaborate plan to murder me. It said that the attack involved a group made up of INLA members and criminals. A source was quoted as claiming: 'There were eight guys, three of them were going to take out the armed gardaí protection on Williams and the other five were going to storm Williams' home and kill him.' It was an extraordinary statement which the gardaí assured me was not true. It claimed that one of the gang members had been arrested in Crumlin village with a loaded handgun. The gardaí said that he was involved in a separate incident. However, many years later a former member of the ERU I bumped into in my local pub volunteered that he and his team had swooped on four guys who were headed to my home around that time and that they had been instructed to keep the information under wraps. But mounting such an attack seemed way over the top and didn't actually make sense. I was only a bloody reporter after all and certainly not worth the carnage. In any event criminals don't like going to a fight where there are guns waiting for them.

A lot of enduring friendships were built over those years with members of the protection team becoming like part of the family. Many of them are still close friends today. They certainly kept the criminals at bay.

On a number of occasions the SDU officers had to pull their guns as a precaution during the time they were with me. The most dramatic incident occurred on 26 February 2004, a few months after the bomb scare, when members of the Byrne crime gang in Crumlin were sent to test the security. At least twice a week I trained in nearby Friarsland Gym in Clonskeagh with my friends Damian Boyle and Seanie Connell. Our routine involved a three-mile run, followed by a weights session. The mob knew it was one of my haunts.

That day detectives John Gleeson and Pat Tobin were with me. John was coming for a run with me while Pat drove along in the escort car. As we were about to leave the gym a thug smashed in the window of a car parked outside. It was later revealed they thought it was mine. He was wearing a motorbike helmet and at the end of the road his partner was waiting on a high-powered bike. We chased the thug as he ran for the bike and they attempted to get away. By that stage Pat had his Sig pistol drawn and was blocking their escape which was across the road from the entrance to the mosque in Clonskeagh.

In the confusion the driver lost control and they fell off the bike and were quickly subdued. I got in on the act and reefed the helmets off their heads. It felt good but it was a total breech of the security protocols – I was supposed to run away and not towards the trouble. The two hoods found themselves facing the business end of two garda pistols. Damian, who was the gym manager, was following us out when he spotted the commotion. As he looked down to the end of the car park he saw Pat pulling his gun. He went back and told the receptionist to phone the police. When he heard the bike crashing he assumed there had been a shooting. The poor girl began to panic when Damian told her to call an ambulance saying: 'I think they've shot Paulie.'

She was crying as she rang 999 and told the operator that 'Paul Williams has been shot'. When that went out over the garda network every cop in the south city seemed to converge on the area. Little Paulie hadn't been shot but the two Byrne associates were under arrest. They could only be charged with causing criminal damage and were subsequently convicted and given a fine.

Garda intelligence later confirmed that they had been sent to test the security and also cause me annoyance with more damage to my car. The driver of the bike is a well-known member of the Byrne/Kinahan gang who is still involved with them today. His accomplice was a disposable drug addict who was used to do the dirty work. After that incident the mob got the message and there were no more attempts to test the readiness of the SDU boys.

A month after the bomb hoax I suffered an episode of post-traumatic stress disorder. It is something that I have never spoken about before, apart from to close friends and family. PTSD is an insidious condition that affects people in different ways. It just creeps up without you knowing. What I found particularly scary was that I didn't realize what I was doing or thinking for a while. It was like a kind of spell of madness where I was gripped by a sense that I had lost all control over my life.

It manifested when something banal triggered an outburst where I verbally abused Brophy and MacGinty. I resigned from my job on the spot which was utterly irrational and inexplicable. On my thirty-ninth birthday in December I organized a mega birthday party. I told everyone I was going to celebrate my fortieth birthday now because I was unlikely to be around in a year's time. To everyone else I seemed my normal self but when I recovered I couldn't understand what had motivated me to blow up. It was utter madness.

The thing was that I was perfectly normal at home with the family but took out my madness on the two men who had done more for me than anyone else.

I didn't realize the magnitude of what was happening to me until Doctor Louis O'Carroll phoned me when he heard what I had done. Louis and his brother Gerry, who I once christened the Sheriff, had been good friends for many years. It was very advantageous having Louis as a friend especially if you were going bonkers – he was considered to be one of the finest consultant psychiatrists in the country. I remember him saying firmly: 'Either you come to see me or I'm coming to see you.' When we met Louis helped me realize that the emotional explosion was caused by a build up of layers of stress over several months and even years. In layman's terms I had effectively blown a gasket in my head. Foley *et al* would have loved to hear that they had succeeded in fucking my head up.

The sense of embarrassment after something like that happens in your life is hard to explain and painful to write about. But with the understanding of my bosses and the support of family, colleagues and friends I got over it, dusted myself off and was back persecuting the gangsters a month or so later. Over the years since I have often helped others who found themselves in the same kind of situation where the world was closing in on them. Once you've been there you recognize the signs in others.

The investigation of the bomb hoax lasted for three months. In the immediate aftermath of the incident Foley put out the word through his network of police informants that it had been done by the INLA. It was well known that Declan 'Wacker' Duffy had a long-standing vendetta against me and had been planning some kind of attack or abduction from his prison cell. But within an hour of finding the device the cops knew who the real culprits were.

The homes of Foley and his associates were searched by gardaí with warrants looking for explosives. The gang members were arrested in February 2004. There was not enough evidence with which to charge any of them, even though Michael Keating had made some admissions. By pure coincidence three years later, almost to the day, Keating was lucky to escape with minor injuries after a gunman fired two blasts from a shotgun at his head. Foley and another sidekick were the last to be arrested on 23 February 2004. The night after they were released from custody, in a final malicious act, they again sent fire engines to our home.

When I reflect back on all that happened I still get goose bumps. It was certainly a white-knuckle ride.

CHAPTER FIFTEEN

THE COST OF FEAR

Making threats is not the only tactic used by gangsters to silence the media. Over the years criminals have sought High Court injunctions to silence crime journalists and newspapers in the High Court through defamation proceedings for the loss of their good names. In the modern age they use the sewers of social media to throw dirt at their enemies in the echo chamber now called X. But in the days before the advent of mass social media they used websites and even the national airwaves to have a go and vent their anger at me. It was all part of the drama. I had a number of memorable confrontations with gangsters in the courts, through the web and on Joe Duffy's *Liveline* programme. The insidious effects of the fear instilled in society by the spectre of organized crime, however, was to impact my life in ways I had not anticipated.

It came back to my old nemesis Martin Foley who wasn't quite finished with me yet. In 2004 I updated the book *Crime Lords* to reflect the momentous events that had occurred in the year since it was first published. In the new version I brought closure to the story of the notorious Westies by writing about their violent demise in Spain in January 2004. In the chapter about the Viper I revealed the background to the acid and hoax bomb attacks and named him as being responsible.

On 3 December I was interviewed about the new edition by Pat Kenny on RTÉ's *The Late Late Show*. As I told the story about the incident a picture of Foley was helpfully emblazoned across the screen which left the viewer in no doubt as to who and what he was. The revised edition of the book was serialized in the *Sunday World* two days later, under the headline: 'Foley's A Dead Man Walking'. The incidents had caused him a lot more bother than he had bargained for.

In the new edition I expressed my strongly held suspicion that Foley was a police informant as a possible explanation as to why he had narrowly escaped being busted with drugs on at least three occasions. Some of my reliable garda sources, who had tried to nab him, had expressed the same view that he was being protected by a senior officer to whom he was providing information. I also revealed how he had been paying the IRA protection money from his drug trafficking operation to ensure they left him alone.

I was told the story drove the Viper ballistic and he decided to take action. The gangster who had already survived three assassination attempts and a kidnapping was afraid that words on a page might provoke another attempt on his life. He had proved adept when it came to provoking murder attempts without any media assistance. Foley had been mistrusted by other villains since the time of Martin Cahill – they didn't need to be convinced by a newspaper.

The continued garda protection meant that he couldn't register his dissatisfaction in the usual way. Instead he reverted to the second line of attack that he had used throughout his career – he instructed his lawyers to shut us up once and for all. He told them to seek a High Court injunction gagging the newspaper from writing about him in the future. The gangster who had shown nothing but contempt for the rule of law was always happy to hide behind it when it suited his own needs.

On 16 December his lawyers went to the High Court to seek leave to apply for an interlocutory injunction against the *Sunday World* on the grounds that our coverage 'gravely compromised his right to life'. An interlocutory injunction would prevent us writing anything else about Foley pending the full hearing of the case, which could take years. The following week the High Court gave the go ahead for the application to be heard.

The injunction was being sought to restrain the newspaper from publishing 'any material concerning Mr Foley which encouraged, advocated, promoted or predicted, explicitly or by necessary implication, an attempt to endanger Mr Foley's life and health'. In a grounding affidavit the Viper's solicitor described the article as 'among the most profoundly irresponsible journalism and editorship of a widely circulating national newspaper that I could conceive of'.

Of particular concern to Foley was a quote from an unnamed retired detective who had known the gangster for many years. He had also dealt with Foley's numerous threats against me over the years. The former cop stated:

> I have always predicted that Foley will not die in his sleep and have told him this on many occasions. The only thing that amazes me is that he has lived for so long.

Foley's lawyers argued that the article exposed him 'to a threat of violence'. The garda's quote could only be read as predicting Foley's 'death by violent methods'. The Viper was, of course, denying all the allegations against him. He was an innocent soul who was being tormented by a dirty tabloid. Like most criminals, Foley wanted to blame someone else for his problems.

When the *Sunday World* was notified of the injunction needless to say we were determined to fight it tooth and nail. The paper's solicitor Kieran Kelly began putting our response together and Colm MacGinty as editor prepared a responding affidavit. Kelly was astonished by the Viper's chutzpah and predicted he was on a hiding to nowhere. The consigliere, as we call him, and our legal team were told that the paper would stand up to the bullying tactic and they forensically prepared for the fight. If anything Foley was actually exposing his criminality even further. The court listed the case to be heard over two days, on 18 and 19 January 2005.

I missed the first day of the hearing because I had agreed to participate in a charity fundraiser for the survivors of the tsunami disaster on 26 December 2004 which killed an estimated 228,000 victims. It was the deadliest natural disaster of the twenty-first century and all around the world a huge effort was being made to raise money to help the survivors and the recovery operation. Prison officers in Cork prison came up with the wheeze of locking up a group of twenty public figures for over twenty-four hours in the former Cork City Gaol. It was organized in conjunction with TV3 (now Virgin Media) and the public pledged cash to keep us inside. They raised a lot of money!

Behind the prison walls we were cut off from the outside world and I was blissfully unaware that the hearing of Foley's injunction application was dominating the news bulletins that day. One of the country's most notorious criminals attempting to silence the country's most popular newspaper whose crime editor he had attempted to intimidate into silence was big news. Foley hired one of the best advocates in the business, senior counsel Michael O'Higgins, to fight his corner. In his former life as a journalist, O'Higgins was the only one who ever got an in-depth series of interviews with Foley's former boss, the General, Martin Cahill.

Michael O'Higgins told the court that his client was seeking the gagging order because, as a convicted criminal, his chance of successfully suing for libel 'was slim'. He said he would also be seeking a declaration that the *Sunday World* article breached Foley's right to life under the Constitution and the European Convention on Human Rights, exposed him to the threat of violence, and infringed his right to privacy. He said the article stated that reliable sources believed Foley was protected by a senior member of An Garda Síochána and that he had astonishingly escaped three major drug busts by leaving the scene minutes beforehand.

This assertion, he said, exposed Foley to danger from 'psychopaths in the criminal underworld who might believe he was a garda informer'. Every citizen had the right under the European Convention of Human Rights that articles which caused a real and substantial risk to their life would not be published. 'It doesn't matter whether Mr Foley was the biggest blaggard or thug, that's not the issue,' O'Higgins said.

In his affidavit Colm MacGinty didn't pull his punches stating:

As indicated by Mr Foley's solicitor there have been three attempts on his life. Foley has also been abducted by the IRA. These incidents have all stemmed from his involvement in criminal activities. Martin Foley is a person who orchestrates and deals in terror and violence. Any threat to his life is wholly attributable to his continued involvement in crime and association with other members of the criminal class.

He said articles concerning Foley's activities were published in the public interest. Colm recounted the high-profile campaign of intimidation that ensued when Foley learned of his inclusion in *Crime Lords*. The incident had 'attracted enormous publicity from all parts of the media'. He said the public was entitled to know about persons such as Foley and his involvement in drug dealing, violence and crime. It was also entitled to know about the efforts of the authorities to deal with his activities.

All of this had been widely reported by the time I was 'released' from custody with my fellow prisoners at 6 p.m. that same day and was covered extensively in the following day's national newspapers. I attended the hearing the next day with Colm and Kieran. Foley did not attend, probably because he knew the media would be there in force to film him. Representing the *Sunday World,* senior counsel Eoin McCullough said Foley did not have an arguable case. He said he hadn't sworn his own affidavit and had got his solicitor to do so instead so that he could avoid being cross-examined under oath. Mr McCullough commented:

> If people had given evidence, he's open to being cross-examined as to how he would realistically say he had any fear of what the *Sunday World* was writing when unfortunately there have been previous attempts on his life in the past.

Ten days later Mr Justice Peter Kelly threw out Foley's application. In what was a landmark judgement, with implications for all media in such cases, he said the newspaper had not encouraged anybody to shoot Foley and was critical that he had not been prepared to be cross-examined in his application. Moreover, he said, the newspaper was entitled to publish facts and opinions about Foley arising from his involvement in serious crime. The judge said:

The three previous attempts on his life long antedate the publication of any material by the *Sunday World* which Martin Foley has identified as offensive. That fact is supportive of the view that any risk to Martin Foley's life or well being comes not from any publication by the *Sunday World*, but rather from his own involvement in criminal activities.

The judge said the information in question was in the public domain and the bringing of the proceedings with its attendant publicity had given the matter 'much wider circulation'. In such circumstances an injunction restraining the newspaper from repeating the information would be of little value.

Mr Justice Kelly said the right to freedom of expression was provided for in Article 40 of the Constitution and Article 10 of the European Convention of Human Rights and was an important right which the courts 'must be extremely circumspect about curtailing', particularly at the interlocutory stage of a proceeding.

It was a spectacular success for the *Sunday World*, and for the media in general, as it supported our efforts to continue shining a light on the underworld. It had also been an expensive error for Foley, a notorious miser, who had to pay his costs which would have been estimated at around €100,000. He was also ordered to pay our costs but he never did. Chasing him for the money would have been more expensive than it was worth. We had our victory. However, by the time the verdict was delivered I didn't have much stomach for celebration. The laws of unexpected consequences had intervened to create a major problem in my personal life.

After the end of the second day of the hearing on 19 January as MacGinty and I were being driven back by the SDU to the *Sunday World*, now based in Talbot Street, central Dublin, I switched on my phone. There were at least a dozen text messages and missed calls from a lawyer I had retained to complete the purchase of our new family home. After a few years of searching we had found our dream home in a small new development of houses in south Dublin. We'd paid the deposit the previous October and were waiting for the house to be completed over the next month or so.

But the lawyer had some very bad news – that morning the developers had returned our deposit cheque by courier and bluntly informed her that they would not be selling to me. It came as a massive shock. The bottom line was that they were afraid that people would be reluctant to buy a house next door to me in case they might get shot or blown up. The wall-to-wall coverage of the injunction hearing the previous day, with all the talk of intimidation, shootings, assassination attempts, bombs and murder, would scare the living daylights out of any potential home buyers.

It caused panic with the sellers and they withdrew the sale of the house to me citing the fact that they had not signed a binding contract for the property. This was a prime example of the kind of ancillary subconscious fear criminals generate in society.

Over many years, and especially in the wake of the publicity around the bomb scare, I heard more times than I can remember how people would get nervous if they found themselves sitting next to me in a bar or restaurant. The proprietor of one of the locals I frequented at the time told other customers that he was considering barring me for safety reasons. He dropped the idea after someone pointed out that with two armed cops outside it was the safest pub in Ireland.

My publishers at the time, Merlin, were told by others in the industry that they were mad to be publishing my books as they too would be in the firing line. A graphic artist turned down the job of designing covers for my books as a result of their irrational fear. A designer would be the last person the mob would have thought about. My editor, Aoife Barrett, was even advised not to meet me to discuss edits on the books. I am glad to say that Aoife is still my editor.

One Sunday evening not so many years ago I got an unexpected call from an old friend who was head of security at one of the country's top banks. He was able to tell me that I was with the wife and kids and we had just sat down in the Merry Ploughboy restaurant in Rathfarnham, south Dublin. He laughed as he explained that the bank's chief executive had recognized me. They were sitting with their family a few tables away. The executive phoned him in a state of urgency to ask if they were in any danger and should they leave! The experienced ex-cop reassured them they had nothing to worry about but gave me the heads up. I pretended not to notice my nervous fellow diners.

Meeting sources was always a hazard. People who contacted me would insist on meeting outside their home areas in case I was spotted and their house was burned down.

When the kids were younger we used to have an awful job trying to get babysitters because their parents were afraid. That was why when we did find a reliable babysitter they were paid well over the hourly rates – we were just so delighted to get them. I remember how we lost one great babysitter after the gardaí arrived at the house one night while we were out. Someone had been spotted acting suspiciously nearby and the cops had been called. They insisted on checking out the house to ensure she was okay. The poor kid freaked out when she saw one of the officers armed with an Uzi submachine gun. Her parents didn't let her come back after that.

Whenever I was invited to speak at an event the organizers would automatically inform their local gardaí out of concern for security. In 2011 a book signing in Easons in Limerick was cancelled at the last minute when a local criminal informed staff that he would be confronting me during the signing. I had no problem with that. Despite reassurances from the local gardaí that armed officers would be there and the guy would not be allowed near the place, the shop management were not prepared to take the risk.

It was also a source of dark humour in my own business. My colleagues in *The Star* used to run a macabre lottery listing the top ten people they reckoned were going to die as a result of violence or some other malady. They used to tell me I regularly got to the top of the list. It was the kind of gallows humour we media people enjoyed behind the scenes which is a byproduct of reporting disasters, tragedies and violence all the time. Other pals used to pretend to duck for cover when I met them in the pub. They called me Dead Man Walking. It was a bit of craic.

I decided that I was not going to easily walk away from our dream house on the principle that I had done nothing wrong to anyone. I understood why neighbours might be worried about having me next door but when I moved in the gardaí would be moving with us and the neighbours would have nothing to worry about. I wasn't prepared to be discriminated against because of my job.

The paper's lawyer Kieran Kelly came to my rescue, as he has done on many occasions over the decades. He argued that we were entitled to buy the house because the *Sunday World*'s security company had been allowed to install security features, including miles of wiring for the CCTV system in the house before the walls had been plastered. We argued that this work and the costs incurred amounted to part performance of the contract. There were a few tense weeks of a standoff before common sense prevailed and the panic abated. As we geared up to do battle the vendors said they would offer me a deal whereby I would pay for the house immediately but stay out of it for three months until the others were sold. We could not agree to that, having set our hearts on moving in, and we wanted the comfort of the added security features so our lawyer was having none of it. It was then agreed that the sale of the house could go ahead without conditions.

I later learned they had also expected that, given the above average chances of me exiting this mortal coil prematurely through violent means, I hadn't a hope of getting life insurance to cover the huge Celtic Tiger mortgage I was drawing down and I would not be allowed to close the deal. Their prescience proved to be true. I discovered that organized crime's corrosive effect on society manifests in many different ways.

By pure coincidence the day after it was agreed for the sale to go through I was the guest speaker at a breakfast gathering of the Irish Insurance Federation in Dublin Castle. I did the gig for free as a favour to an old friend. Every insurance company in the country was represented at the event where I gave a talk on the state of organized crime. I remember staying on much longer than scheduled to pose for pictures with the cream of Ireland's insurance industry. As I was talking and posing for pictures my broker went out to find me an insurance package to cover the mortgage.

By 4 p.m. that afternoon every one of the companies represented at the breakfast function had blankly refused to give me cover. The broker told me that when he rang each company and mentioned my name he got short shrift. They wouldn't even consider the proposal. They reckoned I was, like my nemesis Foley, a dead man walking. It was another manifestation of discrimination that I could do nothing about. Telling them I had police protection and the threats had subsided cut no ice with actuarial calculations. It was devastating news. But I wasn't finished yet.

Between the broker and INM we eventually put together a hotchpotch of policies, including my death in service company insurance, to cover the borrowed money. The balance was made up with a policy from Lloyds of London, the only company willing to take on the risk. In April 2005 when we finally moved into our lovely new home we became something of a curiosity in the locality.

I later heard that one local who lived on a nearby road came around to see what kind of car I was driving. If it was the same model as his he intended changing the car in case it was mistakenly targeted. Not even the criminals could get things that badly wrong.

Fear makes people do irrational things. The other houses were sold and our little enclave, with its garda presence, became an oasis of calm. I always understood the reasons for the initial concerns and anxiety. It was a bizarre and highly unusual situation for anyone to find themself in. The neighbours became great friends and remain so twenty years later. We often laugh about it now. In the meantime I continued doing my job. The criminals had not given up the battle.

———

Around the same time I became embroiled in an unexpected spat with a flamboyant English con man called Giovanni Di Stefano. The Italian-born career fraudster arrived in Ireland in 2005 in a flourish of publicity claiming to be a lawyer who would singlehandedly overturn the convictions of some of the country's most notorious gangsters. The bombastic Walter Mitty character thrived on publicity and could deliver alternative facts – lies – with the same aplomb as the king of grifters, Donald Trump.

Di Stefano gained international notoriety acting on behalf of some of the world's biggest monsters, mass murderers and perverts. He relished his reputation as the 'Devil's Advocate'. Di Stefano's disreputable list of 'clients' he claimed to represent included Osama bin Laden, Saddam Hussein, Slobodan Milošević, Serbian warlord Arkan, aka the Butcher of Bosnia, and UK serial killers Harold Shipman and Ian Brady. He also claimed to be on first name speaking terms with the likes of New York mob boss John Gotti and Iran's Ayatollah Khomeini. In a 2003 BBC documentary, *The Devil's Disciple*, he caused universal outrage when he claimed that if he had been around during the Second World War, he would have ensured Hitler was never convicted of killing Jews. Di Stefano declared that he would represent Satan because he saw himself as 'defending the indefensible'.

He variously described himself as a multi-millionaire entrepreneur, a Hollywood studio boss, a player in the Balkan war and the founder of a political party. The truth was that he was a charlatan and a criminal who had absolutely no legal qualifications.

His first Irish client was Patrick 'Dutchy' Holland, the serial hit man hired by John Gilligan to murder Veronica Guerin. While there was not enough evidence to charge him with the murder due to intimidation of witnesses, Holland had been convicted of drug trafficking in 1997. He was initially sentenced to twenty years but it was reduced to twelve years on appeal. The Devil's Advocate rolled into town in the run up to Holland's release from prison and launched a campaign to clear the name of the sixty-seven-year-old veteran assassin.

He was also 'hired' by other notorious criminals including members of the McCarthy/Dundon mob serving life for the Kieran Keane murder. Di Stefano also declared that he would overturn John Gilligan's conviction for drug trafficking. Hindsight would show that the con man conned the cons so to speak – and took large amounts of cash from them in the process. When it came to ripping people off Di Stefano did not discriminate.

Certain elements of the Irish media loved Di Stefano because he provided plenty of colourful copy and they were hoodwinked into believing his lies. At one stage he announced that he was even planning to buy Shelbourne Football Club. In 1999 he had tried to buy Dundee Football Club in Scotland but the deal fell through when fans protested and his criminal past was exposed. The same thing happened when he tried to buy two other UK clubs. There was plenty of evidence in the public domain to show that everything about Di Stefano was a lie.

A judge in London's Old Bailey had once described him as 'one of nature's fraudsters' and a 'swindler without scruple or conscience'. He had been banned from the United States in the 1980s after being involved in a bogus bid to buy MGM Studios in Hollywood. He was also banned from entering New Zealand as a prohibited immigrant and had spent a total of eight years in Irish and UK prisons for fraud and deception.

In September 2005 he appeared on *The Late Late Show* to announce his campaign for Dutchy Holland and John Gilligan. I was brought on as a guest in the audience to challenge him on the facts surrounding the Guerin case and blow holes in his preposterous claims. I knew that he was talking rubbish and pointed out on the show how Gilligan and Holland had intimidated vital witnesses who were too terrified to testify. It was the reason, I said, that neither of them were charged with the murder.

The media continued to describe him as a 'controversial UK-based lawyer' even though the Irish Chief Justice John Murray had demanded that Di Stefano produce evidence of his legal qualifications, which he never could and never did. It arose at a hearing on 13 March 2006 when Dutchy Holland applied to have him recognized by the court as his legal representative in a miscarriage of justice case dreamed up by the con man.

He had also attempted to mount spurious legal proceedings on behalf of Limerick psychopaths Anthony 'Noddy' McCarthy and Dessie Dundon. The con man became a regular visitor to Portlaoise prison to meet his various 'clients' including John Gilligan. He claimed that he could get Gilligan's conviction overturned because his case was 'flawed' even though the mobster had been represented by some of the country's top – and real – lawyers who had already launched unsuccessful appeals.

Chief Justice Murray objected to a letter he had received from the fraudster. The judge said that the letter, which contained outrageous and false allegations about members of the legal profession, was a stunt designed to distract from Di Stefano's failure to provide proof of his legal qualifications. The judge accused the con man of being ignorant of Irish law.

The grifter then used his website to announce that he was going to issue defamation proceeding against the Chief Justice in the UK courts. The announcement was dutifully reported in the media. In fairness it was an eye-catching story.

When Dutchy Holland was released from prison a month later, in the early hours of Saturday 7 April 2006, Di Stefano ensured that he received maximum media coverage. He collected the soft-spoken assassin at the gates of Portlaoise prison in a limo and brought him to the upmarket Merrion Hotel in central Dublin. The bill was being paid by the *News of the World* after Di Stefano negotiated a financial deal with the paper for Dutchy to tell his exclusive story of being framed by the State.

That afternoon he flew Dutchy to Rome to take a lie detector test that would prove he was a victim of a miscarriage of justice. Needless to say Holland passed the test which had no legal standing in Ireland or the UK. Di Stefano was doing his best to make a mockery of the law. It was pure theatre.

The day after his release I published a front page story and inside feature reminding the public of how Dutchy Holland had gotten away with murder. He had been involved in the planning of the murder from the beginning. Shortly after Dutchy shot Veronica Guerin six times Gilligan laughed and joked down the phone, telling the killer: 'I hear you put a smile on her face. I wonder who she will be investigating now she is in heaven.' The planning and aftermath of the murder had been witnessed by Carol Rooney, Gilligan's teenage lover, who was put on a plane to Australia by Gilligan. She later told police how Dutchy had warned her that it was in her best interests to forget about everything she had witnessed. When gardaí eventually found her she was too terrified to testify in court. If she had, Gilligan and Holland would certainly have been convicted of the murder. Her evidence could have provided crucial affirmation for the otherwise uncorroborated testimony of a supergrass in the trial. I was able to reveal the details of what she said when I got my hands on the content of her explosive statement from one of my sources.

The following week I decided to further balance the media books by writing details of a major investigation exposing Di Stefano's criminal past and lack of legal qualifications. A source had slipped me a copy of a confidential report by Eurojust, the European Union's Judicial Co-operation Unit. The report, which had been sent to the Department of Justice, cleared up any doubts about the Devil's Advocate. It stated: 'Mr Di Stefano is not, according to Italian Police inquiries, entitled to practice as a lawyer in Italy.' It also revealed that he had a criminal record for 'the crimes of issuing uncovered cheques, fraud, use of cloned credit or payment cards and documents' for the purpose of obtaining money.

Enquiries with the Registry of Lawyers in Rome showed that there was actually no one by the name of Giovanni Di Stefano registered with them. It continued: 'In view of the penal records [criminal record] of Di Stefano, it seems not possible that he could legally practice law in Italy or any other country.'

I contacted the Law Society of England and Wales which confirmed that they were well aware of Di Stefano. A spokesman told me: 'Mr Di Stefano has no legal qualifications or status whatsoever.' At the time the Law Society had called in the police to investigate his false claims.

As part of the same probe I contacted colleagues in Scotland and London who had previously investigated the Devil's Advocate and exposed his criminal past. Di Stefano subjected the journalists at the *Guardian* and *Scotland on Sunday* newspapers to menacing threats and malicious slurs on their characters. He mounted the attacks from his website in the days before Twitter/X and the use of social media by criminals.

Di Stefano issued 'press releases' containing wild and unfounded allegations about the journalists and also claimed to have hired private detectives to investigate their private lives. The aggressive campaign of vilification caused the reporters concerned a lot of distress. It was intimidation designed to silence them. I could relate to their upset as the modern use of social media to attack journalists and identify their homes has a chilling effect. I understood how stressful it could be.

After the exposé Di Stefano turned his attentions to me. The day after the *Sunday World* appeared he announced on his website that he was going to sue senior gardaí and me for defamation. He then embarked on a full-on assault on my character which continued for months. He accused me of every possible vice he could dream up in his warped mind. I was a cocaine addict, an extortionist, a paedophile, a user of prostitutes, a serial philanderer and a perjurer. He even claimed that I had been responsible for causing the murders of a number of criminals, a spurious claim that gangsters and their families had used against me over the years as they tried to find someone else to blame.

I was well used to criminals trying to impugn my reputation but what was shocking was that some elements of the media gave credibility to Di Stefano for reasons I still cannot fathom. The *Sunday Tribune* was the only newspaper to run a story highlighting the outrageous invective in an attempt to undermine my integrity and even put it on the front page. The paper effectively guided its readership to the website to read the defamatory material for themselves. It made the newspaper just as guilty of libel as Di Stefano. They either completely ignored or were blissfully unaware that the facts showed Di Stefano up as a liar and a hoodlum. By implication it suggested that there was no smoke without fire. We were being attacked from our own backyard yet again. It emboldened Di Stefano to put the boot in even further.

I got a call from a *Tribune* reporter on the Saturday morning to ask me for a quote about Di Stefano's attacks. My position was to publicly ignore his invective and not dignify it with a response, although I asked if they were seriously considering running a story based on the rantings of a notorious criminal with form for similar attacks on journalists in the UK. My objections were ignored.

The story caused intense anger amongst the management of INM and in the *Sunday World*. For a second time the *Tribune* had launched an attack on the integrity of another paper in the same media group. I was advised that I was well within my rights to sue the paper for what was an even more blatant libel than the one before. The allegations they amplified in public were of the most egregious nature. My lawyer fired off a letter informing the newspaper of the seriousness of what they had done.

Michael Brophy contacted Mick Roche, the *Tribune*'s managing director, to complain about the article. Mick then called me to offer an apology which I accepted. On a back channel he told Brophy that if I did launch an action the paper would be prepared to make an immediate settlement of €20,000. He acknowledged that publishing the story was highly libellous and malicious.

For the same reasons as before I decided not to proceed. The paper had been dying a slow, agonizing death for years, despite INM throwing good money after bad to keep it afloat. The original strategy of using it to prevent the expansion of the *Sunday Times* in the market was not working. Tony O'Reilly and the INM board were facing a dilemma about what to with it because it was a huge drain on the organization's bottom line. I felt that the libel might be used as the final straw. I didn't want to be associated in any way with a move that left colleagues without livelihoods. The *Tribune* struggled on until February 2011 when it was finally shut down.

In the meantime Giovanni Di Stefano continued to attack me on a daily basis coming up with even more lurid allegations. But as time went on it was clear that the man was actually mad. When Kieran Kelly notified the host platform in the USA it dropped Di Stefano's website and he moved to a server in Eastern Europe.

Other journalists who began writing stories about his criminal past, particularly Jim Cusack at the *Sunday Independent*, came in for similar treatment. At one stage during Di Stefano's campaign, leaflets containing some of his more lurid accusations and lies were distributed by Dublin criminals in my home town of Ballinamore, County Leitrim. Apart from cocaine and women, I apparently abused the English language, the media and the Irish public! It illustrated the lengths some of the thugs were prepared to go to when they couldn't get to me in person. To get them that riled I must have been doing something right.

Di Stefano's campaign to empty Irish prisons of some of its more illustrious thugs fizzled out pretty quickly. His attacks abated because they were getting no traction and other media outlets began telling the truth about him. He also ran into trouble and steered clear of Ireland after the McCarthy/Dundons realized that he had ripped them off for large undisclosed sums of money. He had ripped off several criminals it transpired, including Gilligan. He was on the run from the UK authorities as well who wanted to arrest him on fraud charges.

The charade of the Devil's Advocate finally came to an inglorious end in 2013 when Di Stefano was sentenced to fourteen years by a London court after being convicted for a string of fraud cases. It had taken the UK police years to get him. Another eight and a half years were added to the sentence unless he immediately paid his victims back over €1.7 million which he took from them while posing as a lawyer. He served eight years behind bars and is now a free man.

Dutchy Holland meanwhile forgot about his attempt to prove his innocence and returned to a life of crime in the UK after his release. Two years later he was convicted of conspiracy to kidnap a businessman in London and was jailed for eight years. Holland died in his sleep in Parkhurst prison on the Isle of Wight in 2009. I wrote his obituary over two pages in the *Sunday World*. It was a fitting finale.

A year after the Di Stefano episode I found myself centre stage in a full-on row with two major gangland figures on national radio. It was to become one of the most extraordinary and dramatic episodes ever heard on Irish radio.

―――――

On 1 May 2007 I was invited onto Joe Duffy's *Liveline* programme on RTÉ radio to debate with Sinn Féin councillor Christy Burke the issue of the connections between organized crime gangs in Dublin and Sinn Féin and the IRA. It was a politically sensitive time as the General Election was due to take place a few weeks later on 24 May. It followed the conviction of notorious north inner-city drug trafficker Christy Griffin for the rape of his partner's daughter. Griffin was a powerful player in organized crime where he was known as Tony Soprano because, like the fictional character, he had invested his loot in waste disposal.

The rape of the child had caused a gang war in the inner-city neighbourhood which claimed three lives and led to several gun and bomb attacks. I interviewed the victim of the gangland paedophile a week before I appeared on *Liveline*. I had also highlighted how

Griffin had been involved in robbing container goods from Dublin docks in conjunction with IRA members who were also members of Sinn Féin.

I was debating with Christy Burke when events took a dramatic turn. An armed robber and drug dealer from Finglas, Alan 'Fatpuss' Bradley, phoned Joe Duffy to put the record straight. Bradley was a member of Martin 'Marlo' Hyland's gang, one of the country's biggest drug trafficking operations at the time.

I had written about Bradley on many occasions including a recent story in which I revealed that he was involved in a row with another dangerous thug called John Daly. Also from Finglas, north Dublin, Daly who was linked to at least three murders, was coming to the end of a nine-year prison sentence and had threatened to get Fatpuss when he got out. In fact it later transpired that he had issued threats to several gangsters demanding money and giving notice that he was going to be taking over once he was released. I also wrote an article that Daly was suspected of orchestrating shootings on the phone from his prison cell. In fact I had been writing for some time about how criminals were running their rackets from prisons with illegal phones.

At the time the Minister for Justice Michael McDowell responded and denied that prisoners had access to phones. When Bradley rang into *Liveline* I made sure to properly introduce him to the listeners as a major criminal:

> This is Alan 'Fatpuss' Bradley we're talking to? Good man Alan. You should introduce yourself to the public and tell them who you are - the criminal figure who is also known as Fatpuss Bradley. Were you told by your republican friends to come on here?

Bradley replied: 'No, I wasn't. Does it upset you that I'm on the air?'

I came back: 'No, absolutely not, I'm delighted to finally get a chance to talk to you Alan.'

A year earlier Fatpuss and his brother had lost a libel action against *The Star* Sunday newspaper after he had been described as someone who struck fear into the community around him.

Bradley was in fighting humour and we went toe to toe as Joe deftly played the role of the ringmaster. Bradley called me a 'lying cunt' and 'fuckin' lowlife' as he turned the air blue on the country's most listened-to radio show. Fatpuss was clearly a follower of Giovanni Di Stefano as he said: 'Was there not something printed about you snorting cocaine somewhere? You should hang yourself... you're making people's lives a misery.'

'Even if I was told it was a miracle cure for cancer I would not snort one line of cocaine because scumbags like you make money from it,' I replied.

Then I laid into him:

> You're a major criminal figure and you're terrorizing the people of Finglas. How come the Criminal Assets Bureau are hitting you for a bill for several hundred thousands of euro? As long as I have breath in my body I will do my utmost to keep space on the front page for you and your criminal associates. You're an absolute cancer in our society. You're a criminal and a thug.

As the showdown continued for several minutes, Bradley hit boiling point:

> You're the lowest form of scum. You only do the police's dirty work. You're a fuckin' lowlife. You should just shut up.

He repeated several times that he was not involved in a row with John Daly. Members of the public phoned in to berate Bradley and call him out. It was radio gold dust.

But then came an even more dramatic twist to the extraordinary confrontation. I was flabbergasted to hear Joe say: 'John Daly's on the line. John, good afternoon to you.' For the first time ever a radio audience was about to hear two dangerous criminals on the airwaves. Daly was extremely agitated and highly strung. It was clear that he wanted to settle the score with me. The call from his prison cell was radio history in the making. The following is a summary of what happened next.

> Duffy: John: How's it going? All right? You're in Portlaoise prison at the moment?
>
> Daly: I'm in Portlaoise right now, yeah. There's only one place I can be. Paul Williams knows that very well.
>
> Duffy: Take your time now, John.
>
> Daly: I will do. How's it going Alan, alright?
>
> Bradley: Not too bad. Yourself?
>
> Daly: Yeah. Thanks for the postcard while you were away. Now, Mr Williams. How many thousands of people would you say read your newspaper every Sunday?
>
> Williams: Almost a million.
>
> Daly: Almost a million? Do you know how much lies you tell every week? Do you know I sent a registered posted letter today with an article from that newspaper that you just wrote saying that I carried out armed robbery when I got out on my review. I did not get arrested for any armed robberies. In 2003 I did not get arrested for any armed robberies
>
> Williams: You're in prison serving how many years?

Daly: It doesn't matter how many years I'm serving.

Williams: Actually, where did you get the mobile phone to ring out?

Daly: (getting agitated) Who told you I had a spat against Alan Bradley who was a friend of mine, who I grew up with? I have a complaint in against you because if I didn't know Alan Bradley and Alan Bradley did not know me, you are kicking off a fucking gangland war.

Duffy: John, the language, the language.

Daly: OK, but that's what his intention is, to kick off war.

Duffy: John, you're in prison at the moment for armed robbery for an Esso station. Isn't that correct?

Daly: Yeah, back in 1999. I was eighteen years of age.

Duffy: And how many years are you serving in Portlaoise?

Daly: Nine years. Finishing off nine years.

Williams: You were let out of prison, then it was re-activated.

Daly: I'm going on holiday with Alan when I get out.

Duffy: You're denying that you threatened to kill Alan Badley?

Daly: Denied? The date, it was all in the *Herald* a week before Williams over in the *Sunday World*. You check that date in that *Herald* and you check this prison of when Alan Bradley sent me a postcard that very same day.

Bradley: [chuckling] And that's someone I left the country over.

Daly: I have to go; I have to go.

Duffy: John Daly, John, are you still on the phone there?

Daly: I can't stay long. I can't stay long. I'm in a cell. Paul Williams, you are a liar. You make up lies to start war. If I didn't know Alan Bradley and Alan Bradley did not know me, you would have kicked off a war there. People would be wanting to get

one person before the other person got the other. Now I'm
going. Get off the phone, you fuckin' liar.

Daly's call from Ireland's most secure prison went dead as warders
who had heard the show rushed in to take the phone. He had just
become a household name as one of the most infamous criminals
in Ireland. Bradley stayed on the line to get the last word and told
me again – 'You're a lying cunt.'

The confrontation had taken up the last hour of the show. As he
was signing off Joe Duffy sighed into the microphone: 'There's a
glimpse of something. Let that invest its way – I-N-V-E-S-T – not
F-E-S-T. Let that invest its way into the election, I hope.'

The drama had just given the astonished public a glimpse
into gangland through the voices of two thugs. It had come as a
complete shock to me but I had enjoyed such a rare opportunity
to confront two notorious thugs in such a public way.

There has never been anything like it on live radio, either
before or since. Some years ago a documentary series about the
social phenomenon that is Joe Duffy and his *Liveline* programme
featured a full episode recounting John Daly's infamous phone
call from prison.

To say that his call had set off an explosion would be putting it
mildly. The show created an unprecedented political storm coming
so close to the election. The following day's edition of the *Daily
Mail* summed up the reaction: 'Day Fatpuss came into Ireland's
living rooms'. The paper carried a mock-up bill declaring:

Mr Joe Duffy's *Liveline* theatre presents: The Most Bizarre Bit of
Radio Ever.
Dramatis personae:
Mr Duffy as himself

Paul Williams as the tabloid hack

Fatpuss as Public Enemy Number One.

The late Gerry Ryan described it as the most compelling and entertaining radio he had ever heard.

As the resulting bushfire engulfed the criminal, law enforcement and political worlds there was another sinister development. Giovanni Di Stefano uploaded three pictures of my home to his website. In a post he claimed that the pictures had been secretly taken by Marlo Hyland four months before he was murdered in December 2006. It illustrated how, despite police protection, the mob were still carrying out surveillance on me. The gardai said they were very concerned about the development and the officers at our home were put on high alert. Di Stefano said the murdered crime boss had given him the snaps and he was happy to publish them as a belated favour.

The fraudster wrote:

> Mr Hyland took the photos because he was sick and tired of Williams giving away the location of certain people which substantially got them killed, and of Williams hiding his whereabouts at the expense of the taxpayer. He wanted to print up 10,000 copies and give them out in Dublin. So to Paul Williams I am sharing the gift that Martin Hyland gave me and from the grave I am fulfilling his wishes!!!

It was an extraordinary development that represented a new level of intimidation. Gardaí said they were very concerned about the development and stepped up security at our home. It was very worrying for the family. I was also glad that I wasn't buying another home at the time.

A month later senior gardaí from the Crime and Security branch contacted me to warn that they had discovered yet another threat from the INLA. As happened so many other times I believe that the cops intervened behind the scenes and the threat subsided.

John Daly could never have imagined the storm of controversy that he was about to unleash when he picked up the phone to 'Talk to Joe'. After the call he was immediately moved to Cork prison as a punishment to serve the final months of his sentence. In many ways the move was as much to protect Daly as it was punishment. The episode was intensely embarrassing for the Department of Justice, the prison service and particularly the voluble minister. I was told by a source that behind the scenes Michael McDowell was threatening to have people sacked.

Within days there was a major clampdown in prisons across the country with hundreds of phones confiscated from prisoners which made Daly very unpopular, especially amongst his fellow inmates like his friend John Gilligan. Daly's call had stoked up a hornet's nest and he suddenly found himself becoming a hated figure. His act of stupidity had cost the other inmates their privileges. When Daly's phone was later analysed it was discovered that he had made 3,500 calls in the previous week alone.

The day after the showdown I was invited back on *Liveline* to reflect with Joe on what we had heard. I spoke again about the problem of the widespread availability of contraband phones in prisons which criminals used to orchestrate drug deals and murders, which had been vehemently denied by Michael McDowell who was then the leader of the PDs.

There was yet another extraordinary sequel to the show. Michael McDowell was given a slot on the following day's *Liveline* so that he could counteract what I had said. Joe Duffy had to sit there as the Justice Minister gave his response. Joe had been instructed that McDowell was not be interrupted and he was not to take any calls from the public. It was unprecedented in broadcasting history and went against everything that one of Ireland's most popular radio shows was about as a forum for ordinary Irish people to share their views and stories. The public service broadcaster had been blatantly bullied by the Government. I can still hear the frustration and anger in Joe Duffy's voice as he had to allow Michael McDowell say his bit.

The fallout from John Daly's phone call loomed over the elections. It had indirectly helped to seal the political fate of the Progressive Democrats and its controversial leader. An unknown volatile gangster had put the final nail in the minister's political coffin. McDowell lost his seat a month later and the PDs were wiped out. I was genuinely sorry to see that happen. Despite the bad blood, McDowell was a politician I always admired, especially his stance on the sinister past of Sinn Fein and the Republican movement. The party was later disbanded altogether. In many ways they were another casualty of the cost of fear. But John Daly had not come out of it too well either.

In the weeks leading up to his release on 14 August speculation was rife that Daly was going to create mayhem when he returned to Finglas. I had heard he was contacting former associates in Hyland's gang, including Bradley, looking for money that he said he was owed. The volatile killer was also promising to settle a number of old scores and was making death threats. The phone incident had helped to convince people that his days were numbered.

After his release gardaí warned Daly that there was a threat on his life. He told them to 'fuck off' and continued throwing his weight around. One detective told me at the time:

> We had received a load of intelligence that there were threats
> all over the place to kill Daly and these were from wholly reliable
> sources. We had information that he wouldn't get up the road
> from Portlaoise. There was a hole dug with his name on it. There
> was a queue of people to kill him.

Daly's fatal mistake was stamping on the toes of the new boss on the block, Eamon 'the Don' Dunne. Dunne, an even more dangerous monster, had organized Marlo Hyland's murder and taken over the gang. The Don's claim to fame is that he became one of the most blood-soaked killers in gangland history before he was assassinated. John Daly was one of Dunne's fifteen victims.

In the early hours of 22 October Daly arrived at his home in a taxi with friends. He was sitting in the front seat putting the fare together to pay the driver. A stolen Land Cruiser pulled up and a lone figure got out. He walked quickly up to the passenger's door and fired five shots into the feared mobster. Daly slumped forward and fell onto the terrified taxi driver as the rounds were pumped into him. He died instantly. Daly's was the fifteenth gangland killing of the year.

For his part Alan Bradley was subsequently convicted of conspiring to commit an armed robbery which took place a month after Daly's demise. He was part of a gang responsible for at least a dozen cash-in-transit robberies with Eamon Dunne. The money was used to finance drug shipments. In 2012 he was sentenced to nine years.

But there was yet another postscript to the story. The murder of Daly had created another forgotten victim – the unfortunate taxi driver. In the huge amount of media coverage of Daly's execution there was little or no mention of the completely innocent man who had narrowly escaped serious injury or death.

A week later he told me how he would never again work as a taxi driver which was how he supported his wife and four young kids who were aged between twelve weeks and ten years. He said he would never be able to get into the car which had been drenched in the gangster's blood. But there was no compensation, no support. An innocent family had become the victims of the gangland madness.

The only thing I could do was highlight their plight.

BACK WHERE IT BEGAN

In July 2015 a phone call I received from an angry farmer in County Tipperary brought me straight back to the first crime story I covered over thirty years earlier – rural crime. Robert O'Shea lived close to the tranquil village of Littleton on the old Dublin to Cork Road, five miles from the town of Thurles. Robert had a remarkable to story to tell. Ever since the village was bypassed by a new motorway it had been besieged by so-called travelling criminals.

Over the previous three years alone the village and its 400 residents had become the epicentre of a crime spree. In that period practically every residence, business premises and farmhouse within a ten-mile radius of the village had been burgled at least once with many being hit on multiple occasions. The scale of the problem was mind-boggling. Robert and a number of other local businesspeople, all of whom had been victims of burglaries, had facts and figures and names to back up the story.

I had sporadically covered the phenomenon of rural crime over the decades, but usually in cases where someone was killed when a robbery went wrong. Thankfully they had been few in number. In terms of crime coverage in the media we had been preoccupied with the antics of the emerging narcos and crime gang wars. In

2015 the issue of crime in sleepy villages and towns in the country did not feature on the national news agenda. In many ways I was one of the many people who assumed that it wasn't a problem anymore. I soon learned how wrong I was.

I spent a day in Littleton and its surrounding lush hinterland where I interviewed about a dozen people whose homes and businesses had been hit. Everyone I met was happy to talk because they wanted the rest of the country to know what was going on. I remember being amazed at the extent of the crime wave. So many people had been affected that I just didn't have the time to talk to all of them. On the August bank holiday I wrote a two-page investigation in the *Irish Independent* about the village besieged by crime.

At the end of the story we issued an appeal for victims of rural crime to contact us in order to gauge if this was confined to one geographical area. The response was phenomenal. Within a few days I received hundreds of emails and phone calls from victims across the country who wanted to tell their stories. A picture quickly emerged of a widespread problem that was undermining the peace and tranquillity of pastoral Ireland. It just hadn't been highlighted. We were going to change that.

The problem of crime had spiralled as budget cuts, particularly in the wake of the economic collapse of 2008, caused the closure of garda stations and shortages of squad cars and personnel in every rural district in the country. The gangs the Travelling community still refer to as 'granny bashers', took full advantage of the policing deficiencies and motorway network as they rampaged around Ireland. The favourite time of year for travelling crimes has always been winter when the long, dark nights provide shelter for the raiders. It is the time of year dreaded by people living alone in isolated areas. Farmyards were a particularly popular target as massive quantities of equipment and machinery were – and still are – stolen for resale at markets around the country. Crimes of burglary and robberies peak in the season of the dark nights.

The gangs travelled in groups in high-powered cars plundering whole communities at a time. Then they would speed back to their bases on the outskirts of Dublin. They also attacked from Limerick and several Midland towns. All of the gangs were interlinked through a nationwide network based on family connections – and crime traditions.

Unofficially garda sources were telling me that some rural counties in the Midlands had just one squad car to cover the entire county. Officially the garda top brass told me there was no problem with resources and no problem with rural crime. The politicians seemed to be of a similar mind. Official Ireland didn't seem to want to know what was happening to the peace-loving country folk. We decided to launch a campaign to tell the public the truth of what was going on. It was a labour of love for something that was close to my heart.

Over the following weeks and months I travelled across the country interviewing dozens of people and community groups who related their experiences. The story of rural crime became a daily staple of the Indo during those months. They just kept coming. It became apparent that Littleton's story was being replicated in every county in Ireland.

I was encountering the same overwhelming sense of despair and fear that I first experienced in Leitrim in the winter of 1984. Elderly people living alone were speaking again about how their peace of mind had been shattered by a visit from the lowest form of criminal life that exists. All the victims shared the same feeling of not being safe in their own homes in the twilight years of their lives. I felt the same surge of anger from all those years earlier.

Many farmers quietly confided, off-the-record, that they had fired shots over the heads of the unwelcome nocturnal visitors. In the absence of a credible deterrent from the State's primary law enforcement agency, taking the law into their own hands seemed the only option for many. I tended not to include the details about the warning shots in the stories because the only garda response would involve them seizing the poor farmer's gun. Preventing the serious injury or death of a thug who was more than prepared to use violence if cornered seemed to be more important than giving their victims some measure of protection.

Apart from the palpable sense of fear there was a perception that the law-abiding, loyal citizens felt they were being forgotten by the gardaí and their public representatives. In the countryside, where traditionally the police always enjoyed high levels of support, people were losing faith in the force's ability to protect them. The crime epidemic was corroding the old bonds of social cohesion.

There was also much anger that they were being taken for granted by a Government that placed the economy before the people they served. The continuing closure of post offices, banks and garda stations, the focal points of a rustic community, were sucking the life out of small villages and towns. The people living there were justified in believing that their way of life was under threat and their plight was being neglected. The travelling crime gangs had inadvertently provided the catalyst for rural Ireland to finally speak out.

The *Irish Independent* campaign gained extraordinary traction and quickly blew up into a major political issue. What began as a report on one village quickly mushroomed into a national talking point and a burning electoral issue which politicians could no longer ignore. It was what journalism in the public interest was all about – giving a voice and highlighting scandals.

The Government and Garda HQ went into defensive denial mode and reacted by claiming that we were making a mountain out of a molehill. At one stage I was invited to Garda HQ in the Phoenix Park to discuss our coverage of the problem with a senior officer. The suggestion was that I was being very unfair to the organization and should maybe go a 'bit easier'. I said that, like a detective, I was going where the evidence brought me. We continued publishing more firsthand accounts of rural crime victims as the emails and phone calls never stopped.

At the Ploughing Championships that year we decided to organize a discussion about rural crime in the *Irish Independent*'s tent. Robert O'Shea and the others who had first alerted me were invited as speakers. They had formed a group called Save our Local Communities (SOS) which we merged with the newspaper campaign. Several senior gardaí came to hear the public's stories and to reassure them. The place was swamped.

Over two hours people took the microphone to share their experiences. As chair of the debate I posed two questions to the crowd. Would they support any farmer or rural dweller who used a licensed firearm to either kill or injure an intruder on their property. Every hand, with the exception of the senior gardai present, was enthusiastically raised in the air. When I asked then for a show of hands from the audience to indicate if they knew their local garda – only three people responded. The evidence was piling up to prove that the official line was nothing more than mere spin.

The publicity dovetailed with the SOS group who asked me to assist in organizing and chairing a public meeting on the subject.

I was happy to oblige. On 8 October 2015 a crowd estimated at over 2,000 gathered for the meeting in the Anner Hotel in Thurles. The hotel function room was stuffed and hundreds more packed into the bars and other conference rooms to watch the debate on TV screens. People came from all over the country. Cars were parked up to a mile away from the venue as the silent majority of rural Ireland came to express their anger and dismay. Every media organization in the country were there to report on the night. Even the BBC sent a news crew.

We had agreed that no politician would be invited to speak. It wasn't a time for political ball playing – it was the people's turn to talk. A line of senior gardai of all ranks sat in the front row, scribbling down notes and looking concerned. For over three hours the men and women of rural Ireland held the microphones in faltering hands to share harrowing stories of being robbed and terrorized in their homes. They spoke of living in fear and when I asked the question again, would they condone shooting an intruder, their unanimous show of raised hands showed no equivocation. The huge media coverage of the event sent a shiver through the Government parties that they were losing the confidence of their most trenchant supporters. Fine Gael was always seen as the farmer's party.

Three days after the monster meeting crime again dominated the agenda when an unarmed garda, Tony Golden, was shot dead by a deranged dissident republican in County Louth. It was another wake-up call. A month later I chaired another public meeting in Trim, County Meath, which was attended by over 1,000 people. Proof that the rural crime campaign had gotten through to the Government was that the Justice Minister of the day, Frances Fitzgerald, twice announced new legislation to put 'repeat offenders' in jail for longer and without the right to bail. Research had shown that the vast amount of rural criminals were recidivists with strings of convictions for burglary, robbery and car theft.

A month later Garda HQ announced the launch of a nationwide anti-robbery offensive with the powerful codename Operation Thor. The operation proved to be a great success, with several gangs caught by a dedicated team of detectives. Press releases were also issued informing the public that more squad cars and personnel were being deployed in counties which had suffered the most crime. Something was being done. The *Irish Independent* and its editor Fionnan Sheehan had thrown the whole weight of the paper behind the campaign. In the truest traditions the newspaper had done the public some service in raising awareness about a hidden scourge. It was one of the biggest honours of my career to have been involved in the campaign.

Several years later there was a postscript of sorts to the story when one of the most prolific gangs who had targeted the people who spoke in Thurles came to a sticky and unlamented end.

———

On 7 July 2021 three notorious thugs who specialized in robbing and terrorizing rural people in their isolated homes were making their way back to Dublin after another robbery expedition. Dean Maguire, Graham Taylor and Carl Freeman, who ranged in age between late twenties and early thirties, had been career burglars since their early teens.

With more than 200 convictions between them, the trio was described in garda intelligence reports as being amongst the most dangerous and prolific travelling criminals operating in Ireland. They were the latest generation of a nationwide network of family-based thieves whose criminal roots could be traced all the way back to when the phenomenon first emerged forty years earlier.

The gang used high-powered stolen cars and the motorway network for their nocturnal jaunts, leaving a trail of victims in their wake. Maguire's modus operandi was to smash his way into a home and threaten his mostly elderly victims with a screwdriver. The gang leader's warning shout became his calling card: 'You know the score, get down on the floor.' In fact his terrifying rhyme was celebrated by his cronies.

Maguire and his associates were top of the garda most wanted list. They were also wanted for similar attacks in rural England. They had regular high speed chases with the police as they raced recklessly to get back to their safe haven in south-west Dublin. On the night of 7 July, they literally ran out of road.

After escaping from a garda chase the three desperados drove in a BMW down the wrong side of the motorway as they made their escape. They had no regard for the safety of others, only contempt. The car smashed into a truck and exploded in flames. The three criminals were burnt to death. Luckily the truck driver escaped physically uninjured though deeply traumatized. It was hard to have sympathy for the manner of their passing. Maguire's subsequent funeral reinforced that feeling. It said everything that had to be said about the class of criminals he came from.

The funeral Mass in St Mary's Priory Catholic church in Tallaght, south Dublin, descended into a shocking and grotesque spectacle as Maguire's admirers eulogized his life of violent crime. Gang members on motorbikes and in cars escorted the hearse carrying his coffin from the funeral home to the church, driving at high speed in convoy through afternoon traffic, while taking over oncoming lanes. The lawless rabble broke lights and endangered everyone in their path. The demonstration of contempt went into overdrive at the church which was crowded by what seemed like hundreds of menacing thugs in hoodies who had little regard for the Covid distancing restrictions in place at the time. That was the least of it.

They were there to celebrate and glorify their pal by giving the two fingers to the rest of society. It played out like a scene from *The Sopranos* only without any pretense of glamour or style. Over fifty years since the evolution of organized crime first began in Ireland, the bad guys no longer felt compelled to remain in the shadows. The mourners recorded everything and put it up on social media for the world to see.

One of the local priests who officiated at the mass later said it was the most disturbing liturgy he had attended. He and his colleague were left feeling intimidated and afraid. As mementos of Maguire's toxic life, a screwdriver and a torch – the tools of his trade – were carried to the altar in the same fashion that a hurl or football jersey is at the funeral of a respected sportsperson.

Floral tributes in the shape of a torch and screwdriver were later placed on his grave as part of the whole tacky affair. Laughter rippled through the congregation as someone recounted his memorable phrase. 'RIP Dean. You know the score, get on the floor, don't be funny, give me the money.' The thugs got up one by one to pay expletive laden tributes to the thug who they promised would not be forgotten. 'Sorry for the language, Father,' a woman warned the priest before declaring, 'Rest in peace, you fuckin' legend.'

Amongst the mourners was the large cohort of Maguire's friends who are still involved in violent home invasions throughout rural Ireland. The sheer numbers of them on display was another reminder as to why decent people don't feel safe in their homes. They were telling the world that they had no intention of going away.

After watching the display I thought: 'Good riddance.' At least there were three less of the bastards in the world. Then my mind wandered back to John Bernard Keaney and his trusty shotgun and how he once sent Maguire's forebears packing on a cold winter's night.

The rural crime spree of 1984 had only been the start. I had witnessed the opening of another new chapter in our rough draft of social history. Like most forms of crime in Ireland by 2024 it has only gotten worse.

It has become a fact of life.